Intention, Character, and Double Effect

LAWRENCE MASEK

INTENTION, CHARACTER,

and

DOUBLE EFFECT

University of Notre Dame Press

Notre Dame, Indiana

University of Notre Dame Press
Notre Dame, Indiana 46556
undpress.nd.edu

Published in the United States of America

Library of Congress Cataloging-in-Publication Data
Names: Masek, Lawrence J., 1976– author.
Title: Intention, character, and double effect / Lawrence J. Masek.
Description: Notre Dame : University of Notre Dame Press, 2018. | Includes
    bibliographical references and index. |
Identifiers: LCCN 2018043825 (print) | LCCN 2018044731 (ebook) |
    ISBN 9780268104719 (pdf) | ISBN 9780268104726 (epub) |
    ISBN 9780268104696 (hardback : alk. paper) | ISBN 0268104697
    (hardback : alk. paper)
Subjects: LCSH: Double effect (Ethics)
Classification: LCC BJ1500.D68 (ebook) | LCC BJ1500.D68 M37 2018
    (print) | DDC 170/.42—dc3.
LC record available at https://lccn.loc.gov/2018043825

∞ This paper meets the requirements of ANSI/NISO Z39.48-1992
(Permanence of Paper).

For Maria and Mark

Contents

Preface

My interest in the principle of double effect (PDE)—which I define as the principle that the difference between intended effects and foreseen side effects is relevant for judging actions—began when I was a graduate student and took an ethics course that covered PDE. The principle interested me because of its applications to fictitious cases of runaway trolleys, flooding caves, and organ transplants, as well as to real cases of war, euthanasia, and pregnancy. PDE seemed intuitively plausible, but I did not think about the basis of these intuitions.

My thinking about PDE, and about moral philosophy in general, changed a few years later when I read Alasdair MacIntyre's *After Virtue*. MacIntyre's book says little about specific questions in applied ethics and nothing explicit about PDE, but he persuaded me that philosophers should not settle for arguments that rely on mere intuitions. Instead of using intuitions to defend a moral theory against its rivals, a proponent of the theory must show that the theory can identify, explain, and overcome limitations of its rivals.[1] For example, someone cannot refute Kant merely by citing the case of lying to a murderer at the door, and someone cannot refute utilitarianism merely by citing the case of framing and executing an innocent scapegoat to prevent deadly riots. I concluded—and I still believe—that mere intuitive appeals cannot settle the debate about PDE. The same cases can elicit different intuitions from different people. Critics cannot design a counterexample that refutes PDE once and for all, and proponents of PDE cannot hope to refine the principle so that it fits everyone's intuitions about every case. To resolve the debate, a proponent of PDE must find the different theories of morality that support these conflicting intuitions and then show which theory is best.

MacIntyre also persuaded me that moral rules make sense only as directions for people to use to fulfill their potential as human beings. This teleological view of moral rules may be unfashionable in contemporary moral philosophy, but MacIntyre argues that philosophers who reject this view cannot explain why people should follow moral rules, given that they have strong inclinations to disobey them.[2] At the time, I did not see MacIntyre's defense of this view of morality as relevant for debates about PDE.

When I applied for jobs a few years later, an interviewer noted that I had published a paper about PDE.[3] He asked why PDE first developed in the Catholic tradition and why it is still more widely accepted among Catholics than non-Catholics. I did not have a good answer at the time. I said that the Catholic tradition includes exceptionless moral rules, such as the prohibition of murder, and that these rules would create inescapable moral dilemmas without PDE. I was unsatisfied with my answer, so my interviewer's question stayed in the back of my mind. I still covered PDE when I taught courses about ethics, but my scholarly work focused on other issues.

A few years later, I read a critique of my paper about PDE.[4] I welcomed the chance to restate and improve my argument, which I had come to see as flawed in many ways, so I wrote a reply.[5] Writing this reply made me think more seriously about PDE, including my interviewer's question about PDE and the Catholic tradition. The close relation between PDE and the Catholic tradition did not seem like a historical accident, but I did not believe that PDE depended entirely on theological premises or appeals to authority. The intuitions that support PDE still seemed clear to me. Further, some philosophers, such as Thomas Nagel and Philippa Foot, accept PDE despite being atheists.[6] (Foot even describes herself as a "card-carrying" atheist.[7]) I wanted to find the basic reasons that people disagree about the relevance of an agent's intention. Assuming that one side of the debate is simply stubborn, confused, or blinded by religious beliefs would have cut off the analysis too soon, before I had any real insight into the disagreement.

One cause of my confusion was that many contemporary philosophers divide moral theories into consequentialism, which says
that the right action is the one that causes the best consequences, and
deontology, which says that people should follow duties or obligations
even when violating them would cause better consequences than following them. PDE does contradict consequentialism, but calling it a
deontological principle is misleading, because the disagreements about
PDE do not line up with the disagreements between deontologists and
consequentialists. Prominent deontologists such as Alan Donagan,
T. M. Scanlon, and Judith Jarvis Thomson reject both consequentialism
and PDE. My thinking about PDE began to focus on finding the basic
disagreement that separates proponents and critics of PDE.

This disagreement came into clearer focus after I studied Philippa
Foot's critique of consequentialism.[8] She tries to explain why consequentialism is plausible and why it is ultimately mistaken. Her
answer is that consequentialists correctly see benevolence as one of
the virtues but that they treat benevolence as *the only* virtue, ignor-
ing justice and other virtues. In other words, she argues that consequentialists confuse part of morality (i.e., causing happiness for other
people) with the whole of morality. I came to believe that contemporary deontologists who reject PDE make a mistake similar to the one
that Foot sees in consequentialism. While consequentialists reduce
acting morally to causing happiness for other people, many contemporary deontologists reduce acting morally to treating other people
properly. Consequentialists reduce all the virtues to benevolence, and
contemporary deontologists reduce all the virtues to justice. Deontologists do not accept consequentialism because they deny that
people may mistreat an individual to cause more happiness. They
agree with consequentialists, however, that whether an action is right
or wrong depends only on its effects outside the agent. According
to this deontological view of morality, the difference between intention and foresight might be relevant for judging the agent's character,
but the difference is irrelevant for judging whether the action itself
is right or wrong. Victims are no worse off when their killers intend
death than when their killers merely foresee death.

An alternative to both consequentialism and deontology is the
view of morality that I accepted after studying *After Virtue*. According

to this view, an action can be wrong because of the way it forms the agent's character, even if the action does not have any other harmful effects. This view explains why the difference between intention and foresight is relevant for judging both actions and agents. I first sketched this account of the basic disagreement about PDE in a paper published in 2010.[9] In this book I develop my argument and explain how many disagreements about PDE arise from disagreements about the nature of moral rules.

After I was convinced that PDE makes sense only if the agent's character is relevant for judging actions, I began to see that confusion results when philosophers set aside the agent and focus on causal relations outside the agent. For example, many proponents of PDE replace the distinction between intention and foresight with a distinction between "direct" and "indirect" actions. Critics of PDE then have an easy time arguing that there is no plausible definition of direct and indirect.

My defense of PDE appeals to the agent both to explain why intentions are relevant for judging actions and to define what agents intend in specific cases. An agent-based version of PDE resolves some controversial issues in debates about PDE, including debates about medical procedures that save a pregnant woman while killing her unborn child. I argue that someone who accepts the view of morality that supports PDE can identify and resolve some problems better than consequentialists and many contemporary deontologists. I use some cases as illustrations, but I do not rely only on intuitions about these cases to defend PDE or to criticize its rivals.

I now have a better answer to the question about why PDE developed in the Catholic tradition. As I explain later, people do not need to be Catholic to accept PDE, but many philosophers and theologians in the Catholic tradition see developing a good character as an important part of living morally. Ultimately, PDE does not depend on appeals to authority or to intuitions about cases. Instead, it depends on a view of morality that treats a person's character as relevant for judging actions, a view that I defend throughout this book.

Acknowledgments

I begin by thanking Michael Dougherty for his comments on early drafts of every chapter of this book. For comments on drafts of chapters and papers that developed into chapters, I thank Brian Besong, Thomas Cavanaugh, Walter Kokernot, Matthew Ponesse, Michael Storck, and Christopher Tollefsen. I thank the late Joseph Boyle and an anonymous referee at *The Philosophical Quarterly* for their comments on a paper in which I first presented a justification of PDE and a definition of intended effects. In the introduction, chapter 1, and chapter 2 I develop the arguments in that paper. My defense of PDE does not depend on the version of natural law theory defended by Boyle and Tollefsen, but their writings, along with those of Germain Grisez and John Finnis, have shaped my views about PDE. Their influence is evident throughout this book.

I further thank participants in a 2013 conference at Franciscan University, where I presented an earlier version of the argument in chapter 1. I thank John Zeis for comments on my article in *American Catholic Philosophical Quarterly*, which presents the genealogy of the trolley problem and the minimalist version of PDE that I develop in chapter 4. I thank Marc Maitre for his help with the figures and illustrations in this book. A sabbatical from Ohio Dominican University enabled me to write chapters 1, 4, and 5.

I am grateful to Matthew Dowd, Stephen Little, and Wendy McMillen at the University of Notre Dame Press, as well as the manuscript reviewers, for their guidance and comments. I also am grateful to Marilyn Martin for her meticulous copyediting of the manuscript.

Finally, I thank my parents, who provided me with the education that makes my work possible, and my wife and children, who supported me throughout this project. As will become clear in my defense of PDE, being a husband and father has shaped my thinking about moral philosophy. I trust that my family will forgive me for all of the unflattering examples about children, parents, and spouses. These examples are, of course, fictitious.

Introduction

According to the principle of double effect, the difference between intention and foresight is relevant for determining whether an action is right or wrong. To illustrate this difference, consider two cases of bomber pilots who kill innocent civilians:

- One pilot targets a hospital so that the deaths of the hospital's patients will weaken the enemy's morale.
- Another pilot targets a weapons factory, despite foreseeing that the explosions will kill some patients at a nearby hospital.

Both pilots kill innocent people, but the first pilot *intends* their deaths as a means of weakening the enemy's morale, while the second pilot *knowingly causes* or *foresees* their deaths as a side effect of destroying the weapons factory. According to PDE, the agent's intention is relevant for judging actions in two ways. First, it is relevant for judgments about how to act (e.g., "I will not drop the bombs because I would intend to kill innocent people" or "The pilot should not drop the bombs because the pilot would intend to kill innocent people"). Second, the agent's intention is relevant for evaluating actions that have occurred (e.g., "The action was wrong because the pilot intended to kill innocent people").

A writer can say little about PDE without stepping into a briar patch of thorny issues. My definition and illustration of PDE already raise some disputed questions. Is PDE one principle or a set of principles? What if a bomber pilot needs only for innocent people to look dead, not to be dead? What about empirical studies in neuroscience and moral psychology that seem to debunk PDE? What if a bomber pilot targets a large man who is stuck in the mouth of a cave where five people who need organ transplants are trying to escape from a runaway trolley? The last question is a parody, but not much of a stretch from cases that philosophers actually use.[1] A writer can discuss only one issue at a time, so I will set aside these questions and many other objections and alleged counterexamples for now, or else my defense of PDE never will begin. For example, I consider the famous trolley problem—which is the challenge of explaining common intuitions about cases in which agents save several lives from runaway trolleys at the expense of one—only after I develop my version of PDE. My delay in considering the trolley problem is intended, not merely foreseen. When I discuss the trolley problem in chapter 4, I explain why confusion results when philosophers assume that PDE is supposed to explain common intuitions about trolley and transplant cases.

To defend PDE, some philosophers rely on intuitions about cases, but I use cases only to illustrate PDE. My main theses are these: (1) the difference between intended effects and foreseen side effects is relevant for judging actions because what people intend forms their character differently from what they knowingly cause, and (2) to define intended effects, someone must consider the action from the agent's perspective, not the perspective of an observer or victim of the action.

Like the bombing cases presented above, many examples of PDE also involve causing death and serious bodily harm:

- Torture is wrong, but causing pain as a foreseen side effect can be right. For example, interrogators may not electrocute a prisoner of war to extract information about a hidden weapons depot. Pilots may, however, bomb power lines to a weapons depot even if they foresee that the bombing will knock down power lines and electrocute an enemy soldier.
- Intending to kill a patient is wrong, but rationing medical care can be right. For example, physicians may not withhold drugs from

one patient so that the patient's death will make organs available for five life-saving transplants. Physicians may, however, ration a scarce drug so that they can save five patients instead of only one.[2]

- Suicide is wrong, but causing one's own death as a side effect can be right. For example, a mother may not kill herself so that her son can collect on a life insurance policy in order to afford medicine that he needs to survive. The mother may, however, run into a burning building to save her son even if she foresees that she will die from smoke inhalation a few hours later.

Some critics challenge common moral intuitions about these cases, and other critics try to explain these intuitions without PDE. For now, I use the cases only to illustrate the distinction between intended effects and foreseen side effects and to show why many people believe that this distinction is relevant for judging actions.

That these cases are interesting is good enough for me, but some critics with more refined tastes urge other philosophers to spend their time on more important topics. I respond to these highbrow critics when I discuss the trolley problem in chapter 4. For now, I note that the link between these cases and real choices is indirect, like the link between an athlete's weight training and a game. Basketball players lift weights to build muscles, not to be ready in case they need to lie down and lift other players off their chests. The point of contrived cases is to analyze moral rules and definitions of terms, not to be ready when a trolley comes speeding down a hill.

Dramatic cases of murder and torture are not the only illustrations of PDE. The distinction between intention and foresight is also relevant in ordinary cases:

- Intending to embarrass an opponent is wrong, or least an example of bad sportsmanship, but knowingly causing an opponent's embarrassment is not. For example, coaches may not run up the score so that an inferior rival will feel embarrassed. Coaches may, however, tell their team to play hard even if they know that doing so will cause a lopsided score that will embarrass their opponent.
- Lying is wrong, but knowingly causing a false belief as a side effect can be right. For example, I may not tell my boss that I was stuck

in traffic when I really overslept. I may, however, apologize for being late and omit the reason why even if I foresee that my boss will assume that I was stuck in traffic.

- Plagiarizing is wrong, but knowingly causing a misattribution of ideas can be right. For example, I may not use Plato's allegory of the cave without citing Plato so that my students will attribute the allegory to me and overestimate my brilliance. I may, however, use the allegory of the cave in a conference presentation without citing Plato so that I do not insult my audience's intelligence, even if I foresee that some students in the audience will attribute the allegory to me and overestimate my brilliance.

- Inciting envy is wrong, but knowingly causing envy can be right. For example, a child may not choose a toy in order to incite a sibling's envy. A child may, however, choose a toy to have fun despite foreseeing that a sibling will feel envy.

PDE seems to explain why the two actions in each pair elicit different moral intuitions even though they have similar effects. In each pair, the first agent intends a bad effect (i.e., embarrassment, a false belief, a misattribution of ideas, or envy) as a means, while the second agent knowingly causes or foresees the same effect without intending it.

Why would a person act wrongly by intending an effect but not by knowingly causing the same effect? In chapter 1 I answer this question by explaining the rational basis of PDE. Agents can act wrongly by corrupting their own character, not only by mistreating other people. Agents have a closer relation to what they intend than to what they cause as a side effect, so intending an effect can corrupt the agent's character even if knowingly causing the same effect does not. For example, intending to embarrass an opponent can block someone from respecting opponents, even if causing embarrassment as a side effect does not. After presenting this agent-based justification of PDE, I argue that proponents of PDE cannot overcome objections if they turn away from the agent's character and appeal to intuitions, exceptionless moral rules, or phenomenological descriptions of intending evil.

How can people draw the line between intended effects and foreseen side effects? In chapter 2 I answer this question by considering actions from the agent's perspective. I argue that an agent intends an effect if and only if it is part of a true and complete answer to the question "What is the agent's goal, and what are all the steps in the agent's plan to achieve that goal?" Instead of defining intended effects from the agent's perspective, some proponents of PDE set aside the agent's perspective and define intended effects by analyzing causal relations outside the agent. For example, some proponents of PDE claim that agents intend all the effects that *closely* or *directly* follow from their actions. These definitions inevitably entail false conclusions because they classify some effects as intended even though the agent regards them as irrelevant or even when the agent works against them—as when a sniper uses a flash suppressor and muzzle to reduce the flash and noise that follow a gunshot more closely or directly than the bullet's hitting the sniper's target.[3] More importantly, these definitions undermine the basis of PDE. When proponents of PDE set aside the agent's perspective to define intended effects, they cut the link between intended effects and the agent's character, leaving them unable to explain why intentions are relevant in the first place. Unlike definitions that refer to closeness or directness, my agent-based definition of intended effects fits the agent-based justification of PDE that I present in chapter 1. One objection to PDE in general is that it is merely a tool for rationalizing moral judgments, because people classify a bad effect as an intended effect when they disapprove of the action and as a side effect when they approve of the action. To support this objection, some critics cite empirical studies in which subjects' moral judgments seem to influence their judgments about what people intend. These studies have flaws, but even if moral judgments cloud some people's judgments about intentions, it does not follow that all people's judgments about intentions merely rationalize their moral judgments.

Do people accept PDE because they confuse judgments of actions and judgments of agents? This challenge strikes at the heart of PDE because it seems to explain both PDE's appeal and its failure. According to the objection, PDE is appealing because intentions are relevant for some moral judgments, but PDE is false because intentions are relevant only for judging agents, not for judging actions. In chapter 3 I argue that this objection arises from an unnecessarily narrow view of morality. The objection seems plausible because the agent's intention is irrelevant for judgments about whether the action treats someone unjustly, but the objection is mistaken because treating someone unjustly is not the only way to act wrongly. The objection also seems plausible because many philosophers, including proponents of PDE, speak about actions as if they existed apart from intentions, as a hammer sits on a shelf apart from a user's intention. Anyone who treats a bent nail as evidence of a bad hammer confuses a judgment of the hammer with a judgment of the user, so treating actions like tools on a shelf exposes PDE to the objection about confusing different types of moral judgments.

What does my version of PDE say about the famous trolley cases? Very little, but I argue in chapter 4 that these cases are widely misunderstood. Many critics assume that intuitions about trolley cases are the only basis of PDE, but PDE predates trolley cases by centuries, and the trolley cases come from critics of PDE, who use them to analyze other moral principles. When philosophers expect PDE to explain intuitions about all the trolley cases, they end up defining intended effects too broadly. Like the proverbial carpenter who has only a hammer and sees every problem as a nail, philosophers who expect PDE to solve the trolley problem end up seeing too many actions as examples of intending evil. When critics assume that PDE depends on intuitions about trolley cases, they end up rejecting PDE too quickly. Some of these critics claim that recent studies in moral psychology and neuroscience debunk PDE by showing that it is the product of unreliable emotional processes rather than more reliable cognitive processes. I challenge these critics' assumptions, especially the assumption that PDE depends on intuitions about trolley cases and other bizarre scenarios.

What does my version of PDE say about the famous case of obstetric craniotomies and other hard cases in war and medicine? Caesarean sections have replaced craniotomies as remedies for obstructed labor, but the principles used to analyze the craniotomy case are still relevant. According to a traditional view of PDE, performing an obstetric craniotomy is wrong because the surgeon directly kills the fetus as a means of saving the mother. The traditional view has been disastrous for PDE's reputation—and, more importantly, for any woman who has died along with her child because her surgeon followed the traditional view and did not take the only action that could have saved at least one life. In chapter 5 I argue that a surgeon can perform a craniotomy without intending death. Many philosophers, including many proponents of PDE, dismiss this conclusion about the surgeon's intention as absurd, but the apparent absurdity results from the assumption that agents do not need to consider their intentions or that someone can set aside an agent's perspective to judge an action. By focusing on causal relations outside the agent, opponents of the craniotomy undermine the rational basis of PDE. They end up with a legalistic view of moral rules that cannot explain why directness or closeness is relevant in the first place. After analyzing the craniotomy and other pregnancy cases, I consider some other alleged counterexamples to PDE from medicine and war. Again, I respond to these cases by defining intended effects from the agent's perspective, not by analyzing causal relations outside the agent. Some critics assert that an agent-based definition of intended effects entails some form of dualism or subjectivism. In fact, I assume nothing about the relation between mental and physical states. What agents intend is one question; how those intentions are related to physical states is another. I also do not assume subjectivism about what is right or wrong. Whether people may intend death is one question; whether a specific person intends death is a separate question.

Throughout this book I use PDE, or "principle of double effect," rather than the equally common "doctrine of double effect."[4] Using "doctrine" implies that the view depends on appeals to authorities in the Catholic tradition, not on rational arguments. Most authors in the Catholic tradition oppose polygamy, but it would be misleading for philosophers to speak of the "Roman Catholic doctrine" that polygamy is wrong. This label creates the impression that no rational argument explains why polygamy is wrong. Philosophers should analyze arguments about polygamy on their own merits, without assuming that opposition to polygamy depends on faith rather than reason. They should do the same with arguments about PDE.

Some authors avoid the theological connotations of the label "doctrine of double effect" by using "double-effect reasoning" to label the principle.[5] This label avoids the theological connotations of "doctrine," but I bow to precedent and custom by using the label "principle of double effect" instead. Also, the label "double-effect reasoning" fits the act of applying a principle better than it fits the principle itself. Other possible labels include the "principle of side effects."[6] I have no serious objections to this label, but precedent and custom again support the label "principle of double effect" instead.

I use "foreseen side effects" to describe effects that the agent knowingly causes but does not intend. The label "merely foreseen effects" suggests that the effects are not serious or that the agent is not responsible. Speaking of effects that the agent knowingly causes would be more precise, because people can foresee effects that they do not cause, but using "knowingly caused side effects" would be more cumbersome than using "foreseen side effects." Some proponents of PDE refer to foreseen side effects as effects that the agent "indirectly" causes, but I argue that PDE's proponents made a wrong turn when they shifted from speaking about the difference between intention and foresight to speaking about the difference between "direct" and "indirect" actions. When proponents of PDE refer to directness and indirectness, they cause confusion about specific cases. They also undermine the basis of PDE by obscuring the agent's perspective.

I define PDE as one principle of the distinction between intention and foresight, but some proponents of PDE treat it as a set of conditions that people must fulfill when they cause foreseen harms. In my view, PDE relates to other moral principles as the rule "To find 25 percent of a number, divide it by four" relates to other mathematical principles. The rule about dividing by four does not require exceptions or additions to mathematical principles. It merely clarifies them and makes them easier to apply in specific cases, such as calculating a discount. Likewise, PDE clarifies moral principles, such as the rule against murder, and makes them easier to apply in specific cases. By itself, my version of PDE does not forbid, excuse, or justify any action. It says only that the agent's intention is relevant for judging actions. When I discuss the trolley problem in chapter 4, I argue that trying to squeeze all moral considerations into a complete checklist leaves PDE vulnerable to counterexamples and motivates some proponents of PDE to define intended effects too broadly. Morality is too complex to be reduced to three or four principles. For now, I note that parents cannot find three or four rules that answer every question about what they should permit a child to do. Living morally is no simpler than raising children.

I am not alone in treating PDE as a single principle. The labels "principle of double effect" and "doctrine of double effect" were first used for a set of conditions that someone must satisfy when causing bad effects, but many contemporary philosophers define PDE as a single principle about the relevance of the agent's intention.[7] Anyone who would reserve the label "principle of double effect" for a set of principles can still see my project as a defense of PDE, because one step toward defending any version of PDE is explaining why the distinction between intended effects and foreseen side effects is morally relevant. The label "principle of double effect" is not essential to my arguments. As noted earlier, someone could call the principle that I defend the "principle of side effects," but this name has not become as common as the "principle of double effect."

To defend PDE, I use several examples about parents and children. If the way that parents raise their children contradicts a moral theory, something has gone awry with the parenting or with the theory. In most cases, I identify the theory as the likely culprit. For example, students in an ethics course might retreat to some form of moral skepticism—for example, asking, "Who's to say what's good and bad?"—when they face an argument that challenges their beliefs. Outside the classroom, however, parents assume that they know quite clearly what is good and bad for their children.[8] There are no moral skeptics in the front seat of a minivan.

Good parents also assume principles that provide a rational basis for PDE. They assume that an action can be wrong because of the way it forms their children's character, not only because of the way that the action affects other people. They also assume that children form their character differently when they intend an effect, such as a sibling's envy, instead of knowingly causing the effect.

Chapter One

The Rational Basis of the Principle of Double Effect

In debates about PDE, philosophers often use fictional cases of violent deaths to illustrate the principle. These cases feature heavy men who suffer untimely deaths as they are pushed off bridges, hit by trolleys, trapped in caves, and blown up by dynamite. I am not squeamish about using macabre examples, as shown by many of the cases discussed in this book, but I make a fresh start here with two bloodless cases:

- A boy and his Swedish friend are bickering about superheroes. After his friend insults Spider-Man, the boy mumbles a racial epithet for his friend, quietly enough that his friend does not hear.
- A boy and his Swedish friend are playing with superhero action figures. The boy chooses to play with Spider-Man instead of Thor, a character based on the Norse god. The boy foresees, but does not intend, that his friend will feel offended.

If I were the boy's father in the first case, I would categorically forbid him to use the racial epithet, even under his breath. If I were the boy's father in the second case, I might tell him to consider a different toy, but I would not categorically forbid him to choose Spider-Man. Mumbling the epithet offends nobody, but choosing Spider-Man offends the boy's friend. Why, then, would a parent forbid the *less* offensive of the two actions?

My cases of the mumbled epithet and the offensive toy do not fit the typical pattern of cases used to illustrate PDE. In these cases, the agent's intention seems to be the only relevant difference between two actions that elicit different moral intuitions. In my cases, the two actions are not similar apart from the boy's intention, and I ask what a parent would forbid, not what is morally right or wrong. Instead of using my cases to make PDE intuitively plausible, I use them to explain PDE's rational basis. In the first section of this chapter, I argue that people can act wrongly by corrupting their own character. In the second section, I argue that what people intend forms their character differently from what they foresee or knowingly cause, so intending an effect sometimes corrupts a person's character even if knowingly causing the same effect does not. In the third section, I criticize justifications of PDE that rely on common moral intuitions. Intuitive appeals can make PDE seem plausible, but critics can argue that these intuitions are unreliable. Also, anyone who bases PDE on intuitions has no principled basis for choosing among different definitions of intended effects. In the fourth section, I criticize attempts to base PDE on exceptionless moral rules. My version of PDE neither assumes nor denies the existence of such rules. In the fifth section, I consider Thomas Nagel's justification of PDE, which contrasts the experiences of intending evil and causing evil. Nagel explains why intending evil feels worse from the agent's perspective, but he does not explain why the agent's perspective is relevant for judging actions. Nagel's justification of PDE falls short because he assumes that all moral rules are based on other people's interests, not the agent's character.

MORAL JUDGMENTS AND THE AGENT'S CHARACTER

Why would a parent forbid a child to mumble a racial epithet that offends nobody and permit a choice of toys that does offend someone? I begin my answer by noting that the problem with the boy in my case is not merely the uttering of certain words. I would not forbid my children to report another person's use of a racial epithet as strictly as I would forbid them to use an epithet themselves, and I would forbid them to use a seemingly inoffensive term (e.g., "black" or "Jew") as an epithet. The problem with the boy in my case is that he intends to denigrate his friend, not that he says something from an index of forbidden words. This intention to denigrate someone—not the effect of causing someone to feel offended—explains why I would categorically forbid the use of the epithet if the boy were my son.

Someone could say that a parent should forbid the mumbled epithet because using it makes the boy more likely to mistreat other people. To see why this explanation is incomplete, suppose that the boy promises that he will use racial epithets only in private and that he will never treat anyone in a racist way. If I were the boy's father, I still would not permit him to mumble the epithet, even if I trusted his promises. Using the racial epithet would encourage him to develop racist character traits, such as feelings of superiority and hostility. These traits would block friendships and peaceful relations with other people. I want my son to have friendships and peaceful relations with other people, so I do not want him to become a racist, even a racist who reliably but grudgingly avoids offending people. To prevent him from forming racist character traits, I would categorically forbid him to mumble the epithet. By contrast, I might not forbid my son to choose a toy that offends his friend because his friend's feeling offended might not be a decisive reason to not choose the toy. The friend might be reacting unreasonably, so forbidding the choice would treat my son unfairly.

My analysis of these cases does not say that mumbling a racial epithet is always more seriously wrong than offending someone. The *strictness* of a rule differs from the *seriousness* of violating it. To illustrate the difference, consider two rules of thumb in chess: "Do not move a pawn in front of your rook on your first move" and "Do not trade a queen for a pawn." The first rule is stricter, because there are few games in which a player should open by moving the rook pawn and countless positions in which the sacrifice of a queen forces checkmate. Violating the second rule is more serious because recovering from a bad opening usually is easier than recovering from a lost queen. For an example of the difference between the strictness and seriousness of moral rules, consider the rules "Do not intend the death of an innocent human being" and "Do not drive a car through a playground" and two actions that violate these rules:

- A woman is suffering from an incurable disease that will kill her soon. To end her suffering, a physician gives her a lethal injection to euthanize her.
- A man wants to arrive at a bar before happy hour ends. He is stuck in traffic, so he cuts through a playground, foreseeing that he will run over and kill some children.

Euthanasia is a controversial issue that I will not try to resolve here. The relevant point for now is that someone can believe the physician acts wrongly and still believe the reckless driver does something more seriously wrong. The rule against murder is stricter, and possibly exceptionless, but violating the rule against driving through playgrounds can be more seriously wrong.

Because of the difference between a rule's strictness and its seriousness, PDE's proponents have no reason to blush about cases in which an agent acts wrongly, even seriously wrongly, without intending a bad effect. Such cases do not refute PDE. They merely illustrate that a sound view of morality needs principles other than PDE, a point that PDE's proponents have no reason to deny.

I claim that people can act wrongly by corrupting their own character. A critic could agree that there is some link between wrongness and the agent's character but still object, "You have it backward. An action is not wrong because it corrupts the agent's character. It corrupts the agent's character because it is wrong." I agree in many cases. For example, reckless driving corrupts a driver's character because reckless driving is wrong. It is not wrong because it corrupts the driver's character. My justification of PDE depends on the premise that the reverse can also be true—that is, that some actions are wrong because they corrupt the agent's character. To defend this point, I need to clarify "corruption." Saying that an action corrupts the agent's character does not always presuppose a moral judgment of the action. Suppose that computer technicians deliver the dreaded news "Your hard drive is corrupt." The technicians clearly are not making a moral judgment. They mean that the hard drive cannot store and read data. Auto mechanics who say that a battery is corrupt are also not making a moral judgment. They mean that the battery cannot hold a charge. The hard drive and the battery are corrupt because they cannot do something that hard drives and batteries characteristically can do. Similarly, when I say that an action corrupts the agent's character, I mean that the action blocks the agent from some good that human beings characteristically can achieve. For example, even if the boy does not cause anyone to feel offended, mumbling a racial epithet corrupts his character by blocking him from the goods of friendships and peaceful relations with other people. I regard these goods as important parts of a happy life, so I would prohibit my son from using the racial epithets.

This view of corruption depends on the premise that something can be good for people even if they do not desire it and even if they never will desire it. Defending this assumption is a larger project than defending PDE, so I try only to make the assumption seem plausible. Suppose that children tell their parents that they do not want any friends and that they plan to become hermits when they grow up. Good parents would not start looking to buy their children a cabin in the woods. They would look for ways to make their children appreciate friendships. Similarly, suppose that children tell their parents that they do not want to be educated. Good parents would not excuse their children from school. They would work on aligning their children's desires with what is good. According to the view of corruption that supports my version of PDE, people can corrupt their character even if they do not frustrate their actual desires. Even if heroin addicts want nothing more than feeling high, they could be missing out on goods that are essential to a happy human life. To use an example more closely linked to PDE, that torturers do not care about friendships and peaceful relations with other people does not rule out the possibility that they could live more fulfilling lives if they stopped torturing people. Adulthood does not confer infallibility on a person's desires.

Someone might object, "These examples about children, drug addicts, and torturers who corrupt themselves are out of place because morality is about treating other people properly, not about doing what is good for oneself." If acting morally were reducible to treating other people properly, then my examples would be out of place, but I see no reason to accept this reductive view of morality. Good parents want their children to treat other people properly and to be happy, so some rules require children to consider each other's interests (e.g., a rule against biting and a requirement to take turns), and other rules are based on children's own interests (e.g., a rule against mumbled racial epithets and a requirement to attend school). Anyone who assumed that *all* of a parent's rules for a child must be based in other people's interests would have an unnecessarily limited view of parenting and would be unable to explain many of a parent's rules. Similarly, morality includes both rules based on other people's interests and rules based on the agent's own interests. A difference in the agent's intention may not affect other people, but the difference can affect the agent's character, as I explain below.

Someone could argue that *all* of a good parent's rules ultimately promote a child's interests. For example, someone could argue that learning not to bite people keeps children open to friendships. I agree, but I have argued only that *some* of a good parent's rules promote a child's own interests. In the mumbled epithet case, other children's interests do not explain the rule against the epithet. Analogously, someone could argue that *all* moral rules, including rules about treating other people properly, ultimately promote the agent's own interests in some way, but my defense of PDE assumes only that *some* moral rules depend on the agent's own interests.

According to the view of morality that supports PDE, moral rules are similar to a parent's rules because both types of rules direct people toward what is good for them. Someone might worry that treating moral rules as analogous to a parent's rules makes moral rules unfitting for rational adults. I disagree. In fact, the analogy may work even better for older parents and adult children, who can follow their parents' rules because they see the wisdom of their parents' advice, not because they fear punishment or want to please an authority.

For convenience, I refer to the view of morality that supports PDE as a "Socratic view" of morality. One advantage of this label is that the views of the historical Socrates are sketchy enough that I can use the label without delving into exegetical questions about what he really believed. The only Socratic principle necessary for my defense of PDE is that people can act wrongly by corrupting their own character, as well as by mistreating other people. My defense of PDE does not depend on other Socratic principles, such as the impossibility of incontinence or the unity of the virtues.

Judith Jarvis Thomson considers the possibility that PDE depends on what I have called a Socratic view of morality. She suggests that many people accept PDE because they accept "an inward-looking" view of morality that "could be described as a form of moral solipsism":

> If you think morality is *wholly* a matter of what makes a person be good or bad—if you suppose it is *wholly* a set of instructions for being virtuous and not being vicious—then it would be no surprise if you thought that one is in breach of morality *only if* one does a thing the doing of which marks one as so far a bad person, i.e., a thing one is at fault or to blame for doing [emphasis added].[1]

I respond in three ways. First, the terms "wholly" and "only if" are unnecessary. That someone can act wrongly by becoming a vicious person does not rule out the possibility that someone can also act wrongly for other reasons. Second, by referring to "moral solipsism" Thomson does not address the possibility that being a good person requires both treating other people properly and developing a good character. Someone who accepts the Socratic view of morality can agree that good people will not spend all their time "looking inward." A good person also will want to treat other people justly. For example, Plato's dialogues portray Socrates as keenly interested both in being virtuous himself and in treating other people justly. Third, Thomson describes the view that acting immorally "marks" the agent as a bad person. If acting with a bad intention merely *marked* a fault, then Thomson would have good reason to regard the agent's bad intention as irrelevant for moral judgments since the agent would already be corrupt by the time of the action. I argue, however, that intending some effects corrupts agents even more than they have already been corrupted. For example, suppose that a girl asks, "May I play with this toy now?" When asked to explain why she wants the toy, she answers, "Because I want to make my brother envious." If I were the girl's father, I would refuse. I might answer differently if she intended to have fun while foreseeing her brother's envy. Choosing the toy to incite envy would do more than simply reveal a pre-existing character flaw in the girl. It would corrupt her character further. If intending to incite envy merely revealed a pre-existing flaw, I might say, "Yes, but we need to talk about envy later." Instead, I simply would forbid her to choose the toy.

I agree with Thomson that people should avoid a narrow view of morality, but this point supports the Socratic view of morality. Excluding principles about character makes a view of morality unnecessarily narrow. To illlustrate this point, consider two actions that seem to be wrong because they corrupt another person:

- A man and his colleague go to a bar for happy hour. The man knows that his colleague is a recovering alcoholic with a distaste for gin and a fondness for tequila. The man considers ordering a martini, which will not tempt his colleague, and a margarita, which will. The margarita is a few cents cheaper, so the man orders it, despite foreseeing that the smell of tequila will tempt his colleague to resume his destructive drinking habit.
- An author of a children's book chooses a name for a story's villain that identifies the villain with an ethnic group. Before the book is published, the author realizes that using this name will encourage her young readers to form negative views about the group. She considers using a word processor's find-and-replace feature to change the name, but she does not bother.

Both actions seem wrong because they corrupt other people. Corrupting other people unintentionally may not always be wrong, but saving a few cents or a few seconds of effort are not good reasons to corrupt a recovering alcoholic or a young reader. Someone could claim that both actions are wrong for some reason other than corrupting another person's character, but this approach would not explain the actions' apparent similarity. These cases illustrate the unnecessary limitations of a view of morality that excludes considerations about people's character. An action can be wrong because it corrupts someone else, so it is arbitrary to deny that an action can be wrong because it corrupts the agent.

So far I have argued that an agent's character is relevant for moral judgments. The next step in my defense of PDE is to explain how intending an effect can corrupt the agent's character although knowingly causing or foreseeing the same effect does not corrupt the agent's character in similar cases.

INTENTIONS AND CHARACTER

Even if people can act wrongly by corrupting their own character, why is the distinction between intention and foresight relevant for judging actions? Proponents of PDE do not need one answer to cover every case. Murderers who intend death and liars who intend to deceive may act wrongly for different reasons. Coaches who intend to embarrass an opponent may act wrongly for another reason, and children who intend to incite a sibling's envy may act wrongly for yet another. I do not analyze every application of PDE or every case in which people act wrongly because they intend a bad effect. Instead I explain why people have a closer relation to intended effects than to foreseen side effects. Because of this closer relation, people sometimes act wrongly by intending an effect even though they would act rightly by knowingly causing the same effect in similar circumstances.[2]

The agent performs the action, but the action also forms the agent. For example, I feared roller coasters as a child. When I finally chose to ride a roller coaster for the first time, my choice showed that my fear had faded (or at least that it had become weaker than my fear of looking like a coward). My first ride did not merely reveal a change in me. It also weakened my fear of roller coasters even more. The first ride was the hardest; the second ride was a bit easier, and so on. (Many years later, being tossed around on a roller coaster seems neither scary nor pleasant.)

This two-way relationship between agents and actions supports PDE because agents have a different relation to intended effects than to foreseen side effects.[3] I define "intended effects" more precisely later. For now I claim only that the agent seeks an intended effect, either as an end or as a means. I also could say that the agent *wills*, *chooses*, *pursues*, *aims at*, or *tries for* an intended effect. By contrast, the agent merely *causes* foreseen side effects. The agent's relation to intended effects is internal, because the agent is related to the effect as a seeker and as a cause. The agent's relation to foreseen side effects is external because the agent is related to the effect merely as a cause. For example, consider the bombing cases that I presented earlier:

- A bomber pilot targets a hospital so that the deaths of the hospital's patients will weaken the enemy's morale.
- A bomber pilot targets a weapons factory despite foreseeing that the explosions will kill some patients at a nearby hospital.

The first pilot has an internal relation to the deaths because the pilot uses the deaths as a means of demoralizing the enemy. The second pilot has an external relation to the deaths because that pilot sets in motion a chain of events that causes the deaths. If both pilots say, "I may be causing the deaths of innocent people, but I am not seeking or trying to kill them," only the second pilot would be telling the truth. This difference in their intentions does not give the second pilot a license to kill innocent people with impunity. The second pilot could act wrongly by treating people unjustly without intending their deaths, and the second pilot also could develop bad character traits, such as recklessness and callousness. Still, intending to kill innocent people changes the first pilot more directly because that pilot has a closer, or more internal, relation to the deaths. The second pilot might be unjustly callous toward other people's deaths, but that pilot does not seek or try to kill innocent people, in the sense that the deaths are neither the pilot's end nor a means to the pilot's end. By contrast, the first pilot does not merely pay too little attention to the deaths of innocent people. That pilot seeks the deaths as part of a plan for weakening the enemy's morale.

Some critics of PDE claim that intending death *as an end* corrupts the agent but that intending death *as a means* does not. According to this objection, the relevant difference in the bombing cases is between pilots who intend death as an end and pilots who do not intend death as an end but might intend death as a means.[4] One problem with this objection is that the line between ends and means is blurry. If a bomber pilot seeks vengeance on a hated enemy, is killing innocent people an end or a means to satisfying the pilot's desire for vengeance? This question has no clear answer. Another problem with this objection is that a mercenary killer seems no better than a malevolent killer. If asked, "Why did you murder those people?," saying "Because I wanted money" seems to be no better an answer than saying "Because I hate them." The end of making money turns the murderer from a malevolent killer into a mercenary killer, but this change does nothing to justify the murderer's action. For less violent examples that do not involve death, I would not permit my children to denigrate a friend's race on a dare or permit them to denigrate a friend's race for its own sake. I also would not permit them to incite a sibling's envy to win a bet or permit them to incite a sibling's envy for its own sake. If intending these effects as ends would corrupt my children's character, so would intending these effects as means. Thus the explanation of how intending death corrupts the agent applies equally well to people who intend death as a means as to people who intend death as an end.

My justification of PDE does not depend on the premise that people who intend death *always* intend something bad. (I agree with that premise, but I do not defend it here.) For example, proponents of euthanasia could claim that intending a patient's death benefits the patient by ending pain. I claim only that intending death and knowingly causing death as a side effect form the agent's character differently.

Someone might say, "Your analysis of the bombing cases explains why the pilots have different relations to the deaths, but you have not proven that these different relations form a pilot's character differently." This objection is not completely wrong. At some point, a justification of PDE bumps up against the limits of rational analysis. My best response to the critic begins with the premises that friendships and peaceful relationships with other people are good and that being malevolent blocks a person from participating in these goods. The bomber pilot who targets a hospital to demoralize the enemy necessarily acts malevolently toward the victims. The pilot cannot will that the victims survive, at least not without hoping for something that would make the bombing pointless. By contrast, the pilot who targets the factory does not necessarily act malevolently, because the victims' survival would not make the bombing pointless. As explained earlier, the pilot who knowingly causes deaths might develop character traits such as recklessness and callousness, and these character traits might also impede friendships and peaceful relations with others. I claim only that intending death is one way that agents can impede friendships and peaceful relations with others, not that it is the only way. Even if a pilot acts recklessly or carelessly, that pilot would not act malevolently, as does the pilot who intends death.

Someone could add, "Your argument is circular. If you define malevolence as intending to harm someone, then of course the first pilot acts malevolently, but acting malevolently is no worse than knowingly causing harm, and malevolence does not corrupt an agent any more than negligence or callousness." If someone insists that intending death and knowingly causing death form the agent's character in the same way, I have no demonstrative reply. I could ask, "As a parent, do you see a relevant difference between your child's intending to incite a sibling's envy and causing a sibling's envy as a foreseen side effect?" I also could ask, "Suppose that I want to be a nastier, more malevolent person. What is a quicker and more reliable way to achieve my goal, becoming a hitman or becoming a bomber pilot?" The answer seems clear, even if I cannot provide a demonstrative proof.

Instead of denying that intention and foresight form the agent differently, someone could challenge my justification of PDE by claiming that the difference between intention and foresight is relevant only for judging agents, not for judging actions. In chapter 3 I respond to this objection by arguing that an action can be wrong precisely because it corrupts the agent.

One proponent of PDE notes that moral judgments apply only to voluntary actions and concludes that it "puzzles and goes against sound taxonomy" to deny that further distinctions among voluntary actions—including the distinction between intending and foresight—also are morally relevant.[5] On the other side of the debate, critics find it puzzling when proponents insist that an action can be wrong because of the agent's intention. One critic imagines considering a pilot's intention to determine whether the pilot may proceed with a bombing and exclaims, "What a queer performance this would be!"[6] Another critic finds PDE not merely false or implausible but "wildly implausible."[7] Why do intelligent people on both sides of the debate find the other side's view puzzling, queer, or wildly implausible?

I begin my answer by noting that it is not always puzzling when someone admits the relevance of a category and then denies the relevance of differences and degrees within that category. For example, someone can admit that only citizens can serve as jurors and deny that further differences among citizens (e.g., immigrants vs. natives) are relevant for jury service.[8] Similarly, there is no logical inconsistency when critics of PDE believe that only voluntary actions can be morally right or wrong and deny that further differences among voluntary actions are relevant for moral judgments. To use an analogy more relevant to debates about PDE, suppose that the police pull me over for speeding. Arguing that the speed limit was not posted or that my car malfunctioned might persuade the police not to give me a speeding ticket because these excuses mean that I did not voluntarily break the speed limit. Suppose, however, that I say to the police, "I was running the engine harder to warm up the car. My speeding was a foreseen side effect." If the police did not laugh in my face, a reply could be "If you were voluntarily speeding, it doesn't matter what you intended." Similarly, someone can say that actions must be voluntary to be morally right or wrong and then deny that the difference between intention and foresight is relevant for judging voluntary actions.

The example about speeding and a driver's intention illustrates a basic disagreement about the purpose of moral rules. The point of most traffic laws is to keep drivers from hurting other people, so the driver's intention is usually irrelevant. (Laws about wearing seat belts may be exceptions.) Philosophers who see moral rules as akin to traffic laws will see no relevant distinction between intended effects and foreseen side effects. Instead of treating moral rules as analogous to traffic laws, I treat moral rules as analogous to a parent's rules. Some rules direct people toward what is good for themselves, not only what is owed to others.

In the following sections I criticize other justifications of PDE that rely on intuitions, exceptionless moral rules, and phenomenological descriptions of intending evil. At first these criticisms might seem unnecessary. Why would I not accept allies wherever I can find them? The problem is that these other justifications leave PDE vulnerable to objections. One objection is that proponents of PDE have no good way to define intended effects. Another objection is that intentions are relevant for judging only agents, not actions. Another objection is that people accept PDE only as a rationalization of unreliable emotional responses to harmful actions. Proponents of PDE cannot overcome these objections unless they base PDE in a view of morality that treats the agent's character as relevant for judging actions, a view that I have labeled the Socratic view.

Intuitive Justifications of PDE

Some proponents of PDE rely on pairs of cases that are designed to elicit different moral intuitions even though they cause similar effects.[9] I already have presented several examples:

- Targeting innocent people versus bombing a weapons factory and killing innocent people as a foreseen side effect
- Torturing an enemy soldier versus attacking a military target and causing an enemy soldier's pain as a foreseen side effect
- Withholding medical care to kill a potential organ donor versus rationing a scarce drug to save several patients instead of one
- Committing suicide so that children can collect on an insurance policy versus causing one's own death as a foreseen side effect of running into a burning building to save children
- Intending to embarrass an opponent versus causing an opponent's embarrassment as a foreseen side effect of playing a game well
- Lying versus telling the truth and causing a false belief as a foreseen side effect
- Plagiarizing versus knowingly causing people to attribute another person's ideas to oneself
- Choosing a toy to incite a sibling's envy versus choosing a toy to have fun and causing a sibling's envy as a foreseen side effect

For an adult version of the cases of inciting envy, consider the following pair:

- A man goes to a party and sees that his ex-girlfriend is one of the guests. The man hears that the bar is running out of Cabernet, his ex-girlfriend's favorite drink. The man goes to the bar and orders Cabernet so that his ex-girlfriend will not be able to enjoy it.
- A woman goes to a party and sees that her ex-boyfriend is one of the guests. She decides that she needs something stiffer than her customary glass of wine, so she orders a Scotch, which happens to be her ex-boyfriend's favorite drink. The bartender says there is only enough Scotch for one serving. The woman wants the Scotch, so she decides to order it anyway, foreseeing but not intending that her ex-boyfriend will not enjoy his favorite drink.

In this pair of cases, the first agent intends a bad effect and seems to act wrongly, or at least rudely, while the second agent foresees the same effect and seems to act rightly.

These cases illustrate why many people find PDE intuitively appealing, and the last few cases show that this intuitive appeal does not depend on unusual cases of life and death, but intuitions alone cannot provide a sound basis for PDE. One problem with relying on intuitions is that critics can simply deny the intuitions that support PDE. Another problem is that proponents of PDE who rely on intuitions have no principle by which to define intended effects. People use "intention" and its cognates in different senses. (Some uses puzzle me, as when I hear that my university will create "intentional experiences" for students.) For example, people sometimes use "intention" to refer only to their end, as when a jogger says, "I am not running for fun. My intention is to stay in shape, not to run." They also use "intention" to include their end and their means, as when a jogger says, "I intend to run because I intend to stay in shape." They even use cognates of "intention" to include side effects, as when a jogger says, "I know that running is hard on my knees, but I am intentionally wearing out my knees because I need to stay in shape." The jogger presumably sees worn-out knees as an unwelcome side effect of jogging, so this use of "intentionally" indicates that the jogger did not accidentally or unknowingly risk a knee injury. Each of the three statements makes sense in context, but each uses a different sense of intention. No version of PDE can include every sense in which English speakers use "intention" and its cognates. To know which sense of intention is relevant for judging actions, proponents of PDE must explain why the distinction between intention and foresight is relevant in the first place. They cannot do so if they rely entirely on intuitions.

I do not deny that appeals to intuitions have a place in moral philosophy. When I was a graduate student, I may have succumbed to the illusion that philosophers can set aside all of their intuitions, develop a moral theory, and apply the theory to specific cases.[10] I no longer hold this view. Intuitions that contradict a moral theory can be mistaken, but they also can reveal a truth that the theory ignores. If a moral theory told me that I might steal lunches from children and torture small animals with impunity, then I would have good reason to doubt the theory. Even if moral philosophers cannot set aside all their intuitions, they should not assume that their intuitions are correct. A principle that seems intuitively plausible in one case might seem implausible in other cases, and even a coherent set of intuitions can arise from a basic error. To provide a sound basis for PDE, its proponents must find the basis of the intuitions that make PDE seem plausible.

ABSOLUTIST JUSTIFICATIONS OF PDE

Instead of relying on intuitions, some proponents of PDE rely on moral absolutism—that is, the belief that some moral rules are exceptionless. I use "exceptionless rule" and "moral absolute" interchangeably. If the labels "absolute" and "absolutism" were not so common, I would not use them at all. One problem with the label "absolute" is that it also describes Platonic forms that exist separately from the things that participate in them, so calling a rule a "moral absolute" seems to separate the rule from what is good for human beings. Another problem with the label "absolute" is that absolutism can be defined as the political theory that the sovereign has unlimited authority, so describing moral rules as "absolute" portrays the rules as decrees that subjects must obey on the basis of authority, not reason.[11] Unsurprisingly, then, one critic of PDE alleges that "a normal person" who accepts a moral absolute "must either have failed to see what it involves or be passively and unquestionably obedient to an authority."[12] Another problem with the label "absolute" is that it obscures the difference between *universal* rules and *exceptionless* rules. The rule "Do not get between a mother bear and her cubs" is good advice in all cultures. The bear does not care whether the potential threat to her cubs is a contemporary American philosopher or a medieval Japanese farmer. Despite being universal, this rule still has exceptions, such as when someone needs to rescue a child who has wandered between a mother bear and her cubs. I avoid this ambiguity by describing rules as exceptionless, not absolute.

According to some proponents of PDE, exceptionless moral rules, such as the rules against murder and torture, make sense only if they refer to intended effects, not to foreseen side effects. Suppose that the rule against murder prohibited any action that results in an innocent person's death, even as a side effect. If I could stop a woman from murdering other people only by murdering the woman's children myself, then I could not avoid breaking the rule. Similarly, suppose that the rule against torture prohibited any action that causes severe pain. If I could stop a man from torturing other people only by torturing the man's children myself, then I could not avoid breaking the rule. Thus, the argument goes, these exceptionless moral rules make no sense without PDE.[13] My defense of PDE neither assumes nor denies the existence of exceptionless moral rules. Even if some moral rules are exceptionless, an absolutist justification of PDE faces four problems.

One problem with absolutist justifications of PDE is that an absolutist must explain why intending death is always wrong even though knowingly causing death is sometimes right. Why make exceptions to the rule against causing death but not to the rule against intending death? Some proponents of PDE avoid this question by denying moral absolutism.[14] According to these versions of PDE, intending death is harder to justify than knowingly causing death, but intending death is not always wrong. The existence of exceptionless moral rules is controversial, so an absolutist justification of PDE merely swaps one disputed point for another.

A second problem with absolutist justifications of PDE is that they depend on the premise that there are no moral dilemmas, or situations in which people cannot avoid acting wrongly. I accept this premise, but other philosophers treat alleged moral dilemmas as a basic fact that a moral theory needs to explain, not as evidence that a moral theory is inconsistent.[15] Again, using PDE to explain the impossibility of moral dilemmas swaps one disputed point for another.

A third problem with an absolutist justification of PDE is that an absolutist does not need PDE to make sense of exceptionless moral rules without believing in moral dilemmas. Instead of distinguishing between *intending* bad effects and *foreseeing* bad effects, an absolutist can distinguish between *doing* something that causes bad effects and *allowing* the bad effects to occur.[16] For example, an absolutist could say that the rule against murder forbids doing something that kills innocent people but does not forbid allowing innocent people to die. According to this absolutist defense of PDE, I can always avoid doing something that kills a person or causes suffering even if I cannot always avoid allowing a person to die or suffer. If I refuse to murder in order to stop a murderer, I allow the victims to die, but I do not kill them. If I refuse to torture in order to stop a torturer, I allow the victims to be tortured, but I do not torture them. I have doubts that the difference between doing and allowing is relevant for judging actions, but the relevant point is that an absolutist can rely on this difference to avoid the conclusion that some agents cannot avoid acting wrongly.[17]

A fourth problem with absolutist justifications of PDE, which I regard as the most serious, is that they do not explain why an agent's intention is relevant in cases that do not fall under exceptionless rules. For example, the rule against intending to run up a score has exceptions. The margin of a victory can break a tie in the standings, and an opponent might deserve a comeuppance. An absolutist version of PDE cannot distinguish between a coach who intends a lopsided score and a coach who causes the lopsided score as a foreseen side effect of playing well.

For another example of cases in which an agent's intention is relevant even though exceptionless rules do not apply, consider a pair of cases of causing pain:

- A mother and son are walking down the street when a pickpocket snatches the mother's purse. The pickpocket threatens to keep the purse unless the woman makes her son cry. The mother pushes her son so that he bumps into a parked car, feels pain, and cries.
- A father and daughter are walking through a narrow hallway when a pickpocket snatches the father's wallet. The father starts to chase him, but his daughter is blocking the hallway, so he pushes her out of the way. The hallway is narrow, so the father foresees that his daughter will hit the wall, feel pain, and cry.

The mother intends her son's pain, but the father foresees his daughter's pain as a result of clearing a path to chase the pickpocket. PDE explains why the mother's action seems wrong, or at least less clearly right than the father's action, even though neither parent violates an exceptionless rule. If the rule against intending pain were exceptionless, then physicians would act wrongly when they intend to cause a patient's pain to diagnose an injury.

An absolutist could try to modify the rule against intending pain so that it prohibits the mother's action and permits the father's. Even with a modified rule against intending pain, an absolutist proponent of PDE cannot explain why the cases of causing pain seem similar to a pair of cases about revealing confidential information:

- On the first day of class, a professor sees a student who earned a low grade in another course. To make other students laugh, the professor says, "It's good to see you again. I hope this course goes better than the other one."
- After a semester ends, several students in a course appeal their grades. The students falsely claim that the class average was a D as evidence that the course was too hard. To respond, the professor reports the correct average, foreseeing that the students will pool their information and figure out that another student in the class earned a low grade.

The first professor intends to reveal a student's low grade as a means of amusing other students. The second professor foresees that a student's low grade will be revealed as a side effect of responding to a grade appeal. Assuming that neither professor breaks an exception-less rule, an absolutist version of PDE cannot distinguish these cases. A rule against intending to reveal some information (e.g., secrets from a confessional) might be exceptionless, but it seems implausible to say that a professor *never* may intend to reveal a student's grade. If someone holds a teacher at gunpoint to learn a student's quiz grade, the teacher does not have a duty to die rather than divulge the secret, and the teacher will not act unjustly toward the student whose quiz grade is revealed.

To summarize, I have used three pairs of cases to challenge absolutist justifications of PDE, or justifications that refer to exceptionless rules to explain why the distinction between intention and foresight is relevant for judging actions:

- Intending to run up the score versus causing a lopsided score as a foreseen side effect of playing well
- Intending pain versus causing pain as a foreseen side effect
- Intending to reveal confidential information versus causing confidential information to be revealed as a side effect of defending oneself against false charges

If the distinction between intention and foresight were morally relevant only because the distinction was necessary for the intelligibility of exceptionless moral rules, then proponents of PDE could not explain why these pairs of cases have a structure similar to other applications of PDE in which exceptionless moral rules are relevant, such as the cases of terror and strategic bombings. PDE becomes too narrow when its proponents tether it to exceptionless moral rules. Someone can disagree with moral absolutism and still recognize that the distinction between intended effects and foreseen side effects is morally relevant.

I have argued that PDE does not depend on absolutism, but PDE and absolutism have a common source. To see why, consider the following case from Bernard Williams:

> Jim is a botanist who wanders into a South American village and finds twenty prisoners lined up against a wall and about to be

executed. The captain in charge informs Jim that the twenty people have been chosen randomly and are scheduled to be executed as a means of deterring future protests. The captain also says that, as an honored guest, Jim has the option of killing one prisoner. If Jim kills one, the others will be set free. If Jim refuses, then all twenty will be killed. All the prisoners beg Jim to accept the offer.[18]

Williams uses this case to criticize utilitarianism, but it also challenges moral absolutism. Someone does not need to accept utilitarianism to say that, all things equal, an action that kills one person is better than an action that results in that death plus nineteen more. In this case, however, all things are not equal. If Jim refuses to murder one person, the executioners, not Jim, will kill twenty people. If Jim accepts the offer, then he will be the one who kills the prisoner. (I assume that Jim must ensure that the prisoner dies, not merely that the prisoner is shot.) An absolutist cannot explain the rule against murder by considering the harm to the prisoners. An absolutist must say something about *Jim*. I do not attempt to prove that absolutism is true, that the rule against murder is exceptionless, or even that Jim may not shoot the prisoner. My point here is merely to explain the relation between absolutism and PDE. Both views arise from the belief that morality includes considerations about agents, not only about what agents owe to other people.

Critics of PDE might ask, "If PDE does not depend on theological premises, then why did it develop in the Catholic tradition?" The examples of Thomas Nagel and Philippa Foot show that being Catholic is not a necessary condition of accepting PDE, but *something* must explain the close relation between PDE and the Catholic tradition. My hypothesis is that the Catholic tradition includes many teachings about the importance of the human person, so being Catholic disposes people to accept a view of morality that includes considerations about agents. The examples of Socrates and Aristotle show that people do not need to be Catholic to accept this view of morality, so the close relation between PDE and the Catholic tradition is neither a historical accident nor evidence that PDE depends on theological premises.

In his widely discussed defense of PDE, Thomas Nagel uses a case of twisting a child's arm to prevent worse harms. I present the case in Nagel's words:

> You have an auto accident one winter night on a lonely road. The other passengers are badly injured, the car is out of commission, and the road is deserted, so you run along it till you find an isolated house. The house turns out to be occupied by an old woman who is looking after her small grandchild. There is no phone, but there is a car in the garage, and you ask desperately to borrow it and explain the situation. She doesn't believe you. Terrified by your desperation, she runs upstairs and locks herself in the bathroom, leaving you alone with the child. You pound ineffectively on the door and search without success for the car keys. Then it occurs to you that she might be persuaded to tell you where they are if you were to twist the child's arm outside the bathroom door. Should you do it?[19]

At first Nagel assumes only that the case is hard, not that twisting the child's arm must be wrong. That the case is hard entails that reasons against intending harm are stronger than reasons against knowingly causing harm. Otherwise, the driver *obviously* should twist the child's arm, since the child's twisted arm would be less serious than accident victims' injuries.

Initially it might seem that Nagel's case illustrates the distinction between doing and allowing, not the distinction between intending and foreseeing. If the driver twists the child's arm, the driver *does* something harmful; if the driver does not twist the child's arm, the driver *allows* the accident victims in the car to suffer harm. Nagel notes, however, that allowing someone else to twist the child's arm seems to be just as wrong as twisting the child's arm oneself, so he treats this case as an illustration of the distinction between intending and foreseeing, not as an illustration of the difference between doing and allowing.[20] Someone could claim that the driver who allows someone to twist the child's arm wrongly cooperates in the other person's wrongdoing. I agree, but a rule against cooperation in wrongdoing does not handle another variation of Nagel's case. Suppose that the grandmother in Nagel's story knocks over a bookshelf while she runs into the bathroom. The bookshelf falls on the child's arm, and the child screams in pain. The driver considers lifting the bookshelf but then realizes that the child's screams might persuade the woman to say where the keys are. Allowing the child to suffer seems morally similar to twisting the child's arm, so the question "Should you allow the child to scream in pain?" seems as difficult as "Should you twist the child's arm?"

To explain why the driver may not twist the child's arm, Nagel argues that someone who intends evil swims "head-on against the normative current" because people should treat evil as repellent, not as something to be pursued, even as a means to a good end.[21] Nagel's metaphor about swimming against the normative current does not make his argument metaphorical, as some critics allege.[22] He continues without the metaphor:

> If you twist the child's arm, your aim is to produce pain. So when the child cries, "Stop, it hurts!" his objection corresponds in perfect diametrical opposition to your intention. What he is pleading as your reason to stop is precisely your reason to go on. . . . What feels peculiarly wrong about doing evil intentionally even that good may come of it is the headlong striving against value that is internal to one's aim.[23]

Nagel clearly explains why intending pain feels worse than causing pain as a side effect, but critics of PDE can dismiss these negative feelings as irrelevant. For example, critics could agree that twisting the child's arm feels wrong but still insist that the driver should set aside qualms about twisting the child's arm and do what it takes to help the accident victims in the car. Nagel anticipates this challenge: "The immediacy of the fact that you must try to produce evil as a subsidiary aim is phenomenologically important, but why should it be morally important?"[24]

To answer this question, Nagel contrasts two perspectives: the agent's perspective and the impersonal perspective of the world in which the action occurs. From the agent's perspective, intending evil feels worse than foreseeing evil. From an impersonal perspective, the difference seems irrelevant. Nagel concludes that "it does not seem irrational" to evaluate actions from the agent's perspective, which includes the intuition that intending evil is worse than allowing evil.[25] Critics can see Nagel's intuition about intending evil as *mistaken* even if they do not see his intuition as *irrational*. For example, some critics have argued that intending evil feels bad because it usually makes the world worse.[26] According to this argument, people form their moral intuitions in usual cases, but these intuitions are not reliable in unusual cases, such as when twisting a child's arm can prevent even greater suffering. If this argument were correct, the intuition about intending evil would be similar to a paramedic's aversion to cracking ribs. When a patient with frail ribs needs CPR, paramedics should set their feelings aside and do what is necessary to save the patient. Similarly, a critic of PDE could claim that people should set aside intuitions about twisting the child's arm and do what is necessary to save the accident victims. According to this objection, intuitions about intending evil make sense from the agent's perspective, but someone should set aside this perspective to determine what is right or wrong.

To explain why the agent's perspective is relevant for judging actions, I have defended the Socratic view of morality, which says that agents can act wrongly by corrupting their own character, not only by mistreating others. Nagel, however, assumes that "moral requirements have their source in the claims of other persons."[27] Because he makes this assumption, he can explain why people have intuitions that support PDE, but he cannot justify these intuitions. A critic can agree that intended evils seem worse than foreseen evils when people consider the actions from an agent's' perspective, but then ask, "So what? Why treat this perspective as relevant for judging actions?" I see no answer if moral requirements have their source in other people's interests. Given this assumption about moral requirements, thinking about the agent's perspective looks like a distraction from doing what morality requires. To explain why the agent's perspective is relevant for judging actions, proponents of PDE must appeal to the agent, not the interests of other people.

I have argued that the distinction between intention and foresight is relevant for judging actions because people can act wrongly by corrupting their own character and because intending an effect can corrupt someone even if knowingly causing the effect does not. Assuming that the distinction between intention and foresight is relevant, another question is "How do you define intended effects and foreseen side effects?" To answer this question, the next chapter defines intended effects in a way that fits an agent-based justification of PDE.

Chapter Two

An Agent-Based Definition
of Intended Effects

Many proponents of PDE stumble when they try to distinguish intended effects from foreseen side effects. To see why, consider a famous case from Philippa Foot:

- A massive man gets stuck in the only exit from an underground cave, which traps the other explorers in his group. Water starts to fill the cave, so the explorers use dynamite to blast the massive man out of the exit so that they can escape.[1]

I replace Foot's "fat man" with "massive man" to use a more polite label and to emphasize that the mass of the man's body, not his being alive, endangers the explorers—a point that I emphasize later when I discuss other cases that involve the mass of someone's body. Further, whether the man is fat is irrelevant; a massive but lean bodybuilder would cause the same problem for the explorers as a fat man. According to Foot, it would be "ridiculous" for the explorers to say that they intend to blast the man out of the cave but not to kill him. She asserts that the man's death follows the action so closely that the explorers must intend his death. She adds, however, that PDE's proponents will have a hard time explaining exactly how closely two effects must be connected so that an agent cannot intend one without intending the other.[2] According to Foot's objection, any definition of intended effects will be either *absurd* or *arbitrary*: absurd if it excludes the massive man's death or arbitrary if it appeals to closeness. This apparent dilemma does not arise only from Foot's contrived case about a flooding cave. Foot designs the cave case to resemble the craniotomy case, in which obstructed labor threatens a woman's life and surgeons can save her only by collapsing the fetus's skull. Ectopic pregnancies also provide real examples of cases in which the location of someone's body threatens another person's life. I discuss these cases at length later.

Some proponents of PDE respond to the problem by refining definitions of "closeness." I take a different approach by defending the allegedly ridiculous conclusion that the explorers can intend to blast the massive man out of the cave exit without intending his death. In the first section of this chapter I propose three criteria for a good definition of intended effects. The definition should be (1) morally neutral, so that people determine what an agent intends before they judge the action, (2) applicable to children's actions, so that the definition is not too narrow, and (3) intelligible to nonphilosophers, so that people do not need expertise in metaphysics or action theory to know what they intend. In the second section I argue that an agent intends an effect if and only if it is part of an honest and complete answer to the question "What is the agent's goal, and what are all the steps in the agent's plan to achieve that goal?" In the third section I criticize proponents of PDE who respond to the (alleged) problem of closeness by trying to define "closeness" more precisely. These appeals to closeness necessarily fall to counterexamples because they classify some effects as intended even when the agent sees the effects as irrelevant or even when the agent works against them. Another problem with appeals to closeness is that they obscure the agent's perspective, which undermines the basis of PDE. In the fourth section I respond to proponents of PDE who define intended effects as all the effects that are the agent's reasons for acting. This definition is too broad in some cases and too narrow in others. More importantly, this definition exposes PDE to the objection that intentions must be irrelevant for judging actions because people cannot control their intentions. In the fifth section I consider empirical studies about how people classify intentions. Some critics of PDE cite these studies as evidence that PDE merely rationalizes people's moral judgments because subjects in the studies seem to classify bad effects as intended when they disapprove of the action and as side effects when they approve of the action. I explain why these studies do not rule out a morally neutral definition of intended effects.

For now, my only goal is to distinguish intended effects from foreseen side effects in the way that is relevant for PDE. I do not try to develop a general theory of intentional actions or to answer basic questions about action theory, such as whether intentions are identical to brain processes and whether intentions are reducible to beliefs and desires.

Three Criteria for a Definition of Intended Effects

For now I set aside the case of the massive man in the cave and focus on cases in which the agent's intention seems clearer. Recall the cases of a bomber pilot who targets innocent people and a bomber pilot who targets a weapons factory. A proponent of PDE can say, "The bombings are morally distinct because only the first pilot intends death. The second pilot foresees death as a side effect of destroying the factory." This response fits common intuitions, but if proponents of PDE "backsolve" from the intuition that an action is wrong to the premise that the agent intends death, PDE becomes merely a fig leaf over intuitions.[3] Proponents of PDE need to define what a specific agent intends *before* they judge an action. In other words, they need a morally neutral definition of intended effects.

When I argue that a definition of intended effects should be morally neutral, I do not rule out thinking about morality when deciding which sense of intended effects is relevant for moral judgments. In the bombing cases, someone could say that neither pilot intends death as an end, unlike a serial killer who kills with no further end in mind. Someone could also say that both pilots intentionally kill innocent people, unlike a clumsy pilot who misses a target and accidentally kills innocent people or a misinformed pilot who unknowingly kills innocent people. Someone could also say that only the pilot who targets the hospital intends the deaths of innocent people as a means. All three claims about the pilots' intentions are true in some sense, but which sense is the one relevant for PDE? To answer this question, proponents of PDE can think about what is morally relevant without presupposing any judgment about specific cases in which the agent's intention is unclear.

Besides being morally neutral, a definition of intended effects should apply to children's actions. PDE applies to children and adults, so a definition of intended effects should do so as well. Some philosophers, however, define intended effects in a way that excludes children's actions. For example, one philosopher asserts: "For it is inadmissible to say that one intends to put a bullet through a man, stab him, crush him, or blow him to atoms but does not intend to harm him."[4] In fact, a child who has no concept of death can still intend to shoot, stab, or crush someone (a good reason to keep children from playing with guns, knives, and heavy machines). Similarly, a child who has watched too many cartoons might believe that someone can be reassembled after being blown to bits (a good reason to keep children from playing with explosives).

Someone could try to sidestep these counterexamples by stipulating that a definition of intended effects applies only to adults. This definition does not accurately describe the relevant phenomena. A five-year-old who has only a dim idea of death and a limited ability to plan for the future cannot intend to kill a person in the same way that a normal adult can, but a five-year-old can intend some effects the same way that adults do. I see no difference between my intending to eat ice cream when I was five and my intending to eat ice cream now. Any differences between the adult and the child who intend to eat ice cream lie in their knowledge and beliefs, not in their intentions. I might know more about how ice cream is made than I did as a child, and I might be able to make more detailed plans about how to get ice cream, but when I put the spoon in the bowl, the statement "He intends to eat ice cream" means the same thing now that it meant when I was five. To insist that only an adult can fully intend to eat ice cream or that children intend to eat ice cream only in an analogous way would draw a distinction where none exists. Besides drawing unnecessary distinctions, an "adults-only" definition of intended effects obscures some necessary distinctions. For example, such a definition cannot distinguish a child's choosing a toy to incite a sibling's envy and choosing a toy to have fun while foreseeing the sibling's envy. The relevant difference between these two actions is the same as the relevant difference between the action of an adult's ordering a drink to keep it away from someone else and ordering a drink to enjoy it while foreseeing that someone else will not have it. Like adults, children can intend or foresee an effect, so a definition of intended effects should not exclude their actions.

Why do many philosophers define intended effects in a way that applies only to adults? One hypothesis, which is not essential to my defense of PDE, is that Michael Bratman's planning view of intention focuses on intentions about the future. In his influential *Intentions, Plans, and Practical Reason*, Bratman treats intentions about the future as the central case of intentions.[5] Bratman's focus on future-directed intentions fits his project of distinguishing intentions from beliefs and desires, but it does not fit applications of PDE. To determine what an agent intends, someone needs to consider the intention at the time of the action. Children cannot plan for the future as adults can, but they can intend effects in the sense that is relevant for PDE.

Besides being morally neutral and applicable to children's actions, a definition of intended effects should be accessible to nonphilosophers. Explaining why murder is wrong might require subtle arguments, but a definition of intended effects should not be so esoteric that only philosophers can know whether they are guilty of murder. Consider three proposed principles for distinguishing between intended effects and foreseen side effects:

- If x and y are descriptions that pick out events, then if x and y occupy the exact same spatiotemporal coordinates, x and y pick out the same events.[6]
- The relation between the intended means and the harm in question is "too close" to allow for application of the intend/foresee

distinction when the relation between the relevant states of affairs is a constitutive one rather than a merely causal one.[7]

- If one exercises a basic power P in circumstances such that one who exercises P in those circumstances normally knows that the occurrence of C is an essential constituent of that exercise of P, then one intends to bring about C, even if one does not plan to do so. . . . An essential constituent of the exercise of a power is a normal part or aspect of the exercise of that power.[8]

If these principles were true, people could not know their own intentions without understanding concepts such as constitutive relations, spatiotemporal coordinates, and basic powers.

I do not reject any definition of intended effects *only* because it includes concepts unfamiliar to nonphilosophers. Like other baroque definitions of intended effects, the three principles quoted earlier face counterexamples. For example, suppose that a chess master is teaching a student. The student moves a pawn diagonally, which captures the master's piece and opens a file for the student's rook. The master asks, "Did you intend only to take my piece, or did you also intend to open a file?" This question makes sense, but someone who accepts one of the three principles quoted earlier cannot distinguish between the player who intends to open a file and the player who intends only to capture a piece and does not care about the open file. Taking a piece with a pawn and opening a file occupy the same spatiotemporal coordinates, taking a piece with a pawn constitutes opening a file, and a chess player normally knows that opening a file is a normal part or aspect of taking a piece with a pawn. Still, a chess player can intend to take the piece without intending to open the file.

Appeals to observable causal relations entail that effects are intended when the agent regards them as irrelevant, and even when the agent actively works against them. For example, suppose that a man with a severe speech impediment decides to testify as a witness at his father's murder trial, even though the man knows that he will stutter while he testifies and that his stuttering will make his testimony sound less persuasive to jurors.[9] The man's testimony and his stuttered words are as closely related as two effects can be because the testimony consists entirely of the stuttered words, but the man does not intend to stutter. On the contrary, he does his best *not* to stutter, despite knowing that his best efforts are bound to fail.

An Agent-Based or "Strict" Definition of Intended Effects

I begin my definition of intended effects by saying that an agent intends an effect if and only if it is part of an honest and complete answer to the question "What is the agent's goal, and what are all the steps in the agent's plan to achieve that goal?" To answer this question, the relevant plan is the one that guides the agent at the time of the action. Suppose that someone plans to rob a bank with no bloodshed but a customer recognizes the robber. The robber then shoots the potential witness to avoid prison. One critic sees this case as a problem because the robber intends to kill the customer despite not planning to do so.[10] I see no problem because plans can change. The robber rejects the original plan for a bloodless robbery and adopts a new plan that includes the customer's death.

I would create a vicious circle if I defined intended effects in terms of the agent's plan and then defined the agent's plan in terms of intended effects. To avoid circularity, I define intended effects more precisely as follows: Agents intend an effect if and only if the effect is their end or is part of their plan to achieve their end—that is, if and only if they seek the effect for its own sake or believe that it is part of the chain of causes and effects that promotes their end in a way that makes the action worthwhile. This definition has been labeled "strict."[11] "Narrow" and "precise" would work, too, but "strict" is already in use, so I use that label.

The final clause of this definition does not use "worthwhile" in a technical way, so to say that agents see an action as worthwhile means that they see the action as being a viable option among other possible actions. To illustrate this final clause, consider two cases in which two chains of causes and effects promote the agent's end:

- A woman and her friend are the final candidates for a job. The interviewer asks the woman, "What are some of your strengths?"

The ability to learn languages is one qualification for the job, so she mentions her fluency in Basque, Swahili, and Kyrgyz. She knows that her answer will remind the interviewer that her friend failed Spanish and French in college.

- A father is playing chess against his seven-year-old daughter. He captures her rook to gain a decisive material advantage. He knows that she will start crying and lose focus, giving him a decisive psychological advantage.

In these cases, it makes sense to ask, "Did you intend to remind your interviewer that your friend failed Spanish and French?" or "Did you intend to make your daughter cry?" These questions would make no sense if agents intended every effect that promotes their end. According to my definition of intended effects, whether the woman intends to remind the interviewers of her friend's linguistic shortcomings and whether the father intends to drive his daughter to tears depends on whether the woman or the father believes that the effect in question makes the action worthwhile. If the woman thinks something like "This answer will make my friend look bad, but I'll set that point aside," then she intends only to emphasize her linguistic skills, not to make her friend look bad. If the father thinks, "Taking the rook will make her cry, but I would be a poor sport if I tried to make her cry; but taking the rook really is the best move here, and I promised her that I would play my best and not let her win," then the father intends only to capture the rook, not to make his daughter cry. If, however, the woman thinks something like "I should take the chance to make my friend look bad," then she does intend to draw the interviewer's attention to her friend's failure. If the father thinks "I'm not sure that taking the rook is correct, but I know that it will drive her to tears, so that's what I'll do," then he does intend his daughter's crying.

What does my strict definition of intended effects say about the bombing cases? In the first bombing case (fig. 2.1), the deaths of innocent people do belong to the chain of causes and effects that includes the pilot's end of demoralizing the enemy. In the second bombing case (fig. 2.2), the deaths of innocent people belong to a chain of causes and effects that diverges from the one that promotes the pilot's end of weakening the enemy's military. Only the first pilot intends to kill

Figure 2.1. The terror bomber's intention

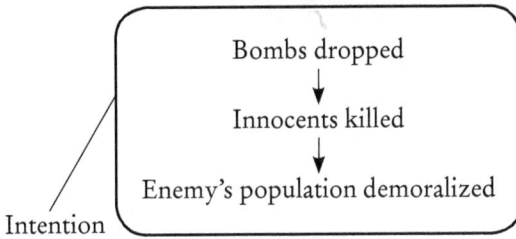

Figure 2.2. The strategic bomber's intention

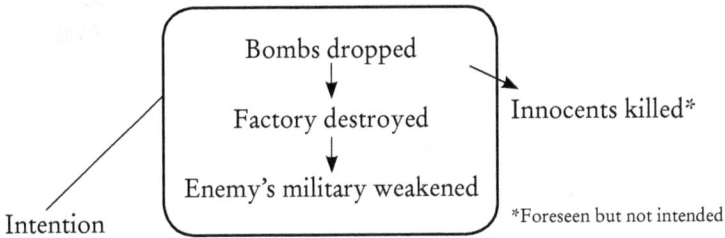

innocent people. The second pilot knows that dropping the bombs will kill them, but their deaths are not part of the chain of causes and effects that promotes the pilot's end of weakening the enemy.

I refer to the first pilot as a terror bomber and the second pilot as a strategic bomber, but I do not mean to excuse so-called strategic bombings that are designed to kill innocent people as a means of weakening the enemy's morale. In the latter case, the label "strategic bomber" is merely a euphemism for a terror bomber.[12] The difference between strategic bombings (e.g., bombing a weapons factory), which are designed to weaken an enemy over the long term, and tactical bombings (e.g., bombing a column of enemy tanks), which are designed to weaken the enemy immediately, is not relevant for my defense of PDE.

To clarify the strict definition of intended effects, suppose that dropping bombs on the factory starts two chains of causes and effects (fig. 2.3) and that each chain is sufficient for the enemy's surrender.[13] To determine whether the pilot in this case intends to kill innocent

Figure 2.3. The case of the overdetermined surrender

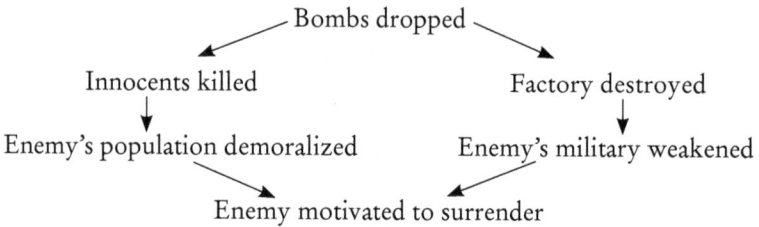

Bombs dropped

Innocents killed → Factory destroyed

Enemy's population demoralized → Enemy's military weakened

Enemy motivated to surrender

people, the relevant question is "Does the pilot believe that killing innocent people and demoralizing the enemy are needed to make the action worthwhile?" If the answer is yes, then the pilot intends both the deaths of innocent people and the factory's destruction. If the answer is no—for example, if the pilot thinks, "Dropping the bombs will kill the civilians and weaken the enemy's morale, but I'll set that point aside because targeting civilians is wrong"—then the pilot does not intend the deaths, even though the pilot believes that the deaths will force the enemy to surrender.[14]

By noting two possible intentions (fig. 2.4), I do not mean that the pilot chooses an action and then chooses an intention. The intention is fixed when the pilot chooses an action. The relevant point is what the pilot considers while deliberating about the bombing, not what the pilot says about the action later. If the pilot decides to bomb in order to kill the civilians instead of setting aside their deaths, no rationalizing after the bombing will change what the pilot intends.

My definition of intended effects fits my agent-based justification of PDE, which says that the difference between intended effects and foreseen side effects is relevant because intention and foresight form the agent's character differently. PDE's proponents cut this link between intended effects and the agent's character when they define intended effects from an observer's perspective. If my definition of intended effects is correct, then an observer cannot determine what an agent intends by looking at an action from the outside and analyzing causal relations among the action's effects. I see this conclusion as a virtue, not a defect. The conclusion that an observer cannot analyze causal relations to determine what an agent intends should

Figure 2.4. Two possible intentions in the case of the overdetermined surrender

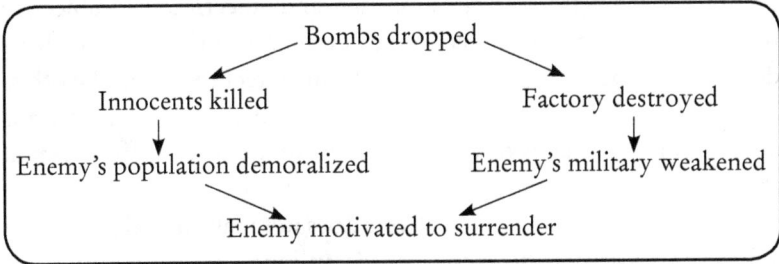

Intention that includes the deaths of innocent people

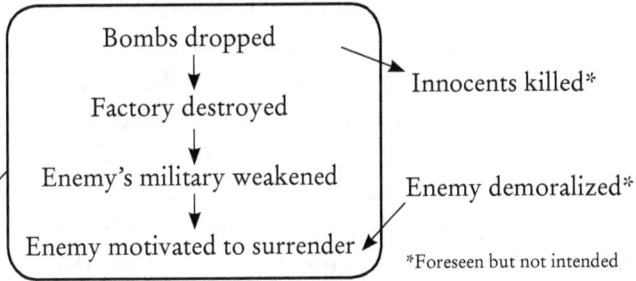

Intention that does not include the deaths of innocent people

be no more surprising than the conclusion that an observer cannot analyze logical relations to determine what a person knows. Oedipus knows that he married Jocasta, and Jocasta is in fact his mother, but he does not know that he married his mother. A logic student might know that "if P, then Q" is true without knowing that "if not Q, then not P" necessarily follows. (Teaching logic would be much easier if students knew all the conclusions that follow from the propositions that they know.) Whether a person knows a proposition is subjective, in the sense that a person can fail to know a proposition that necessarily follows from a proposition that the person knows, but there is a truth of the matter as to whether a person knows something, even if the person lies or pretends not to know. For example, a student who knows a logical truth might feign ignorance about modus tollens to avoid looking smarter than other students. Similarly, whether an agent intends an effect is both subjective and objective. It is subjective because a close causal connection, or even an identity, of two effects does not compel an agent who intends one effect to intend the other. Still, whether an agent intends an effect is objective because there is a truth of the matter as to whether the agent intends an effect, even if the agent pretends otherwise.

My definition of intended effects does not make moral judgments subjective. Whether the agent intends an innocent person's death is one question; whether murder is wrong is a different question. The answer to the first question depends on the agent's perspective, but the answer to the second question does not. Thus proponents of PDE can define intended effects from the agent's perspective and still agree that some actions are wrong regardless of what the agent believes.

According to some critics, the strict definition of intended effects entails that the terror bomber does not intend to kill innocent people because the terror bomber needs only to make the victims appear dead.[15] I agree that the mere appearance of deaths would promote the terror bomber's end, but the terror bomber in this case intends to make the civilians appear dead by making them dead. I discuss more sophisticated versions of the terror bombing later, but I assume that the terror bomber in this case thinks something like "I'll drop the bombs so that innocent people will die so that the enemy will be demoralized and surrender." If the terror bomber later says, "I was only trying to make them appear dead," this attempted rationalization will not change what the bomber intended. The relevant point for my definition of intended effects is the plan that the agent follows, not what the agent or anyone else says about the plan.

My analysis of the bombing cases does not depend on asking the counterfactual question "If everything about the case were the same except that the effect did not occur, could the agent's plan still succeed?" Someone cannot answer this question without presupposing an idea of the agent's plan, so using the question to define the agent's intention would make my definition of intended effects circular. Although I do not use counterfactuals to define intended effects, answering the counterfactual question can clarify what agents intend.

For example, suppose that everything about the bombings were the same except that the innocent people somehow survived both bombings. Their survival would thwart the terror bomber's plan but not the strategic bomber's. Similarly, suppose that the innocent people died just before the bombing. Their deaths would make the terror bombing pointless, but the strategic bombing still would serve the purpose of destroying the enemy's factory. These counterfactuals confirm that only the terror bomber intends to kill innocent people.

My strict definition of intended effects fulfills all three criteria for a good definition. First, it is morally neutral. Whether the agent's plan includes an effect is one question; whether the agent acts wrongly is another. Second, it applies to children, as shown by the cases about choosing toys. Third, it does not include any concepts that require special expertise to understand. The concept of a plan is enough for a rough idea of the strict definition (i.e., the answer to the question "What is the agent's goal, and what are all the steps in the agent's plan to achieve that goal?"). The concepts of beliefs, causes, effects, and good reasons are enough for the more precise statement of the definition. Despite these virtues, many philosophers, including proponents of PDE, reject my version of the strict definition and other similar versions.

One common objection is that the strict definition is *too* strict. Critics who present this objection often rely on bluster and assertion in place of argument. They assert that an agent *clearly* intends an effect that does not satisfy the strict definition, or they say that it would be *ridiculous* to deny that the agent intends the effect. Instead of responding to every alleged counterexample, I focus on two cases that are supposed to show that the strict definition is not just mistaken but *obviously* mistaken: the case of blowing up the massive man in the cave and a case of shooting a bullet through a person.

Foot describes the view that the explorers do not intend the massive man's death as ridiculous. I agree that the explorers would say something ridiculous if they said, "We hope that the man survives being blown to bits" or "We won't be causing the man's death." Suppose, however, that the explorers say, "We need to move the man to clear the cave exit before we all drown. Our plan will work exactly the same way if he dies of natural causes or if, *per impossible*, he

Figure 2.5. The explorers' intention in the cave case

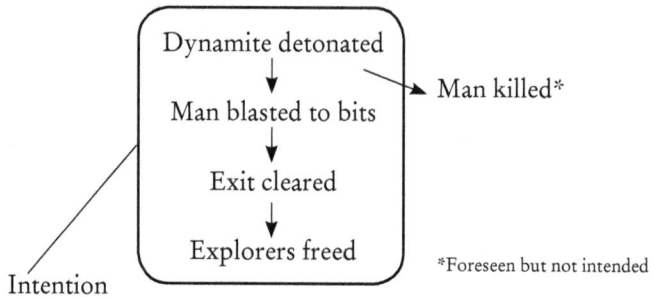

Dynamite detonated
↓
Man blasted to bits → Man killed*
↓
Exit cleared
↓
Explorers freed

Intention

*Foreseen but not intended

somehow survives being blown to bits." Critics of the strict definition need to explain exactly what is wrong with this statement from the explorers. I see nothing false, let alone ridiculous, about the claim that Foot dismisses. Blasting the man to bits will have two effects: the exit will be cleared, and the man will die. The man's death will do nothing to further the explorers' plan, so they do not intend his death. Perhaps the explorers' claim that they do not intend the man's death (fig. 2.5) seems ridiculous because people often contrast what agents intend with what they cause accidentally. As noted earlier, the explorers would say something ridiculous if they denied causing the man's death, but the strict definition entails no such claim.

The counterfactual question "If the man survives being blown to bits, could the explorers' plan still succeed?" clarifies why the explorers do not intend the massive man's death. This question might sound ridiculous because it is ridiculous to think that the man could survive. Suppose, however, that the man dies of a heart attack as the explorers set up the dynamite. One explorer says to the others, "He's already dead. How do we need to change our plan now?" The correct answer is that the explorers do not need to change their plan at all. Detonating the dynamite has exactly the same point as when the man was alive: clearing the cave exit. The man's death does not promote this end in any way, so the explorers do not intend it. For another example, suppose that the massive man tries to crawl through the exit feet first. He gets stuck so that his head is still inside the cave. He sees the rising water, has a heart attack, and loses consciousness. The explorers do not know whether he is dead. They do not bother to find out, because they realize that he will be dead in a few minutes, either from the rising water or from the dynamite. Just before the explorers detonate the dynamite, the man moves slightly. One explorer asks, "How do we need to change our plan now?" Again, the explorers do not need to change their plan at all, just as they do not need to change their plan if the man unexpectedly dies. The man's death contributes nothing to their plan, so they do not intend it.

Recall the assertion that it is "inadmissible" (not merely false) to say that someone "put a bullet through a man" without intending to harm him. Even adults can intend to shoot through someone without intending death. For example, consider two cases of bank robberies:

- A bank robber is holding the bank's guard and customers hostage. The robber says to a hostage, "Shoot the guard in the chest, or I'll kill both of you and three more hostages." To fulfill the robber's demand, the hostage shoots the guard, hoping that the bullet will miss the guard's vital organs but knowing that the bullet most likely will kill the guard.

- A sniper takes aim at a bank robber who has threatened to detonate a bomb. At the last second, a child steps in front of the robber so that the sniper cannot hit the robber without hitting the child first. Thinking that the child will die if the robber detonates the bomb, the sniper shoots through the child to hit the robber.

A definition of intended effects should distinguish these cases from that of the terror bombing, because it would make sense for the hostage to hope that the guard survives and for the sniper to hope that the child survives. It would even make sense if the hostage and the sniper tried to save the guard and the child after shooting them. For the terror bomber, however, it would make no sense to hope that the civilians survive or to try to save them after the bombing because their survival would thwart the bomber's plan to weaken the enemy's morale. To identity this distinction, proponents of PDE can say that the terror bomber intends deaths and that the hostage and the sniper knowingly cause death as a side effect. Someone could use other terms to identify this distinction—for example, saying that the terror bomber "directly" intends death while the hostage and the sniper "indirectly" or "obliquely" intend death—but the important point is that the distinction depends on the steps in the agent's plan, not on causal relations outside the agent. I believe that speaking of directness and obliqueness causes more confusion, so I say simply that the terror bomber intends death and that the hostage and the sniper do not intend death.

Some critics allege that the strict definition classifies an effect as intended only when an agent desires it for its own sake, as in the case of serial killers.[16] At one time, this objection baffled me. Suppose that a woman kills her husband to collect on a life insurance policy. I could not understand why anyone would deny that the woman needs her husband to die for her plan to work. I now see the point: his death is not the only way that she could get money, because she could win the lottery or inherit a fortune from a wealthy uncle. Outside the agent, there is no necessary connection between the man's death and his wife's having money. From the woman's perspective, however, his death is necessary because she could not get the money *as planned* without causing her husband's death. Cutting her husband's brake lines (or poisoning his food, paying a hitman, etc.) would be pointless if the action did not result in her husband's death. Other cases in which people intend death as a means are not rare at all. For example, someone might kill to

- Eliminate a rival for his or her love
- Eliminate a successor to a throne
- Obtain an inheritance
- Eliminate a witness to a crime to avoid prison
- Scare potential witnesses
- Complete a gang initiation
- Appease the gods through a ritual sacrifice
- End someone's suffering
- Avoid the responsibility of caring for an elderly parent
- Avoid the responsibility of caring for a child
- Gain sole custody of a child by killing the child's other parent
- Satisfy a morbid curiosity about how it feels to murder

I stop here, but this list is not exhaustive. Some of the cases are rare, but none of them are ridiculous. The strict definition of intended effects explains what all these agents have in common: they intend death because death is a necessary step in their plans, even if they could achieve their goals by following different plans.

As explained earlier, people can use counterfactuals to clarify what an agent intends, but they must frame the counterfactual question correctly.[17] To determine whether an agent intends an effect, the relevant question is not "Could the agent's end be achieved if the effect did not occur?" Instead, the relevant question is "Could the agent's end be achieved *according to the agent's plan* if the effect did not occur?" For example, suppose that the terror bomber does not kill any innocent people. After the bombing, an earthquake kills innocent people, and their deaths demoralize the enemy. In this case the terror bomber's end is achieved, but not in the way that the bomber planned. People who ask the relevant counterfactual question ("If the effect did not occur, could the agent's end be achieved as the agent has planned?") must have an idea of the agent's plan, so people cannot use counterfactual questions to define intended effects. I use these questions only to clarify what agents intend in specific cases.

According to one critic, I hold "that anything lying outside the intended end and the narrowly construed causal sequence leading to it is strictly unintended."[18] I do not describe the relevant causal sequence as "narrowly construed." The relevant causal sequence is as narrow or broad as the agent takes it to be. When I flush the toilet, I intend to raise the flapper and to pour water into the toilet bowl. If children do not know how a toilet works, then they do not intend this effect. Someone could say that the raised flapper is "strictly unintended" by children, but I would simply say that the children do not intend to raise the flapper. They cannot intend an effect if they have no idea what the effect is. A confused person also might believe that flushing the toilet sends an email to a plumber, who flips a switch that sends a signal to a satellite, which sends a signal to a motor in the toilet, which opens the flapper, which causes water to pour into the toilet bowl. This person would intend a broader causal sequence. Again, the strict definition of intended effects does not say that the relevant causal sequence is either broad or narrow. It says that the relevant causal sequence depends on the agent, who can understand it broadly or narrowly.

Some critics of the strict definition assert that it enables people to avoid responsibility for their actions because they can "redescribe" an action in positive terms or "gerrymander" their intentions to exclude bad effects.[19] These critics assume that their description is the correct starting point for analyzing the agent's intention, so that anyone who disagrees is redescribing the action or gerrymandering the intention. For example, I do not begin with the assumption that the cave explorers intend to kill the massive man and then redescribe their action so that an act of murder becomes something else. Instead I deny that the explorers ever intended the man's death. Similarly, when I analyze the craniotomy and other pregnancy cases, I do not begin by assuming that the surgeon intends death and then describe it in more favorable terms so that death changes from an intended effect into a foreseen side effect. Instead I deny that the surgeon intends death in the first place. By asserting that I am redescribing or gerrymandering the surgeon's intention, critics assume that people should begin with the premise that the surgeon intends death, which is exactly the point in dispute. Agents cannot change what they intend by redescribing their intentions, just as they cannot change what they foresee by redescribing their knowledge. For example, suppose that a gangster slices a potential witness's neck and says that he intended only to move a knife through a particular space, which happened to be occupied by the potential witness's neck.[20] The gangster is almost surely lying. I say "almost" because one could intend to move a knife through space, or even someone's neck, without intending death—which explains why parents do not allow children to play with knives. Presumably the gangster had no reason to move the knife through this space at this time before the gangster decided that doing so would silence the potential witness. Assuming that there was no such reason, the gangster is lying if he says, "I was curious to see what it feels like to move a knife through that specific space at that specific time, which at that moment just so happened to be occupied by the neck of someone who just so happened to be a potential witness against me." Likewise, the gangster is lying if he says, "I had no idea that slicing this person's neck would cause death." According to the strict definition of intended effects, the gangster's claim about his intention is no less false than his claim about his knowledge. The example of the gangster shows that observers can give evidence about what an agent intends that contradicts the agent's claims. The gangster might lie to others about his intention, or even delude himself to rationalize his action, but the relevant point is what he intended when he sliced the victim's neck. No matter what the gangster says, moving the knife through the space occupied by the victim's neck served no purpose apart from killing a potential witness. Someone could change the case so that the gangster sought merely to draw blood or so that the gangster was a child or an insane person who did not realize that slicing a neck would cause death, but the gangster who seeks to silence a witness intends death as a means. Nothing about the strict definition contradicts this conclusion. If anyone is guilty of redescribing or gerrymandering, it is opponents of the strict definition who use amorphous criteria about closeness or immediacy to draw a jagged line around intended effects in a way that includes some effects that play no role at all in the agent's plan.

Observers can dispute a description of what an agent intends—for example, by noting that the gangster's action would serve no purpose if it did not kill a potential witness—but the evidence available to observers is not always decisive. Consider the example of a soccer player who scores a goal, which one critic of the strict definition uses to deny that agents have access to their intentions in a way that is unavailable to observers.[21] An observer who sees the player kick the ball into the net would have strong reasons to infer that the player intended to score a goal, but this inference about the player's intention might be incorrect. For example:

- A clumsy soccer player tries to pass the ball to a teammate near the goal but misses the target and scores a goal accidentally.
- A malicious soccer player wants to hurt the opposing goalie. The player kicks the ball at the goalie, but the goalie ducks, and the ball sails into the net.
- A child who has not learned the rules of soccer and does not know what a goal is kicks a ball that happens to end up in the net.

In all these cases, the player would appear to external observers to be someone who intended to score a goal. The example of seeing someone score a goal does not refute the strict definition of intended effects. Instead the example supports the strict definition by illustrating that well-founded inferences based on external observations can be false in some cases.

Another objection to the strict definition of intended effects is that it depends on some form of mind-body dualism or Cartesianism because it focuses on the agent's perspective.[22] I agree that mind-body dualism is mistaken, but my definition of intended effects says nothing about the relation between mental states and brain states. Suppose that a brain scan could distinguish between a child who takes a toy to incite a sibling's envy and a child who takes a toy to have fun. The brain scan would not rule out using "intention" and "foresight" to name the different neural states or rule out treating the difference between the neural states as relevant for moral judgments. The brain scan would also not make it possible to define intended effects by analyzing causal relations outside the agent.

Another objection to the strict definition of intended effects, which I take as the strongest objection, is that anyone who accepts this definition cannot explain why some people seem to act wrongly for the same reason. For example, consider two cases in which a physician procures vital organs for life-saving transplants:

- Five patients urgently need different vital organs. An anesthesiologist who knows about the five patients learns that a woman is in the hospital for a surgery that requires anesthesia. The anesthesiologist also learns that her organs are a match for all five patients. The hospital's surgeons will not remove organs from living patients, so the anesthesiologist poisons her to make her organs available (fig. 2.6).
- Five patients urgently need different vital organs. A surgeon learns that a patient who is on the operating table for a routine surgery has organs that are a match for all five patients. To save the five, the surgeon removes the healthy man's organs and transplants them into the five (fig. 2.7).[23]

Figure 2.6. The anesthesiologist's intention in the transplant case

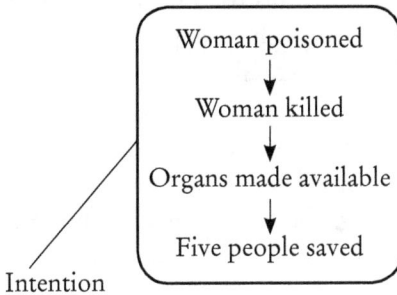

Figure 2.7. The surgeon's intention in the transplant case

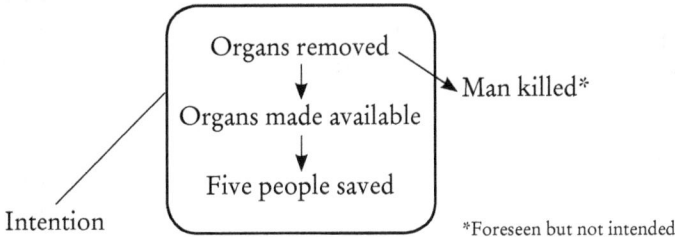

*Foreseen but not intended

In the first case, the anesthesiologist needs the woman to die before surgeons at the hospital will use her organs. If she were already dead, poisoning her would be pointless. If she survived, poisoning her would not make the organs available. In the second case, however, the surgeon does not need the man to die to make his organs available. If he were already dead or if he survived because another surgeon were standing by with replacement organs, cutting out his organs still would make them available for transplants. (I specify each victim's gender only to keep the cases distinct.) The surgeon can answer the question "What is your goal, and what are all the steps in your plan to achieve that goal?" without including the victim's death. The anesthesiologist cannot do the same, so only the anesthesiologist intends death. The objection to my definition of intended effects is that it prevents me from explaining why the anesthesiologist and the surgeon act wrongly *for the same reason*.[24] My response is that they do act wrongly for the same reason. Both of them treat their victims unjustly because they force the victims to give up their organs, and thus their lives, as a means of saving other people.

The strict definition does not entail that the anesthesiologist's intention makes the action worse than the surgeon's action. As I explained in my analysis of a child's racial epithet, a rule's strictness differs from a rule's seriousness, so treating someone unjustly can be as wrong as, or even worse than, intending death. The reason that an action falls under a strict rule, such as the rule against intending death, is not always the most serious reason that the action is wrong. Not everyone who acts wrongly intends a bad effect, and trying to stretch the definition of intended effects so that PDE explains intuitions about actions like the vivisecting surgeon's action exposes PDE to counterexamples. The surgeon and the anesthesiologist procure organs in different ways, and the strict definition of intended effects identifies the difference. The strict definition does not entail that one action is better or worse than the other.

To clarify my analysis of these cases, I do not assume that the agents have only one intention.[25] The surgeon *could* intend both the removal of vital organs and the patient's death, but the question for now is whether the surgeon who intends to remove vital organs also *must* intend the patient's death.

I should emphasize three claims about these cases that I do *not* deny. First, I do not deny that the surgeon who steals organs acts intentionally, unlike a surgeon who accidentally nicks an artery. For my version of PDE, the relevant distinction is between what an agent intends and what the agent knowingly causes, not between what the agent does intentionally and what the agent does accidentally. Second, I do not deny that the surgeon is fully responsible for killing the patient. Agents can be responsible for effects that they do not intend. In cases of negligence, such as drunk driving, they can even be responsible for effects that they do not knowingly cause. Third, I do not deny that the surgeon should be found guilty of murder. The legal definition of murder can apply more broadly than my version of PDE. I do not address legal issues here, but I have no objection to John Finnis's suggestion that the legal definition of murder should include both intending death as an end or a means and also "doing without lawful justification or excuse an act which one is sure will kill."[26] I claim only that the surgeon does not intend death in the same way that the anesthesiologist intends death and that the difference between intended effects and foreseen side effects is a consideration relevant for judging actions. Other considerations (i.e., the injustices that they commit) explain why the surgeon and the anesthesiologist act wrongly for the same reason.

THE PROBLEM OF CLOSENESS

After Foot asserts that the explorers must intend the massive man's death because it so closely follows blasting him out of the cave opening, she asks, "What is to be the criterion of 'closeness' if we say that anything very close to what we are literally aiming at counts as if part of our aim?"[27] I deny that the question has an answer, but other proponents of PDE accept Foot's challenge and try to explain when an effect follows an action so closely that the agent must intend it. These attempts do not end happily for proponents of PDE. To see the problems that result when proponents of PDE appeal to closeness, consider Anscombe's statement of the cave case. She writes, "Imagine a pot-holer stuck with people behind him and water rising to drown them. And imagine two cases: in one, he can be blown up; in the other, a rock *can* be moved to open another escape route, but it will crush his head."[28] Anscombe makes two assertions that require comment: (1) if the explorers do not know that moving the rock will crush the man's head, then they could intend to move the rock without intending to crush his head, and (2) whether the explorers intend the man's death depends on the distance between the rock and the man's head. Regarding the first assertion, there is no reason to consider what the agent foresees and then disregard what the agent considers relevant. Before commenting on the second, I express it in Anscombe's words: "Let us now consider the case where the result is not so immediate—the rock you are moving has to take a path after your immediate moving of it, and in the path that it will take it will crush his head. Here there is indeed room for saying that you did not intend that result, even though you did foresee it."[29] Suppose that the man begs the explorers to move the rock, both because he wants them to live and because he prefers being crushed to drowning. According to Anscombe, if the rock is next to the man's head and if the explorers want to avoid committing murder, they must resign themselves and the man to deaths by drowning, deaths that they could avoid if only the rock had to roll a bit further.

I say more about Anscombe's analysis of the cave case later, but she does not always define intended effects in terms of closeness. In a different context, she considers a case of a man who does his job by pumping poisoned water into a house even though he knows that the water is poisoned. She notes that "the man's intention might not be to poison [those inside the house] but only to earn his pay."[30] To illustrate this point, she imagines a case in which the man says, "I didn't care tuppence one way or the other for the fact that someone had poisoned the water, I just wanted to earn my pay without trouble by doing my usual job."[31] From the outside, the pumping of the water is as close as can be to the pumping of the poison. In fact, an observer could say that pumping the water *is* pumping the poison. Still, Anscombe agrees that the man can intend to pump the water without intending to pump the poison.

When Anscombe analyzes the case of pumping water, she adds that the man must intend to do whatever is a means to his end. This point does not support the conclusion that the explorers intend to kill the man in the cave. In the cave case, the disputed point is not whether the explorers intend what they do as a means of escaping. The disputed point is whether their means include the man's death. Proponents of PDE have no reason to admit that the man in the pumping example can pump the water without intending to pump the poison and then to deny that the explorers can blast the man out of the cave exit without intending to kill him.[32] By hypothesis, the explorers regard the man's death as irrelevant, just as the water pumper does not "care tuppence" about the poison. The explorers simply want to get the man's body out of the way before they all drown, and his death does not further their plan in any way.

Appeals to closeness do not merely entail *false* conclusions; they entail *contradictory* conclusions. Suppose that the stuttering man who testifies for his father rubs a good luck charm in a desperate, but predictably futile, attempt to minimize his stuttering. Philosophers who appeal to closeness must say that the man speaks with the intention of stuttering and simultaneously rubs his good luck charm with the intention of not stuttering. Other cases in which the agent struggles against an effect that follows closely, or even immediately, are not hard to find:

- Competitive weightlifters eat a high-calorie snack to offset burned calories from exercising so that they do not drop into a lower weight class before a competition.
- Carpenters wear earmuffs while using a circular saw to muffle the saw's noise.
- People turn on a bedside reading lamp and then turn up the air conditioning so that the lamp's heat does not make the room too warm.
- Snipers use flash suppressors and silencers so that the muzzle flash and sound of the gunshot do not expose their position.

In all these cases—and I could easily find others—the agents intend one effect and try to prevent another effect that has an even closer causal relation to the action than any effect that the agent intends. In the case of using a flash suppressor, the light that the sniper tries to prevent occurs *before* the bullet hits its target. Fortunately, proponents of PDE have a simple way to avoid the conclusion that these agents both intend an effect and work against the same effect: they can define intended effects by considering the agent's perspective, not by appealing to closeness.

Beside these cases of agents who work against an effect that follows their action more closely than any intended effect, appeals to closeness cannot handle unusual cases in which agents intend something that people who perform similar-looking actions do not intend. For example, suppose that football fans wear lucky hats so that their favorite team will win. Ordinarily, people wear hats to stay warm or to cover their heads, and there is no real causal connection between wearing a hat and a football team's victory, but the fans in this example wear the hats to make the team win. This intention is irrational, but it is their intention, so a definition of intended effects that excludes the agent's perspective entails false conclusions about this case, and about all the other cases in which humans act irrationally. There is no reason to admit the agent's perspective when analyzing the lucky hats case and then exclude the agent's perspective when analyzing the cave case and other alleged counterexamples to the strict definition of intended effects. One virtue of the strict definition is that it applies equally well to fully rational adults, irrational adults, and children. A definition of intended effects that applied only to fully rational adults would be unnecessarily limited. Such a definition also would not apply to many common applications of PDE. In the heat of battle or in an emergency room, politicians, soldiers, doctors, and patients may not be fully rational, so proponents of PDE cannot dismiss cases of agents who are not fully rational.

Philosophers could try to refine appeals to closeness to handle some of these counterexamples, but even these refined appeals would not apply to children's actions. They would also make it impossible for nonphilosophers to know what they intend. Further, these refined appeals to closeness cannot overcome the fact that no causal relation between two effects compels an agent who intends one to intend the other, as no logical relation between two propositions compels someone who knows one proposition to know the other.

I have presented many (perhaps too many!) counterexamples to definitions of intended effects that refer to closeness. These definitions have a more serious problem than counterexamples. If agents intend effects that they regard as completely irrelevant, or even effects that they work against, then proponents of PDE cannot refer to the agent's character to explain why the distinction between intended effects and foreseen side effects is relevant for judging actions. To illustrate this problem, recall Anscombe's case of the explorers who contemplate moving the rock that will crush the massive man's skull. According to Anscombe, the distance between the rock and the man's head is relevant for determining the explorers' intention. Even if Anscombe were correct on this point, why would the difference in the explorers' intention determine whether they act rightly or wrongly? The man will be just as dead if the rock must roll a bit before crushing his head as if his head is wedged under the rock, so the distance makes no difference to the man stuck in the exit from the cave. The explorers want to escape the flooding cave, so the distance also makes no difference to them. A proponent of PDE could say that the distance is relevant because the explorers do not violate the rule against murder when the rock has to roll a bit, but what is the point of this rule? A proponent of PDE cannot explain the rule by appealing to the good of the man's life, since the path does not affect him. The proponent of PDE also cannot appeal to considerations about the explorers, since they will have exactly the same states of mind if the rock crushes the man immediately as they will if the rock has to roll a bit. Divorced from any connection to the massive man's life and to the explorers themselves, the rule against murder appears pointless. Setting aside the agent's perspective results in a view of moral rules that is legalistic in the sense of telling people to follow moral rules even when following the rules does not serve any purpose.

The danger of making moral rules pointless looms for anyone who sets aside the agent's perspective and tries to define intentions from the outside. To see why, consider the case of a sniper who shoots a bank robber before the robber can detonate a bomb, but suppose that the bank robber is standing in front of the child instead of standing in back of the child:

- The sniper takes aim at the bank robber who has threatened to detonate a bomb. At the last second, the robber steps in front of a child. Given the caliber of the rifle and the size of the bullet, the sniper knows that the bullet will travel through the robber and hit the child standing behind the robber. Thinking that the child will die if the robber detonates the bomb and knowing that there is no time to switch to a different rifle or bullet, the sniper shoots the robber, foreseeing that the bullet also will hit the child.

According to the strict definition of intended effects, neither the sniper in this example, who shoots through the robber and hits the child, nor the sniper in the earlier example, who shoots through the child and hits the robber, intends the child's death, because the child's death is not part of either sniper's plan to keep the robber from detonating the bomb. If the child somehow survived or if the child were already dead, each sniper's plan could proceed the same way. According to some proponents of PDE, the fact that one sniper hits the child before the robber entails that the sniper must intend the child's death.[33] Suppose that a critic of PDE hears this claim and asks, "Even if only one sniper intends death, why is this difference in the snipers' intentions relevant for judging the two cases?" By hypothesis, the alleged difference in intentions does not affect the robber or the child, who is killed in both cases. The alleged difference also does not affect the snipers, both of whom could say, "To me, it's irrelevant whether the child is in front or in back of the robber. All I care about is shooting the robber so that he doesn't detonate the bomb." Given that the alleged difference in intentions does not affect anyone in the case, why would the difference be morally relevant? Once proponents of PDE set aside the agent's perspective, they cannot answer this question by referring to the agent. They are left with a definition of intended effects that fits their intuitions about some cases but that makes the distinction between intention and foresight seem irrelevant. Critics of PDE then have good reason to accuse their opponents of sophistry, or at least of backsolving from their moral judgments to judgments about what the agent intends.

INTENDED EFFECTS VERSUS REASONS FOR ACTIONS

According to Anscombe, intentions explain why an agent acts in a certain way.[34] Following Anscombe, some proponents of PDE define intended effects as the effects that provide the agent's motivating reasons for carrying out an action or as the effects that explain the action.[35] This definition fits an agent-based justification of PDE, and it is simpler than the strict definition. It is also morally neutral, applicable to children's actions, and intelligible to nonphilosophers. Despite these virtues, defining intended effects as reasons for actions creates problems.

One problem is that people cannot always choose, or even know, the reasons for their actions. Subconscious motives and desires can influence actions. Sometimes a cigar is just a cigar, but a man might smoke a cigar because of a subconscious desire to act like his grandfather. Defining intended effects as reasons for actions makes it impossible for some agents to know or control their intentions. I return to questions about choosing intentions later.

Another problem is that defining intended effects as reasons for actions is too broad. People can be motivated by an effect that they cause even if they do not intend the effect. For example, consider the case of a physician who must decide how to ration a life-saving drug:

- The physician has two patients who have been bitten by a deadly snake, but only one dose of the antidote. The only relevant distinction between the two patients is that Patient A's organs are a match for five other patients who urgently need vital organ transplants, while Patient B's are not. Because A's death would save five lives, while no further good would come from B's death, the physician gives the antidote to B.[36]

Does the physician intend A's death? On one hand, the physician sees A's death as a reason to treat B instead of treating A, because A's death would make organs available. On the other hand, if someone asked the physician, "What is your goal, and what are all the steps in your plan to achieve that goal?," the physician could give a complete and honest answer without including A's death: "I am giving this patient an antidote so that the patient will survive." A's death and the resulting availability of organs explains why the physician treats B instead of A, but A's death does not explain why the physician sees treating B as a worthwhile option in the first place. Because A's death is neither an end nor a means, the physician does not intend it.

Someone could claim that the physician in this case intends the complex end of saving B and also saving five other patients and that the physician intends A's death as a means of saving five patients. This complex intention is possible, but the details of my case do not require the physician to intend A's death as a means of achieving the complex end. The physician could think, "I need to save one of these patients, but I can't save both. Which one should I save? The only relevant difference is that A's death would make organs available, so I'll save B." After deciding to save B, the physician could think, "I'll do everything I can to save both people, I'll try sucking out the venom from A. It's a long shot, but if it doesn't work, at least A's organs will be available." If the physician's intention included A's death, then the physician would intend contradictory effects: *kill A* so that organs will be available and *save A* by sucking out the venom. I avoid saying that the physician has contradictory intentions by classifying A's death as a motivating side effect rather than as an intended effect.

Besides attributing contradictory intentions to the physician, defining intended effects to include motivating side effects also results in implausible moral judgments. If physicians may not intend to kill patients as a means of making organs available, what should the physician in my case do? By hypothesis, the physician knows that A's death will make organs available. To avoid intending death, the physician could toss a coin. If B wins the coin toss, the physician will not act wrongly by treating B instead of A. Why, then, should the physician toss a coin instead of considering the effects of the two options? Tossing the coin would not change the fact that the physician wants to treat B instead of A, so insisting that the physician ignore the possibility of saving lives seems pointless. According to my definition of intended effects, the physician is motivated by A's death but does not intend A's death. My distinction between intended effects and motivating side effects can support unsound rationalizations, but even classifying all foreseen effects as intended would not prevent agents from pretending not to foresee bad effects. Possible abuse does not make a distinction irrelevant.

I have argued that moral judgments about these cases are one reason to favor the strict definition over some rival definitions, but my argument does not prevent the strict definition from being morally neutral. Someone can use the definition to determine what the physician intends *before* judging that the action is right or wrong.

The distinction between intended effects and motivating side effects is not an ad hoc distinction. Consider a case that does not raise any difficult moral questions:

• A woman decides to throw a party for herself and her friends to have fun. She then foresees that having a party will create a mess in her home. She also foresees that her friends will feel indebted and help her clean up, so she decides to stick with her decision to throw a party.[37]

The woman does not throw the party to make her home clean, because the party causes a mess. She also does not throw the party to make her friends feel indebted. By hypothesis, she throws a party to have fun and considers her friends' feelings of indebtedness only when she considers the party's side effects. Although she does not intend these feelings, they still play some role in her decision, so these feelings are motivating side effects, not intended effects.

The difference between intending an effect (i.e., doing something in order to cause the effect) and being motivated by an effect (i.e., doing something because it will cause an effect) is shown when agents consider an effect that offsets an action's negative effects. For example:

- A man and woman want to have a baby, so they analyze their finances to see whether they should try now or wait until next year. They sadly conclude that a baby would be too expensive this year. The next day, they realize that they forgot about a $1,000 child tax credit. They then begin the pleasant work of trying to start a family.

The tax credit plays some role in the decision to start a family, but the man and woman do not intend to have a child as a means of getting the $1,000 tax credit. They already wanted a child, and no financial advisor would treat a child as the best way of saving $,1000. The $1,000 tax credit is a motivating side effect, not an intended effect.

One critic of PDE proposes (before rejecting) the "doctrine of triple effect" to account for intended effects, motivating side effects, and other foreseen side effects.[38] To see why I do not accept the doctrine of triple effect, consider the following case:

- A physician has two patients who have been bitten by a rattlesnake, but has only one dose of the antidote. Patient A's organs are a match for five other patients who urgently need vital organ transplants, while Patient B's are not. Also, Patient A is Asian. The physician hates Asian people and thinks, "I don't care one bit about procuring organs, but here is a chance to kill an Asian person without being guilty of murder." With this thought in mind, the physician gives the antidote to Patient B.

Someone could suggest that the physician intends the end of saving B and killing A, but the physician can truthfully say, "I decided to give the antidote to A or B, and the fact that A is an Asian person merely broke the tie between these two options." As more evidence that the physician does not intend A's death, suppose that, as a last resort, the physician tries to suck the venom out of A, thinking, "I want this Asian person to die, but I'll do my duty as a physician." Someone who insists that the physician intends to kill A must say that the physician intends to *kill* A at the same time that the physician sucks out venom to *save* A. Classifying A's death as a motivating side effect avoids attributing contradictory intentions to the physician. Thus the racist physician has a bad motive, not a bad intention. This bad motive does not make the physician's action wrong. If the physician asks, "What should I have done differently?" the correct answer is, "You acted rightly by deciding to give the antidote to B, but you should have had a different motive." In general, a good person can be motivated by an effect that would be wrong to intend, but the good person will not desire the effect for its own sake. Instead, the morally good person will see the effect as desirable only because it causes a good effect. For example, the physician in the first scarce antidote case is motivated by A's death, but only because A's death makes organs available for life-saving transplants. By contrast, the racist physician sees A's death as desirable in itself. Neither physician intends a death, but the physician in the second case has a bad motive for saving one patient instead of the other.

I have distinguished judging the action from judging the agent and the agent's motives, so a critic of PDE might object, "If you admit that motives are relevant only for judging the agent, why not say that intentions also are relevant only for judging the agent?" I see this objection as the most serious objection to PDE, so I respond to it at length in chapter 3. For now I repeat that my definition of intended effects includes only the effects that are part of the agent's plan as an end or as a means, not all the effects that motivate the agent. People can speak in a way that identifies the agent's motive with the agent's end, but proponents of PDE must be more precise. Even common ways of speaking distinguish motives from intentions. For example, people might say that greed motivated a thief or that insecurity motivated a bully, but it sounds odd to say that a thief intends greed or that a bully intends insecurity. Because motives differ from intentions, proponents of PDE can argue that motives are relevant only for judging agents, while intentions are relevant for judging both actions and agents.

In the cases of the scarce antidote, the messy party, and the tax credit, defining intended effects as reasons for actions is too broad. In other cases, this definition is too narrow. For example:

- An eccentric zoo owner promises to donate to famine relief, which will save many lives, if and only if a man sneaks into the zoo at night and kills the first mammal he sees. The man sneaks into the zoo. The first mammal he sees is the zookeeper, so he shoots and kills the zookeeper.[39]

The man does not regard the zookeeper's being human as a reason for shooting the zookeeper, but it still seems that the man is guilty of intending to kill a human being. Before analyzing the man's intention, I should note that he could violate a rule other than the rule against murder, such as a rule against causing death unjustly. Still, this man is guilty of murder, even though his reasons for shooting the zookeeper do not include a human being's death. That the mammal is human is not one of the man's reasons for killing it, but he still knows that his target is a human being. To see why this point is relevant, suppose that someone intends to kill a mammal *without* knowing that the mammal is human:

- A zoo owner tells a woman that some mammals at the zoo are infected with a deadly virus. The owner then hires the woman to wait in the parking lot at night and to kill any mammal leaving the zoo. In fact, the zoo owner's estranged wife performs a show while wearing a gorilla suit. He knows that she will wear her costume when she walks to her car after work. Events unfold according to the owner's plan, and the woman shoots the owner's wife.

Like the man in the previous case, the woman in this case sets out to kill a mammal. Unlike the man, however, the woman does not know that her target is a human being, so she does not break the rule against murder, even if she does break rules about negligently shooting guns. This case shows that whether the agent commits murder depends partly on whether the agent knows that the victim is a human being. The rule against murder can be interpreted so that it forbids people from intending the death of an organism they know to be human, not only from intending the death of an organism because the organism is human. The broader interpretation seems more plausible. For example, suppose that a gangster kills someone to silence a witness to his crimes so that the witness cannot testify against the gangster. The gangster might not care whether the victim is a human, a talking parrot, a robot, or an extraterrestrial, but the gangster still intends to kill the witness and knows that the witness is a human being. The gangster's action seems to be a paradigm case of murder. With a broader interpretation of the rule against murder, someone can accept the strict definition of intended effects and still say that both the gangster who kills a witness and the man who shoots the zookeeper are guilty of murder because they intend the death of someone known to be human.

Defining intended effects as reasons for actions does not exclude the agent's perspective, so it does not undermine the basis of PDE as appeals to closeness do. Defining intended effects as reasons for actions also satisfies the three criteria that I proposed earlier: it is morally neutral, applicable to children's actions, and intelligible to nonphilosophers. Despite these advantages, defining intended effects as reasons for actions is both too broad and too narrow: too broad because it includes motivating side effects (e.g., the death of a potential organ donor in the case of the scarce antidote) and too narrow because it excludes the deaths of victims who are not killed because they are human (e.g., the death of a human mammal in the case of the eccentric zookeeper). Another problem is that defining intended effects as reasons for actions makes PDE vulnerable to the objection about confusing judgments of actions and agents, an objection that I discuss in the next chapter.

THE KNOBE EFFECT IN EMPIRICAL STUDIES

A good definition of intended effects must be morally neutral, but some critics of PDE cite empirical studies to argue that people's judgments about intention follow their moral judgments of actions, not vice versa. Consider the following story from Joshua Knobe, which I present in his own words:

- The chairman of the board of a company has decided to implement a new program. He believes (1) that the program will make a lot of money for his company and (2) that the program will also produce some other effect x. But the chairman doesn't care at all about effect x. His sole reason for implementing the new program is that he believes it will make a lot of money for the company. In the end, everything proceeds as anticipated: the program makes a lot of money for the company and also produces effect x.[40]

In this story, effect x seems a clear example of a foreseen side effect because the story stipulates that the chairman does not care at all about the effect.

Knobe and other researchers presented subjects with one of two versions of this case. In the first version, effect x—that is, the effect that the chairman did not care about—was *harming* the environment. In the second version, effect x was *helping* the environment. Of the subjects who considered the first version, 81 percent said that the chairman *harmed* the environment intentionally. Of the subjects who considered the second version, 77 percent said that the chairman did *not* help the environment intentionally.[41] This study suggests that people's moral judgments drive their judgments of what an agent intends. This influence of moral judgments on judgments about intentions has acquired the label of the "Knobe effect." Some critics cite the Knobe effect as evidence that PDE is "more rationalization than rational argument."[42]

One problem for critics of PDE who cite the Knobe effect is that the statements "The chairman doesn't care at all about harming the environment" and "The chairman doesn't care at all about helping the environment" are open to different interpretations. Some philosophers hypothesize that test subjects classify the effect as intentional if they believe that the chairman considers the program's effect on the environment but decides that other factors outweigh the effect. By contrast, subjects classify the effect as unintentional if they believe that the chairman does not even consider the effect.[43] On this hypothesis, most subjects say that the chairman intentionally *harms* the environment because they assume that he considers the harm but decides to proceed with the project anyway. By contrast, most subjects deny that the chairman intentionally *helps* the environment because they assume that the chairman does not even consider this effect. If the chairman did consider helping the environment, presumably he would see it as a positive effect of the program and advertise the effect rather than saying that he doesn't care at all about it. Subjects' statements about what the chairman intends could result from different ways of resolving the ambiguity in the claim that the chairman "doesn't care at all" about harming or helping the environment. Thus these apparently contradictory statements provide no evidence that people's judgments about intentions merely rationalize their moral judgments.

This hypothesis seems plausible, but there is another ambiguity in Knobe's study. Subjects in the studies were asked whether *actions* are intentional, not whether *effects* are intended. A subject's claim that the chairman "intentionally" harmed the environment could mean that the harm was a step in the chairman's plan. On this interpretation, the 81 percent of subjects who said that the chairman intentionally harmed the environment would make an implausible claim. A subject's claim that the chairman intentionally harmed the environment could also mean, however, that he *knowingly caused* the harm, as opposed to *accidentally causing* the harm. As noted earlier, people sometimes use "intentionally" as the opposite of "accidentally" or "unknowingly," as when a jogger says, "I intentionally wore out my knees because I need to stay in shape." If "intentionally harmed" means something like knowingly caused harm, 81 percent of subjects did not make an implausible claim when they said that the chairman intentionally harmed the environment. They could have meant that the chairman's harming the environment was not accidental in the sense that spilling coffee or bumping into someone is accidental. In later studies, researchers presented subjects with different options for describing the chairman's action. The researchers then asked which description of the chairman's action was "most accurate." The results were as follows:

12 percent: "The CEO willingly harmed the environment."
86 percent: "The CEO knowingly harmed the environment."

    1 percent: "The CEO intentionally harmed the environment."
    1 percent: "The CEO purposefully harmed the environment."[44]

In this study, only 1 percent of the subjects said that the chairman "intentionally" or "purposefully" harmed the environment. The vast majority of subjects said that the chairman "willingly" or "knowingly" harmed the environment. Someone who accepts the strict definition of intended effects can agree with both claims, although I prefer "knowingly" to "willingly" because there is no reason to believe that the chairman's will would have been frustrated if the harm did not occur. When discussing these studies, philosophers and psychologists often describe *actions* as intentional or unintentional rather than describing *effects* as intended effects or foreseen side effects. By talking this way, they assume that one can identify an action by identifying the agent's bodily movements and other observable effects without considering the agent's intention. The Knobe effect arises at least partly from an imprecise way of describing the distinction that PDE treats as relevant, so critics of PDE cannot use the Knobe effect as evidence that people *inevitably* define intended effects to rationalize their moral judgments.

To see a more basic problem for critics who cite the Knobe effect as evidence against PDE, suppose that *most* subjects believe that the chairman intends harm to the environment only because they disapprove of the chairman's action. Some subjects still set aside their moral judgments when they analyze the agent's intention. After all, 81 percent, not 100 percent, of Knobe's subjects said that the chairman intentionally harmed the environment. Perhaps the other 19 percent of subjects thought more clearly than the 81 percent. No study about the Knobe effect shows that *all* definitions of intended effects are merely rationalizations of moral judgments.

I have defined intended effects and responded to some objections, but I still have not responded to what I regard as the most serious objection to PDE: that no matter how people define the difference between intended effects and foreseen side effects, the difference is relevant only for judging agents, not for judging actions. I turn to this objection now.

Chapter Three

The Strongest Objection to
the Principle of Double Effect

In a ruling that struck down a law against physician-assisted suicide, an American court rejected PDE by finding "little, if any, difference for constitutional or ethical purposes" between a physician's providing drugs that kill a patient as a means of ending pain and a doctor's providing painkillers that have the foreseen side effect of shortening a patient's life.[1] A dissenting judge responded with a counterexample: "When General Eisenhower ordered American soldiers onto the beaches of Normandy, he knew that he was sending many American soldiers to certain death, despite his best efforts to minimize casualties. . . . The majority's theory of ethics would imply that this purpose was legally and ethically indistinguishable from a purpose of killing American soldiers."[2] This example of Eisenhower provides strong support for PDE. After all, who wants to say that the heroic general murdered his own soldiers on D-Day? Not the U.S. Supreme Court, which quoted the Eisenhower example in a decision that upheld a law against physician-assisted suicide.[3]

The Supreme Court enjoys the final word about federal law in the United States, but moral philosophy falls outside the Court's jurisdiction. Judith Jarvis Thomson tries to turn the Eisenhower example against PDE. She imagines that Eisenhower confesses on the brink of the Normandy invasion that he intends to kill American soldiers, not to liberate Europe.[4] She also imagines that Eisenhower has planned the invasion exactly as someone who wanted to liberate Europe would have planned it, so that his invading to kill American soldiers and his invading to liberate Europe will cause exactly the same effects. Thomson denies that the fictional Eisenhower's bad intention would be a good reason to cancel the invasion. His bad intention would not make the Allied soldiers any more dead or the need to defeat the Nazis any more urgent. According to Thomson, the bad intention would reveal Eisenhower as a bad person but would not make the invasion morally impermissible.

Thomson uses this example to argue that PDE seems plausible because many people fail to distinguish judging *actions* from judging *agents*.[5] According to this objection, someone who intends a bad effect might be a worse person than someone who merely foresees the same effect, but a bad intention does not make the action itself morally impermissible. This objection threatens to deal a fatal blow to PDE. The best objections explain both why a belief is attractive and why the belief is ultimately mistaken. Thomson seems to pull off this feat. If she is correct, PDE seems plausible because the distinction between intention and foresight is morally relevant in some way, but PDE is mistaken because this distinction is relevant for judging only agents, not actions.

I try to turn the tables again by explaining why this objection seems plausible even though it is ultimately mistaken. It seems plausible because the agent's intention is irrelevant for judging whether the action mistreats other people, but it is mistaken because someone can act wrongly without mistreating other people. In the first section of this chapter I clarify the terms of the debate. The main disputed point about PDE is whether an agent's bad intention can make an action wrong, so philosophers beg the question if they assume that a description that excludes the agent's intention (e.g., "ordering the Normandy invasion") gives enough information to determine that the action is right. In the second section I explain why the agent's character is relevant for judging both actions and agents. People who intend some effects might reveal a bad character, as Thomson says, but they also corrupt their character further, and this further corruption can make the action wrong. In the third section I explain why my version of PDE does not completely deny the difference between judging actions and judging agents. People can determine that an action corrupts the agent without judging the extent of the corruption and without comparing the agent to other people. In the fourth section I respond to the argument that intentions cannot be relevant for judging actions because agents cannot choose an action and then choose an intention for it. This inability to choose an intention after choosing an action would be a problem for PDE only if actions existed separately from the agent's intention. Finally, in the fifth section I criticize some attempts to preserve PDE's intuitive appeal while excluding the agent's intention. These alternatives to my version of PDE entail implausible conclusions for anyone who believes that following moral rules must serve some purpose other than mere obedience to the rules.

The Terms of the Debate

Critics of PDE often speak of "moral *assessments*" instead of "moral *judgments*" and describe actions as morally *"permissible"* or *"impermissible"* instead of morally *"right"* or *"wrong."* The term "moral assessment" makes the assessment seem similar to an auditor's assessment of a home. Because an auditor can assess a home by analyzing observable data (e.g., square footage), speaking of moral judgments as "assessments" makes it easier to assume that people can judge actions by considering only observable effects. The labels "permissible" and "impermissible" fit best in legal contexts because most laws concern the ways that actions affect other people, not the ways that they form the agent's own character. Paying taxes to stay out of prison is no less legal than paying taxes to fulfill one's civic duty. As long as the checks arrive on time, Uncle Sam does not care why. Because intentions are irrelevant for many legal judgments, describing actions as "permissible" and "impermissible" makes it easier to dismiss intentions as irrelevant for moral judgments.

To see another way that common ways of framing the issue tilt the debate against PDE, suppose that someone asks, "Is moving one's head up and down right or wrong?" The correct answer is "It depends." A muscle spasm is neither right nor wrong. Even among voluntary movements, a birdwatcher's moving her head to track a falcon differs from a gangster's nodding his head to order a hit. The description "moving one's head up and down" does not come close to picking out a suitable object for a moral judgment. I take this point to be uncontroversial, but consider a more detailed description: "Eisenhower's moving his head up and down in response to an officer who asks, 'Should we proceed with the invasion?'" or simply "Eisenhower's ordering the Normandy invasion." According to Thomson and other critics of PDE, people can determine that an action identified as "Eisenhower's ordering the Normandy invasion" is morally right without considering his intention. If his ordering the Normandy invasion in order to liberate Europe would have been right, so would his ordering the Normandy invasion in order to kill American soldiers. Critics who present this objection presuppose that people can pick out a suitable object for moral judgment and determine that the action is right without referring to the agent's intention. This assumption is exactly the disputed point in debates about PDE.[6]

To illustrate my argument that critics of PDE use terms that slant the debate against PDE, suppose that someone asks, "Is it permissible to kill a person in a way that causes more happiness than unhappiness?" A consequentialist might say yes, assuming that the action really does cause more happiness than unhappiness. A deontologist, however, will ask for more information about the action. (The terms "consequentialist" and "deontologist" can obscure important disagreements in moral philosophy, but I use these terms here only for convenience.) For example, many deontologists, including critics of PDE, agree that a physician may ration a scarce drug to save five people instead of one, even though a physician may not kill one person to make organs available for five life-saving transplants.[7] Suppose that a consequentialist insists on describing both actions only as "killing a person in a way that causes more happiness than unhappiness." Further, suppose that the consequentialist accuses the deontologist of confusing the question "Is the action morally right or wrong?" with the question "Does the action violate any duties or infringe on anyone's rights?" The deontologist should challenge the assumption that these questions are completely separate. The consequentialist believes that an action is wrong only if it causes more unhappiness than happiness, but the deontologist believes that an action also can be wrong because the agent violates a duty or infringes someone's rights. Of course the consequentialist can argue that the deontologist is mistaken, but the consequentialist should not simply assume that someone can determine that an action is morally right without considering the duties and rights that the deontologist sees as relevant. By making this assumption, the consequentialist in this story begs the question against the deontologist.[8] Similarly, critics of PDE should not assume that someone can determine that an action is morally right without considering the agent's intention. For example, they should not assume that the description "Eisenhower's ordering the Normandy invasion" gives enough information to determine that Eisenhower acted rightly. (Someone could determine that Eisenhower acted *wrongly* by treating people unfairly or by breaking a rule that did not refer to his intention.) In analyzing Thomson's cases about the Normandy invasion, proponents of PDE should not concede that the real Eisenhower from history and the evil Eisenhower from Thomson's case performed the same action with different intentions. Instead they should insist that different intentions make different actions, so the two Eisenhowers performed superficially similar but morally distinct actions.

Unfortunately, some proponents of PDE treat actions as bundles of bodily movements and observable effects that can be defined and judged from an observer's perspective. For example, some proponents of PDE argue that an obstetric craniotomy or salpingotomy causes death so directly or immediately that the surgeon must intend death. I discuss these cases later. For now I note that these arguments depend on the view that someone can identify the object of the moral judgment in terms of bodily movements and observable effects without identifying the agent's intention. Other proponents of PDE claim that a type of action, such as dropping bombs, is permissible if the agent could act with a good intention.[9] According to this version of PDE, the relevant question is what the agent *could* intend, not what the agent *does* intend. Again, this version of PDE treats the relevant type of action as something that exists separately from an agent's intention. This version of PDE might fit common intuitions about some cases, but someone who accepts this version will have a hard time explaining why possible intentions are relevant for judging actions in the first place. If actions existed apart from intentions, then people could determine that an action is right without considering the agent's intention, and critics would have good reason to say that proponents of PDE confuse judgments of agents and judgments of actions.

Another potentially misleading practice is describing actions as intentional under some descriptions but not under other descriptions. I say that this practice is *potentially* misleading because talking about actions apart from intentions is unobjectionable in some contexts, as when astronomers speak of the moon's action on the oceans or when historians say, "Eisenhower ordered the Normandy invasion." In debates about moral philosophy, however, PDE's proponents guarantee their own defeat when they speak as if actions could be separated from the agent's intention. Someone can judge a hammer's quality without judging the user's skill, and my bending a nail or hitting my thumb does not make a hammer defective. If actions existed separately from intentions as tools exist independently of the users, then someone could judge an action independently of the agent, and a bad intention would not make the action bad.

The view that actions are intentional under some descriptions comes from Anscombe.[10] I do not refer to Anscombe's view to determine whether an agent intends or foresees an effect. If one general invades Normandy to liberate Europe and another general invades Normandy to kill Americans, the generals perform different actions with the same observable effects. They do not perform the same action, which is intentional under some descriptions and unintentional under different descriptions. I argue only that Anscombe's view can be misleading, not that her view is false. Someone would not make a mistake by saying that the historical Eisenhower's order to invade Normandy was intentional under the description "liberating Europe" but unintentional under the description "killing thousands of Allied soldiers." I suspect, however, that speaking of an action as intentional under some descriptions but not under other descriptions causes confusion about PDE, because speaking this way makes it easier to assume that actions are identical to bodily movements or that someone can set aside an agent's intention and still have enough information to determine that an action is morally right. Proponents of PDE must reject both assumptions (which I do not attribute to Anscombe), or else they will not overcome the objection that PDE seems plausible only because people confuse judgments of actions and of agents.

A Basic Disagreement about Morality

Critics of PDE might say that I have spent too much time quibbling about terms. Someone can agree that the evil Eisenhower from Thomson's story and the good Eisenhower from history perform different actions when they order the invasion and still claim that both Eisenhowers do something morally right. After all, it seems absurd to cancel the Normandy invasion and leave Europe to the Nazis all because of the inner workings of Eisenhower's mind.

Even if President Roosevelt heard about the evil Eisenhower's intention, he would not need to cancel the invasion. He could share Eisenhower's intention that the American soldiers invade Normandy without sharing Eisenhower's intention that American soldiers die on the beaches. Roosevelt's plan works equally well regardless of Eisenhower's intention.

Setting aside Roosevelt's options, the intuitive force of Thomson's story about the evil Eisenhower comes from a typical person's strong interest in defeating the Nazis and weak interest in Eisenhower's character. (I assume that few Nazi sympathizers spend their time reading scholarly debates about PDE.) On the other hand, Eisenhower's wife and parents likely would take a keen interest in whether their husband and son is a war hero who intends to liberate Europe or a wicked man who intends to kill his own soldiers.

These different perspectives for evaluating actions reveal a basic disagreement about morality, a disagreement that forms the basis of the debate about PDE: whether an action can be wrong because it corrupts the agent, apart from its effects on the world outside the agent. This issue pits utilitarians and critics of PDE who reject utilitarianism against those who accept some version of the Socratic view of morality that I defended earlier. For philosophers who reject this view of morality, the distinction between intention and foresight seems irrelevant. Suppose that I play loud music at night despite knowing that the noise will keep my neighbors awake. If I would treat my neighbors unjustly by intending to keep them awake, I also would treat them unjustly by keeping them awake as a side effect. My intention makes no difference to my bleary-eyed neighbors. According to the Socratic view, however, my action can be wrong for two reasons: because I treat my neighbors unjustly and because I corrupt myself by intending to harm my neighbors. The corruption of my character can make my action wrong, even if I do not achieve my goal of keeping my neighbors awake at night. For example, suppose that my neighbors go on vacation without my knowledge, so that my loud music does not bother them one bit as they sleep soundly in a luxurious hotel room, blissfully unaware of the racket outside their home. According to the Socratic view, I can act wrongly even if I do not harm my neighbors. Similarly, suppose that my loud music wakes up my neighbors, who smell smoke and put out a fire before it burns down their house. According to the Socratic view, I can act wrongly even though I benefit my neighbors.

I have argued that the basic disagreement about PDE is a disagreement about whether acting morally is reducible to causing certain types of effects (e.g., effects that do not mistreat other people or effects that promote aggregate welfare). In his widely discussed argument against PDE, Thomas Scanlon diagnoses the basic disagreement differently. He suggests that proponents of PDE understand the principle as a criterion for subjective rightness or moral goodness, not as a criterion for moral permissibility.[11] According to Scanlon's view, I might act *badly* when I try unsuccessfully to harm someone, but I do not act *impermissibly*. Contrary to Scanlon, I do understand PDE as a criterion for moral permissibility—although I prefer the term "moral rightness," for the reasons explained earlier—but my defense of PDE does not separate questions about permissibility from questions about the agent's character. An action can be wrong or impermissible because it corrupts the agent, not only because it mistreats other people.

To support his conclusion that intentions are irrelevant for assessing actions, Scanlon uses an example about attempting to harm a rival by sticking pins in a doll.[12] According to Scanlon, the agent might believe that sticking pins in the doll is impermissible, but doing so is actually harmless and thus permissible. He notes that proponents of PDE might disagree, and he takes this disagreement as evidence that proponents of PDE think about "something closer to an idea of subjective rightness" rather than permissibility.[13] I do not share Scanlon's view of the disagreement. If I saw one of my children sticking pins in a doll to cause a classmate's suffering, I would not permit the stabbing to continue while I waited for an appointment with a psychiatrist to discuss problems with my child's character. I would make the appointment, but I would not permit the child to stab the doll in the meantime. Stabbing the doll would not merely reveal malevolence in the child's character but would develop the malevolence, making the child even more malevolent than before. For a similar example, recall the child who mumbles a racial epithet. As I would not permit my children to stab a doll to harm a classmate, I would not permit them to use racial epithets, even in private, while I worked to fix whatever made the epithet attractive in the first place. I would simply forbid use of the epithet. These examples about stabbing voodoo dolls and using racial epithets show that parents want more than children who treat other people justly. Parents set some rules (e.g., "Share your toys" and "No biting") to keep children from treating other people unjustly, but set other rules (e.g., "Do not stab voodoo dolls" and "Do not mumble racial epithets") because they want their children to develop certain character traits. Parents have no good reason to dismiss a child's character when considering which actions to permit or forbid. Likewise, philosophers have no good reason to dismiss the agent's character as irrelevant for questions about moral permissibility. Some actions are wrong because they corrupt the agent, and some actions are wrong for other reasons.

In another widely discussed argument against PDE, Jonathan Bennett challenges character-based defenses of PDE by comparing a terror bomber, who kills civilians to weaken the enemy's morale, and a tactical bomber, who bombs a military target and foresees the deaths of civilian bystanders.[14] According to Bennett, the civilian deaths gladden both bombers. The terror bomber is glad because the deaths promote the bomber's end, and the tactical bomber is glad because they show that the bombs hit the target. The two bombers do not feel glad for the same reasons. The terror bomber feels glad because of what follows the deaths, while the tactical bomber feels glad because of what precedes the deaths, but Bennett notes that the bombers "do not differ, however, in how greatly glad they will be, or, therefore, how greatly they will hope for and want civilian deaths."[15] He concludes that there is no morally relevant difference between the terror bombing and the tactical bombing even if there is a relevant difference between these two types of bombings and a malevolent bombing.

This objection blurs the distinction between intentions and feelings. According to the strict definition of intended effects that I defended earlier, people do not intend every effect that gladdens them or even every effect that motivates them. They intend only the effects that are their ends or steps in their plans to achieve their ends. Thus the terror and tactical bombers have different intentions even though they feel similarly about innocent people's deaths. The terror bomber intends to kill innocent people as a means of weakening the enemy's morale, but the tactical bomber kills innocent people as a foreseen side effect of destroying a weapons factory. Because they have different intentions, the two bombers perform different actions, which form their characters differently.

ASSESSING ACTIONS VERSUS ASSESSING AGENTS

The Socratic view of morality that supports PDE does not completely erase the distinction between judging actions and judging agents. Before people can determine that an action is morally right, they need to ask, "Does the action make the agent worse?" They do not need to ask, "How much worse?" or "How good or bad is the agent?" or "How does the agent compare to other people?" To illustrate what is relevant for judging actions, consider the statement "Selling real goods for counterfeit bills makes the seller less wealthy." This statement says nothing about how much the seller lost, nothing about the value of the seller's remaining assets, and nothing about how the seller's wealth compares to other people's wealth. It says only that the seller's net worth is lower than it was before the sale. Likewise, saying that an action corrupts the agent's character says nothing about how much the action corrupts the agent, nothing about how good or bad the agent is after the action, and nothing about how the agent compares to other people. It says only that the agent's character has changed for the worse.

The objection about confusing different types of moral judgments might seem plausible because people can do the right thing for the wrong reason. When considering this possibility, it seems tempting to reject PDE and to say that intentions are relevant for judging agents but not actions. In fact, neither PDE nor the Socratic view of morality denies that people can do the right thing for the wrong reason. Someone needs to consider the agent's *intention* to have enough information for a moral judgment, but someone does not need to consider the agent's desires or the reasons that motivate the agent to choose one end over other ends or one set of means over another set of means. Different intentions entail different actions, but different motivating reasons and desires do not. For example, suppose that a miserly physician must decide whether to give a scarce drug to A or to B and that the physician gives the drug to B because B owes the physician $100, not because A's organs can save five people. Like the racist physician discussed earlier, the miserly physician acts rightly for the wrong reason. If either physician asks, "What should I have done differently?," the correct answer is "What you did was morally right, but you should have decided on that action differently." These cases illustrate that someone can accept PDE without denying that people can do the right thing for the wrong reason. In these cases, the problem lies in the reason that the racist physician or the miserly physician picks one action over other possible actions, not in the action that the physician chooses.

As explained earlier, philosophers cause confusion when they speak as if actions existed separately from intentions. For example, suppose that one person says, "I'm sorry" to express remorse over acting wrongly and that a second person says, "I'm sorry" to express sympathy. They do not do the same thing with different intentions. They say the same words, but their actions are different. The first person apologizes, but the second person does not. I do not deny, however, that different agents can perform the same action, or at least similar actions, with different motives. For example, the racist physician and the miserly physician both give the antidote to Patient B, but they have different motives. Intentions are not separable from the action, but the reasons that motivate the action are separable from the action.

Choosing Intentions

Suppose that the fictional Eisenhower in Thomson's story says to a friend, "I plan to order the Normandy invasion to kill American soldiers, but what do you think I should do?" It seems implausible to say that the friend must advise Eisenhower to cancel the invasion, which is the best chance to liberate Europe, all because of Eisenhower's bad intention. The friend might be tempted to say, "You should choose a different intention for invading Normandy," but this answer makes sense only if people can choose an action and then choose an intention for the action. Critics of PDE are correct when they deny this possibility.[16] These critics do not deny that agents can work at changing what they see as reasons for or against an action. For example, the racist physician could read books about admirable Asians so that he will not see an Asian's death as a positive effect, and the miserly physician could start performing works of charity so that he will come to desire saving lives more than having money. When they act, however, the physicians cannot choose reasons that they do not already see as good reasons. The racist physician cannot think, "An Asian's death is really the only good reason to save the other person, but I'll save the other person for some other reason." Similarly, the miserly physician cannot think, "I don't see any good reason to save this person's life except that I'll get $100, but I'll save this person because saving lives is good, not because I'll get $100."

I agree that people cannot first choose an action and then choose their intention, but I do not separate actions from intentions.[17] Actions are not merely bodily movements and observable effects that exist separately from intentions, so choosing a different action is choosing a different intention. In Thomson's story, Eisenhower must choose between two different actions, ordering the Normandy invasion to liberate Europe and ordering the Normandy invasion to kill American soldiers, not between two different intentions for the same action. Instead of advising Eisenhower to choose a different intention for the action that he already has chosen, Eisenhower's friend should say something like, "You should invade Normandy to liberate Europe. You should not invade Normandy to kill American soldiers." Eisenhower's friend can give this advice without assuming that people can choose an intention for the action that they already have chosen. The two actions require identical observable bodily movements, but identical observable movements do not make actions identical. If they did, it would make no sense for a parent to ask, "Did you choose that toy to have fun or to cause envy?" or for a chess teacher to ask, "Did you make that move to capture a pawn or to open a file for your rook?" As explained earlier, actions are not analogous to tools that sit on a shelf apart from the user's intention. From an observer's perspective, invading Normandy to liberate Europe looks the same as invading Normandy to kill American soldiers. From Eisenhower's perspective, the actions look quite different. Eisenhower can think to himself, "Invading Normandy to kill American soldiers would be wrong, so I'll rule out that plan. But if I don't invade, Europe will remain in the hands of the Nazis, unless the Soviets march all the way to the Atlantic. Is there anything else I can do? Yes, I can invade Normandy to liberate Europe."

Critics might find it sophistical to treat Eisenhower's ordering the invasion of Normandy to kill American soldiers and his ordering the invasion to liberate Europe as different actions instead of treating them as the same action done with different intentions. The disagreement runs deeper than a disagreement about how to label actions. The basic disagreement is about whether someone can exclude the agent's intention and still have enough information to say that an action is morally right. To illustrate this basic disagreement, consider evaluations of chess moves. In some positions, there is a correct move that an observer can identify simply by analyzing a position on the board. Suppose that moving a pawn both opens a file and captures a piece. An observer can identify this move as the correct one without asking why the player makes the move. Moving the pawn is the correct move, even if the player makes it for the wrong reason—for example, if the player moves to capture a piece without seeing that a rook can use the open file to checkmate the opponent's king. The player's intention is relevant for judging the player's skill, not for judging the move. An observer who judges the player's skill usually will assume that the player is trying to win, or at least to force a draw. Suppose, however, that the player is a teacher who wants to give a student more practice. In this case the teacher might move a rook and think, "I forgot that moving my rook to that square forces a checkmate on the next move. I should have played a different move to make the game last longer."[18] When a player wants to win, a computer can identify the player's correct move. When a player has another goal, an observer must know the player's intention to know whether the player made a mistake. Reducing morality to treating other people properly makes moral judgments analogous to evaluations of chess moves when both players want to win. As someone can evaluate the chess move merely by analyzing the board, someone can judge an action merely by considering its effects. By contrast, the Socratic view treats moral judgments as analogous to evaluations of a chess teacher's moves. As someone must look inside the teacher to know whether a move is correct, someone must consider the agent's character to know whether an action is right.

When critics deny the possibility of "looking inward" at an agent's intentions to determine whether an action is right or wrong, the critics assume that the only correct viewpoint for judging actions is outside the agent. This assumption would be correct if morality consisted entirely of principles about treating other people properly—or of what we owe to each other, to use the title of one of Scanlon's books.[19] If morality also includes principles about character formation, then people must look both inward and outward to judge actions. For example, suppose that Eisenhower's friend advises him to invade Normandy to liberate Europe and that Eisenhower responds, "I don't care much about liberating Europe. All I really care about is killing American soldiers. Would my action be morally right?" Assuming that generals may not intend to kill their own soldiers, the answer to Eisenhower's question should be no, but the friend should try to persuade Eisenhower to choose a different action: that is, invading Normandy to liberate Europe. If Eisenhower stubbornly

refuses to give up his intention to kill American soldiers, the problem lies with him, not with a view of morality that treats the agent's
character as relevant for judging actions. Critics correctly note that
people cannot choose an action and then choose their motive or the
reason for the action, so PDE collapses without a clear distinction
between what an agent *intends* and what an agent *desires*. I argue only
that agents can control their intentions by choosing different ends or
different means of achieving their ends. I do not argue that agents can
choose their desires.

PROBLEMS FOR INTENTION-NEUTRAL VIEWS

I have argued that proponents of PDE should not rely entirely on
intuitive appeals, but one advantage of PDE is that it explains common intuitions about many pairs of cases. To overcome PDE's intuitive appeal, critics must either reject common intuitions about these
cases or find principles that explain these intuitions better than PDE.

Scanlon takes the second approach. In the bombing cases he
accepts the common intuition that the strategic bombing can be right
even if the terror bombing is wrong. He then denies that the agent's
intention is the relevant difference. Instead, he proposes a rule that says
nothing about intentions, which I present in Scanlon's own words:

> In war, one is sometimes permitted to use destructive and poten-
> tially deadly force of a kind that would normally be prohibited. *But
> such force is permitted only when its uses can be expected to bring
> some military advantage*, such as destroying enemy combatants or
> war-making materials, and it is permitted only if expected harm to
> noncombatants is as small as possible, compatible with gaining the
> relevant military advantage, and only if this harm is "proportional"
> to the importance of this advantage [emphasis added].[20]

For debates about PDE, the key part of Scanlon's rule is the condition that warring parties may use lethal force only when they expect
to gain a military advantage. In the bombing cases, the terror bomber
does not gain a military advantage by killing innocent people, but the

strategic bomber gains a military advantage by destroying a factory. Thus only the strategic bomber satisfies Scanlon's proposed principle for the permissible use of lethal force. I describe the principle as "proposed" because Scanlon does not try to justify this principle or to defend it against every possible objection. He uses it only to show that one can reject PDE and still accept a principle that explains common intuitions about the terror and strategic bombings.

Scanlon's analysis of these cases raises several questions. First, why not count the deaths of innocent people as a military advantage? The terror bomber expects that weakening the enemy's morale will weaken the enemy's ability to support an effective military. Second, even if the terror bomber does not gain a military advantage, why not make more exceptions than Scanlon's rule allows? Someone could propose a principle that permits the use of deadly force in war when it results in a military advantage or when it weakens the enemy's morale. With an exception for weakening morale, the amended principle would permit the terror bombing and the strategic bombing. Third, what if killing civilians results in the military advantage? A terror bombing could kill the children of enemy soldiers so that their grief distracts the soldiers on the battlefield. People in the military would need to resolve these questions before they could adopt Scanlon's rule, but Scanlon does not present the principle to resolve debates about military ethics.[21] The important question is whether people can reject PDE and still explain the common intuitions that seem to support PDE. To answer this question, I focus on a problem that arises precisely because Scanlon's rule does not refer to the agent's intention.

An intention-neutral principle like Scanlon's rule about lethal force sometimes has the perverse feature of treating harmful effects as reasons in favor of an action. I describe this feature as "perverse" since it sometimes favors an action because it causes a harmful effect, not merely despite its causing a harmful effect. In other words, an intention-neutral principle sometimes says that an action is wrong even though adding another harmful effect *while holding everything else constant* would make the action right. Illustrating this feature necessarily requires analysis of some complicated cases. Before presenting the cases, I should note that they are not necessary for my justification of PDE, which does not depend on intuitions. I present them only as evidence that an agent-based version of PDE is more intuitively plausible than its alternatives.

The problem for Scanlon's rule about lethal force results from the fact that the military advantage might result from an effect that the agent sees as irrelevant. For example:

- A general has reliable intelligence showing that an enemy's morale is teetering on the verge of collapse. The general orders bomber pilots to target an apartment building where many soldiers and their families live. He orders the bombing for noon, when the soldiers will be on patrol and only their families will be home (fig. 3.1 and table 3.1). He intends that the deaths of the innocent civilians will motivate the enemy to surrender.

Weakening an enemy's morale does not count as a military advantage, or else Scanlon's rule would not serve its purpose of distinguishing the terror bombing from the strategic bombing. Because the general does not expect to gain a military advantage, the order to bomb the apartment building violates Scanlon's rule. Now consider a similar case:

- A general has reliable intelligence showing that an enemy's morale is teetering on the verge of collapse. The general orders bomber pilots to target an apartment building where many soldiers and their families live. He orders the bombing for midnight, when the soldiers and their families will be at home (fig. 3.2 and table 3.1).

Figure 3.1. The general's intention in the noon bombing

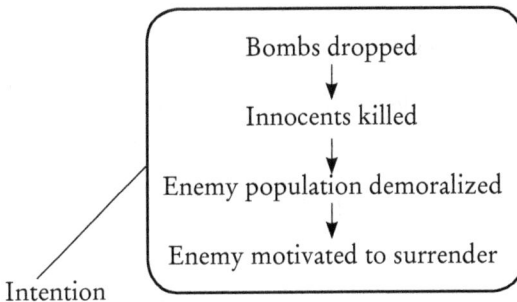

Bombs dropped
↓
Innocents killed
↓
Enemy population demoralized
↓
Enemy motivated to surrender

Intention

He intends that the deaths of the innocent people will motivate the enemy to surrender. The general foresees that the bombs will kill and incapacitate many of the soldiers who live in the apartment building, but he regards this effect as irrelevant.

The midnight bombing satisfies Scanlon's rule, assuming that killing or incapacitating soldiers counts as a military advantage and that the harm satisfies Scanlon's clause about proportionality. By hypothesis, however, the general does not care about this military advantage, so he has exactly the same intention in both cases. As shown in the

Figure 3.2. The general's intention in the midnight bombing

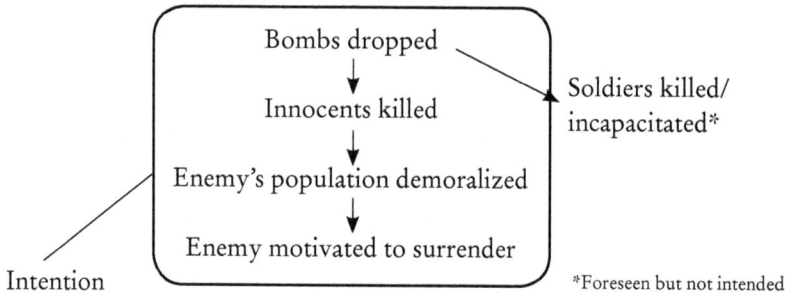

Table 3.1. The noon and midnight bombings

	Intended effects	Relevant foreseen side effects*
Noon bombing	Soldiers' families killed Enemy's population demoralized Enemy motivated to surrender	[None]
Midnight bombing	Soldiers' families killed Enemy's population demoralized Enemy motivated to surrender	Soldiers killed or incapacitated

* Irrelevant foreseen side effects include effects such as burned grass outside the building.

nearby table, the *only* relevant difference between the noon and midnight bombings is that the midnight bombing will cause *more* harm (i.e., killing and incapacitating the soldiers, not just their families). Someone who accepts Scanlon's rule must say to the general, "Instead of bombing at noon, wait until midnight. The delay will not make any difference to you, the delay will not affect the outcome of the war, and the delay will not benefit anyone in any way whatsoever. The delay will kill and injure some soldiers who would not be killed or injured if you bombed at noon." By contrast, someone who accepts PDE can say that the general acts wrongly in both cases because the general intends to kill innocent people.

Someone could claim that the soldiers deserve whatever comes to them, so their deaths and injuries are not bad effects at all. I do not regard the enemy soldiers' culpability relevant for analyzing this case, but someone could modify the case so that the soldiers are children who have been brainwashed or threatened into fighting.

My objection to Scanlon's rule about military force is not merely that it favors a more harmful action over a less harmful alternative. Many principles have this feature. For example, many philosophers who do not accept consequentialism agree that an agent should refuse to murder or torture one person even if doing so is the only way to prevent someone else from murdering or torturing several people. My objection to Scanlon's rule is that it favors a more harmful action over a less harmful and *otherwise identical* alternative. The principle treats the extra deaths and injuries in the noon bombing as effects that count in favor of the action, not as effects that count against it. This feature is a problem because a moral principle should serve some purpose. Defending the premise that a moral principle should serve some purpose is difficult because it seems axiomatic to me. The alternative is a legalistic view that people should obey moral rules simply for the sake of obedience, not for the sake of any other good, such as respecting another person's rights or preserving one's own character. Parents might say, "Because I said so" when they cannot explain the point of following a rule, but they still should have some reason. If I tell my children, "When you wake up in the morning, count to five and slap each other in the face," they, along with my wife, will expect that I have some point in mind. If my rule serves no purpose, then my children will have no good reason to follow it. My objection to Scanlon's rule about lethal force depends on the premise that following a moral rule must serve some purpose other than mere obedience. Scanlon's rule requires the general to make the bombing more harmful, but following the rule serves no other purpose. Any philosopher who accepts a rule other than a consequentialist principle faces the question "What is the point of following the rule when violating it would have better consequences?" The philosopher should have some answer other than simply, "Morality requires it." The philosopher could answer that the more harmful action will respect someone's rights or that it will avoid treating someone simply as a means or that it will avoid corrupting the agent's character. All of these answers are controversial, but all of them are defensible, and all of them avoid making moral rules pointless. By contrast, I see no way to answer the question "What is the point of the general's delaying the bombing?" other than saying that the delay makes the bombing conform to Scanlon's rule about using lethal force.

In response to my argument that following a moral rule should serve some purpose, someone could say, "*I* agree, but *other people*, such as Kant, believe that we should follow moral rules for no reason other than obedience itself." I disagree with this interpretation of Kant, but I do not try to resolve exegetical questions about Kant here.[22] I also do not try to prove that following moral rules must serve some purpose other than obedience, so anyone who finds a legalistic view of moral rules plausible will not be persuaded by my objection to Scanlon's rule about lethal force. I present the objection only as evidence that Scanlon's rule fails to preserve PDE's intuitive appeal.

My objection to Scanlon's rule about lethal force applies to any principle that treats an agent's actual intention as irrelevant. For example, consider FitzPatrick's version of PDE, which considers what the agent could intend, not what the agent actually does intend. This version of PDE supports the same conclusions as Scanlon's rule. At night, the general could intend to incapacitate enemy soldiers instead of intending to weaken the enemy's morale by killing civilians. During the day, the general must intend to kill civilians, or else the bombing would be pointless. Because of this difference in what the general could intend, FitzPatrick's version of PDE favors the midnight bombing over the less harmful and otherwise identical noon bombing.

My objection is not nitpicking that could be addressed by refining Scanlon's rule about using lethal force or FitzPatrick's version of PDE. An intention-neutral principle that is meant to preserve PDE's intuitive appeal will require pointless harms whenever the following three conditions are satisfied: (1) An agent has two options that involve intending harm, (2) one of these options could be justified for a reason that the agent sees as irrelevant, and (3) the circumstances that result in this justification also make the justified option more harmful than the unjustified option.

The problem for intention-neutral principles does not occur only in military cases. Again, finding illustrations of the problem requires analyzing some complicated cases. I begin with simple cases of withholding and rationing a scarce drug and then move to a more complicated case:

- A physician has five patients who need vital organ transplants and one patient whose organs are a perfect match for all five but is sick and needs a drug to survive. The physician withholds the drug so that the one patient's death will make organs available for five life-saving transplants (fig. 3.3).
- A physician has five patients who need one dose of a drug and one sicker patient who needs five doses. To save five lives, the physician gives one dose to each of the first five patients. The physician foresees that the sicker patient will die without the drug (fig. 3.4).

PDE explains the intuition that a physician may not intend to withhold drugs to make organs available, even though the physician may ration drugs in a way that results in one patient's death. The first physician intends death as a means of saving five people. The second physician merely foresees the patient's death as a side effect of saving five people. Scanlon agrees that the physician may not withhold

Figure 3.3. The physician's intention in the drug-withholding case

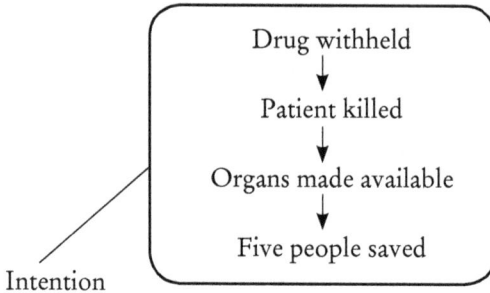

Drug withheld
↓
Patient killed
↓
Organs made available
↓
Five people saved

Intention

Figure 3.4. The physician's intention in the drug-rationing case

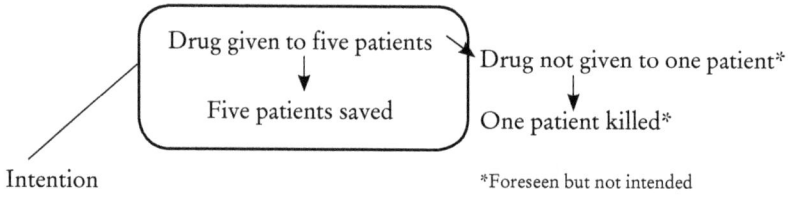

Drug given to five patients
↓
Five patients saved

Drug not given to one patient*
↓
One patient killed*

Intention

*Foreseen but not intended

the drug but may ration the drug. To distinguish the cases without referring to intentions, Scanlon proposes another principle, which I present in his own words:

> If we have some obligation to a person so long as he is alive, the advantages of our being relieved of this obligation by his dying do not justify an exception to the principle requiring us not to kill that person or to save that person's life when we can easily do so.[23]

The physician who withholds the drug from the sick patient violates this principle, because this physician seeks the advantage of making organs available that will result from the patient's death. The physician who rations the drug does not violate Scanlon's rule, since the patient's death does not provide any advantage. In the drug-withholding case, the patient's death saves the five other patients (by making organs available). In the drug-rationing case, the scarce drug saves the five other patients.

Like his rule about using lethal force, Scanlon's rule about killing and saving patients sometimes requires a more harmful action over a less harmful but otherwise identical alternative. To see why Scanlon's rule has this feature, consider the following hybrid case:

- A man has been bitten by a rattlesnake, which injected him with venom and caused a nasty bacterial infection. After being hospitalized, he is receiving two drugs intravenously: an antidote to the snake's venom and an antibiotic for the infection. He needs both drugs to survive. His physician also discovers that his organs could be used for five life-saving organ transplants, so she decides to kill him. The physician does not know that the antibiotic is a scarce drug that could be used to save several other patients.

The unlucky patient in this case has three problems: (1) a snakebite that puts him in need of an antidote, (2) a bacterial infection that puts him in need of an antibiotic, and (3) a physician who wants to kill him for his organs (figs. 3.5 and 3.6).

This hybrid of the drug-withholding and drug-rationing cases is supposed to illustrate an objection to intention-neutral alternatives to my version of PDE, not to resemble any real situation that physicians will face. The physician's intention is the same in the hybrid case and in the drug-withholding case. Given that she has decided to kill her patient by withholding a drug, the physician has two options, and both options have the *unforeseen* side effect of making the antibiotic available for other patients:

Option 1: Disconnect the patient from the antidote, which will cause him to die painlessly as the venom shuts down his nervous system.
Option 2: Disconnect the patient from the antibiotic, which will cause him to suffer from the infection before dying.

As shown in the nearby table (table 3.2), both options also have the unforeseen side effect of making the antibiotic available for five other patients, so the only relevant difference is that withholding the antibiotic will cause more pain than withholding the antidote. If the

Figure 3.5. The hybrid of the drug-withholding and drug-rationing cases

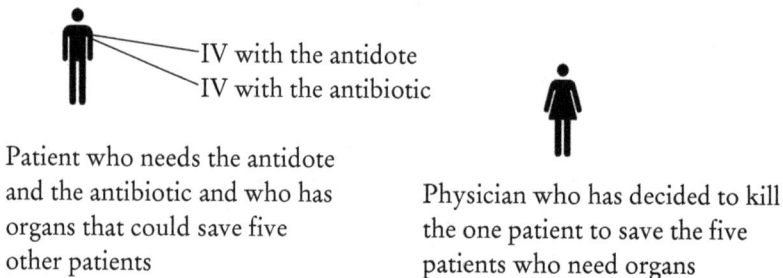

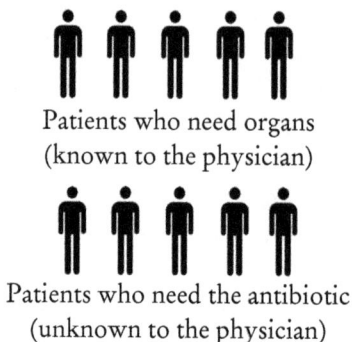

IV with the antidote
IV with the antibiotic

Patient who needs the antidote
and the antibiotic and who has
organs that could save five
other patients

Physician who has decided to kill
the one patient to save the five
patients who need organs

Patients who need organs
(known to the physician)

Patients who need the antibiotic
(unknown to the physician)

Figure 3.6. The physician's intention in the hybrid case

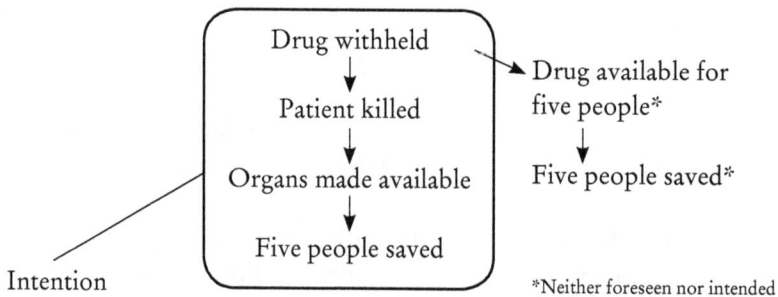

Drug withheld
↓
Patient killed
↓
Organs made available
↓
Five people saved

Drug available for
five people*
↓
Five people saved*

Intention

*Neither foreseen nor intended

Table 3.2. The physician's options in the hybrid case

	Intended effects	Relevant foreseen side effects
Option 1	Antidote withheld One patient killed Organs made available Five patients saved	One patient's pain relieved
Option 2	Antibiotic withheld One patient killed Organs made available Five patients saved	One patient's pain not relieved

physician chooses option 1, then she violates Scanlon's rule, because making organs available does not justify an exception to her obligation to treat the patient. If making organs available did justify an exception, then Scanlon's rule would not distinguish between the drug-rationing and the drug-withholding cases—precisely the distinction that Scanlon designed the principle to make. If the physician chooses option 2, then she does not violate Scanlon's rule because the other patients will benefit from the antibiotic, not the patient's death. The problem for Scanlon's rule is that option 2 (withholding the antibiotic) will cause more suffering than option 1 (withholding the antidote), but option 2 does not serve any other purpose beyond making the action conform to Scanlon's rule. Someone who accepts Scanlon's rule must say to the physician, "Withhold the antibiotic instead of the antidote, even though doing so will cause the patient suffering that you could prevent by withholding the antidote. Withholding the antibiotic will not benefit you, the patient, or anyone else, but withhold the antibiotic anyway."

FitzPatrick's version of PDE has the same feature as Scanlon's rule. The physician could not withhold the antidote without intending to kill the patient because withholding the antidote would be pointless if the patient survived. The physician could withhold the antibiotic to make it available for five other patients, but the physician in the story does not know about these five patients. She withholds the antibiotic instead. Because of this difference in what the physician *could* intend, FitzPatrick's version of PDE approves the more harmful withholding of the antibiotic over the less harmful, but otherwise identical, withholding of the antidote.

A critic of PDE could try to turn the tables by arguing that my objection to Scanlon and FitzPatrick applies to my version of PDE. Suppose for the sake of argument that the physician may not intend to kill her patient to make organs available. Given this rule, someone who accepts my version of PDE must say that the physician should withhold the antibiotic, even though doing so will cause more suffering than withholding the antidote. When combined with a rule against intending death, my version of PDE seems to have the same perverse feature as the alternatives that I have been criticizing: it favors a more painful action over a less painful alternative. My response is that changing the agent's intention prevents the cases from being similar in all respects other than that of the extra harm. When I criticized alternatives to an agent-based version of PDE, the cases were similar apart from the extra harm. Unlike Scanlon's rules and FitzPatrick's version of PDE, the rule against intending death does serve a purpose in these cases. By following the rule, the physician avoids corrupting herself by becoming a murderer. (I should also add that the physician could withhold the antibiotic and then prescribe a painkiller, or the physician could withhold both the antibiotic and the antidote so that the patient does not suffer. In either case, the physician would not intend the patient's death.)

The proposals from Scanlon and FitzPatrick might fit intuitions about some cases, but this intuitive appeal comes at a steep price. Excluding the agent's intention makes it impossible to explain the point of following Scanlon's rules or FitzPatrick's version of PDE. Other philosophers may have different intuitions about the cases in this section, but my version of PDE does not rest on intuitions. Ultimately, my version of PDE depends on the view of morality that treats the agent's character as relevant for judging actions.

So far I have focused on theoretical questions about PDE. The first chapter explained why the distinction between intended effects and foreseen side effects is relevant, and the second chapter defined intended effects from the agent's perspective. In this chapter I have explained why the agent's intention is relevant for judging both actions and agents. In the next two chapters I consider specific applications of PDE, starting with the trolley cases that have made PDE famous in contemporary moral philosophy and have also caused confusion about PDE.

Chapter Four

Trolley Cases and an Objection from Neuroscience and Moral Psychology

My defense of PDE would be incomplete, and less interesting, if I did not discuss the trolley cases that have become the most famous illustrations of PDE. In these cases someone saves several people (five is the standard number) from being killed by a runaway trolley in a way that causes the death of one person. The "trolley problem" has become the standard label for the challenge of explaining common intuitions about these cases and about other cases in which someone saves several lives at the expense of one life. Some critics treat the trolley problem as a litmus test for PDE, so they try to find intuitions about trolley cases that PDE cannot explain. Other critics use evidence from moral psychology to show that common intuitions about trolley cases, the intuitions that are (allegedly) the only basis of PDE, are unreliable.

I argue, however, that no trolley case or psychological study of moral intuitions can refute PDE. The first section of this chapter presents a genealogy of trolley cases. Contrary to a common assumption, proponents of PDE rarely use intuitions about trolley cases as evidence for PDE. The cases originated with PDE's critics, not its proponents, and these critics introduced the cases to analyze other moral principles, not to defend PDE. The anachronistic view that PDE is meant to solve the trolley problem makes it easier to dismiss PDE as superfluous or confused. In fact, trolley cases make poor illustrations of PDE because they focus attention away from the agent and onto an innocent victim. The second section explains why trolley cases are not a waste of time even if many of them make poor illustrations of PDE. Some philosophers urge their contemporaries to stop "obsessing" about trolley cases and to focus on more realistic cases.[1] Trolley cases are not akin to fire drills that prepare people for emergencies. I explain that the purpose of trolley cases is to analyze different principles, not to practice for real decisions. The third section defends my version view of PDE, which treats PDE as a single principle about intention and foresight. I describe my view as "minimalist" because I do not attempt to provide a complete checklist for acting morally—that is, a set of conditions that are individually necessary and jointly sufficient to determine that an action is morally right despite causing a bad effect. My minimalist version of PDE does not solve the trolley problem, but no principle or list of principles can handle every case. The fourth section analyzes Thomson's famous loop case, an alleged counterexample to PDE. My analysis of this case relies on the Kantian rule about treating humanity as an end, not simply as a means, but this rule does not make PDE superfluous. Finally, the fifth section responds to psychologists who argue that PDE seems plausible only when people follow their emotionally charged intuitions, such as the intuitions about trolley cases that seem to support PDE. I explain why studies in neuroscience and moral psychology have not debunked PDE and why no similar studies can debunk PDE.

A GENEALOGY OF TROLLEY CASES

Philippa Foot presents the first case of a trolley or "tram" (which sounds as foreign on this side of the Atlantic as a cricket match, Yorkshire pudding, and warm beer). Foot contrasts a judge who frames an innocent person to prevent riots by a mob with a pilot who steers a disabled airplane away from a more crowded area toward a less crowded area. To make the cases more similar, Foot supposes that the mob has taken five people hostage, and she replaces the airplane with a trolley. The result is the original trolley case:

- A runaway trolley is speeding toward five track workers who cannot escape. To save the five, the trolley driver steers onto a sidetrack, foreseeing that the trolley will hit and kill one worker on the sidetrack.[2]

Both the judge and the trolley driver save five people in a way that results in the death of one innocent person. According to Foot, PDE supports the common intuition that the judge acts wrongly, even though the pilot could act rightly: the judge intends to kill the scapegoat as a means of appeasing the mob, but the driver does not intend to kill the one worker on the sidetrack. Foot finds this appeal to PDE plausible at first, but she proposes an alternative. According to her, the duty not to kill is stricter than the duty to save. The judge kills one to save five, but the driver would kill five by staying on the main track. (I disagree, but this point will become moot shortly.) Foot assumes that the driver cannot avoid killing one or five, so she concludes that the driver may minimize harm by killing one.

The original trolley case comes from Foot, but Judith Jarvis Thomson is responsible for making the trolley cases famous. She introduces some macabre twists to Foot's cases. First, she replaces the judge's legal machinations with a more violent way of saving five people at the expense of one:

- Five hospital patients urgently need different vital organs. A surgeon learns that a healthy person has organs that are a match for all five patients. To save the five, the surgeon takes the healthy person's organs and transplants them to the other five patients.[3]

The surgeon's intention does not matter to Thomson. She contrasts the transplant case with the case of the trolley driver and asks why the driver may turn the trolley even though the surgeon may not cut up the healthy person. She adds, "I like to call this the trolley problem, in honor of Mrs. Foot's example."[4] Thomson then argues that Foot cannot solve the problem by distinguishing the duty not to kill from the duty to save. According to Foot, the driver cannot avoid killing either the five or the one, but Thomson changes the case so that a passenger diverts the trolley:

- A runaway trolley is speeding toward five track workers who cannot escape, and the driver has fainted. A passenger grabs the steering wheel and turns the trolley onto a sidetrack, foreseeing that the trolley will hit and kill one worker on the sidetrack.[5]

In this version of the trolley case, the trolley already threatens five people, so the passenger would not kill anyone by doing nothing. Because the passenger does not face a conflict between the duty not to kill and the duty to save, it seems that the passenger kills one person to save five, as does the surgeon in the transplant case. Why, then, may the passenger divert the trolley onto the sidetrack to save five people on the trolley tracks, even though the surgeon may not cut out the healthy person's organs to save five people who need transplants?

Besides replacing the judge with the surgeon and the trolley driver with the trolley passenger, Thomson delivers a masterstroke with the most famous trolley case of all. She moves the man from the exit of a flooding cave to a footbridge over the trolley tracks. The result mixes farce, violence, and a puzzle for moral philosophers:

- A bystander and a massive man are standing on a footbridge over the trolley tracks when they see a runaway trolley speeding toward five track workers who cannot escape. The bystander, an expert in trolleys, realizes that the only way to stop the trolley is to drop a heavy object in its path. To save the workers, the bystander pushes the man onto the tracks, foreseeing his death (fig. 4.1).[6]

Again I use "massive man" instead of "fat man" both to avoid offending anyone and to emphasize that the bystander uses the man's mass, not the man's death, to stop the trolley. The label "massive" is also

Figure 4.1. The case of the bystander on the bridge

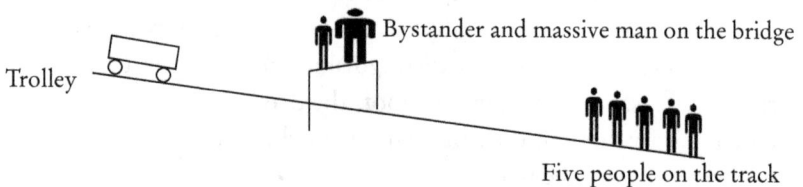

Trolley

Bystander and massive man on the bridge

Five people on the track

more accurate. As in Foot's case about the flooding cave, whether the man is fat is irrelevant, because a massive but lean bodybuilder would stop the trolley as effectively as the man in Thomson's example. Thomson does not assume that the bystander intends the man's death because she uses the case as an example of killing one person to save five people, not as an example of intending death. (I return to this point when I discuss the purpose of the footbridge case.) Thomson does assume that the bystander on the footbridge acts wrongly by pushing the massive man onto the tracks, so she asks why the passenger may turn the trolley to save people while the bystander on the footbridge may not push the man in front of the trolley. Both the bystander and the passenger stop a trolley in a way that saves five people and kills one person. The passenger moves the trolley toward one person, while the bystander moves one person toward the trolley, but both the passenger and the bystander kill someone, and the massive man is no worse off than the person who is run over by the trolley on the sidetrack. Why, then, may the passenger turn the trolley onto a sidetrack, even though the bystander may not push the massive man onto the trolley tracks?

In a later discussion of the trolley problem, Thomson pairs the footbridge case with a case that looks even more similar. She takes the job of diverting the trolley away from the passenger and gives it to a bystander who sees the threat to the five people and who happens to be near a switch in the tracks:

- A runaway trolley is speeding toward five track workers who cannot escape, and the driver has fainted. A bystander sees the danger to the five. The bystander throws a switch in the tracks to divert the trolley onto the sidetrack, foreseeing that the trolley will hit and kill one worker on the sidetrack (fig. 4.2).[7]

Now the challenge to explain common moral intuitions about the trolley cases is even stronger because the switch case resembles the footbridge case even more closely than it resembles the cases of the trolley driver and the passenger. Both bystanders stop a trolley from killing five people, and both of them stop the trolley in a way that kills one innocent person. Neither bystander would kill

Figure 4.2. The case of the bystander at the switch

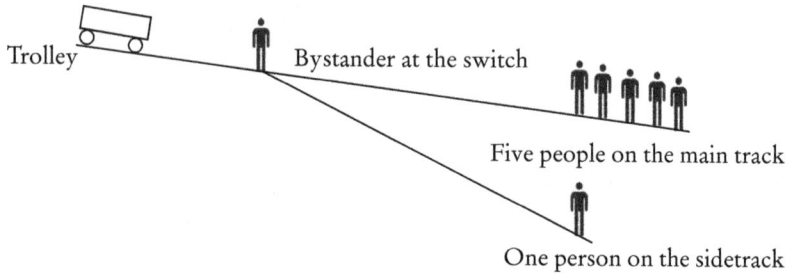

Trolley

Bystander at the switch

Five people on the main track

One person on the sidetrack

the five by doing nothing, so neither would violate the duty not to kill by doing nothing. Why, then, may the bystander at the switch divert the trolley onto the sidetrack to save five people even though the bystander on the footbridge may not push the massive man onto the tracks to save five people? Thomson's footbridge and switch cases have become the most common illustrations of the trolley problem.

Looking back years later, Thomson regrets "having muddied the water" by using the trolley problem in different ways: in one, explaining why the driver may divert the trolley, and in the other, explaining why the bystander at the switch may divert the trolley.[8] Thomson notes, however, that the muddy waters do no harm, because the cases are closely related. Philosophers do cause harm, or at least confusion, when they treat these cases as illustrations of PDE. Thomson does not make this mistake. She emphasizes the point that she does not use the trolley cases to defend or to criticize PDE:

> It may be worth stressing that what I suggest calls for attention is not (as some construals of "double effect" would have it) whether the agent's killing of the one is his means to something, and not (as other construals of "double effect" would have it) whether the death of the one is the agent's means to something, but rather what are the means by which the agent both kills and saves.[9]

Despite Thomson's disclaimer about the purpose of trolley cases, many philosophers and moral psychologists treat Thomson's cases as illustrations of PDE, sometimes even as paradigm illustrations. According to this common view, many people find PDE plausible because it seems to solve the trolley problem. The alleged solution is that the surgeon and bystander on the footbridge act wrongly because they intend to kill one person as a means of saving five, while the driver, the passenger, and the bystander at switch kill someone only as a foreseen side effect.[10]

PDE predates the trolley problem by centuries, over seven centuries if one treats Aquinas as the first one to state PDE.[11] Someone might assume that people *now* accept PDE because they believe that it solves the trolley problem, even if people in the past accepted PDE for other reasons. In fact, critics, not proponents, are the ones who assume that PDE is supposed to solve the trolley problem. After creating this straw man, critics explain why PDE does not solve the problem and conclude that there is no good reason to accept PDE. When critics make this case against PDE, they do not cite proponents of PDE who rely on the trolley problem or consider justifications of PDE that do not rely on intuitions. To show that I am not attacking a straw man myself, consider some quotations from PDE's critics. After contrasting the footbridge and the switch cases, one critic writes: "But as far as I know—as far as anyone knows—the venerable Doctrine of Double Effect has no justification beyond the fact that it is supported (imperfectly) by some of our intuitions."[12] Another critic asserts: "Proponents of the Doctrine maintain the dialectical advantage of offering answers to the Trolley Problem and related intractable cases."[13] Someone who knew PDE only from contemporary debates could be forgiven for thinking that proponents of PDE rely on intuitions about trolley and transplant cases or on arguments that PDE solves the trolley problem. In fact, the most prominent proponents of PDE barely mention trolley cases, and they do not rely on intuitions about specific cases to justify PDE.

I do not survey every defense of PDE, but consider Foot, Anscombe, Boyle, Nagel, and Cavanaugh. Foot uses the original trolley case to introduce PDE before arguing against it. In a later paper, she endorses PDE but says nothing about trolleys. To my knowledge,

Anscombe does not discuss the trolley problem at all, and her justification of PDE relies on moral absolutism, not on intuitive appeals.[14] Boyle presents both absolutist and agent-based justifications of PDE. Neither of these justifications relies on intuitions, and he mentions the footbridge case only in a footnote.[15] Nagel focuses on the case of twisting a child's arm, not on trolley and transplant cases.[16] In his book that defends PDE, Cavanaugh also does not mention the trolley problem or any trolley cases at all. Instead he argues that different types of willing must be morally relevant because morality applies only to voluntary actions.[17] To summarize: none of these proponents of PDE argues that PDE solves the trolley problem, and none of them treats intuitions about trolley and transplant cases as the main justifications for PDE or even as one justification for PDE. I do not know why the view that PDE is supposed to solve the trolley problem has become so widespread among contemporary philosophers. No matter why critics assume that PDE is supposed to solve the trolley problem, PDE's proponents have different reasons for treating the distinction between intention and foresight as relevant, reasons that many critics overlook or dismiss as merely metaphorical. Critics can reject the different justifications for PDE, but it is simply false to assert that "as far as anyone knows" PDE "has no justification beyond the fact that it is supported (imperfectly) by some of our intuitions."

Attributing PDE's appeal to the trolley problem is not merely a mistake about history. If philosophers assume that PDE is supposed to solve the trolley problem, they will end up dismissing PDE as confused, incomplete, or superfluous. My version of PDE cannot explain intuitions about all the trolley and transplant cases, but this inability is not a defect. No one principle can handle every case.

I have already mentioned a related problem about using trolley and transplant cases as illustrations of PDE: none of the cases are clear examples of intending death. Whether PDE is defined as a single principle or as a set of principles, the distinction between intention and foresight is essential to any version of PDE, yet none of the trolley and transplant cases include an agent who clearly intends death. In some cases, the agents clearly do *not* intend death because the death is irrelevant to their plans for saving five people:

- The trolley driver steers away from five people and toward one.
- The trolley passenger steers away from five people and toward one.
- The bystander throws a switch in the trolley tracks to divert the trolley away from five people and toward one.

In other cases, some philosophers assume that the agents intend death:

- The surgeon cuts out a healthy person's organs to save five people.
- The bystander pushes a massive man off a footbridge to save five people.

The assumption that the surgeon and the bystander intend death is certainly controversial and arguably false. When Thomson presents the transplant case, she is not concerned about PDE, so she does not specify whether the surgeon kills the healthy person before cutting out the vital organs. The surgeon could simply take the organs and leave the healthy person to die. The surgeon's plan would work just as well if the person were already dead or if another surgeon were standing by with replacement organs. In the footbridge case, the bystander needs the trolley to hit the massive man, not to kill him. Someone could insist on a definition of intended effects that includes the deaths of the healthy person and the massive man, but I do not repeat my defense of the strict definition and my criticisms of appeals to closeness. For now, the important point is that illustrations of PDE should include *clear* cases of intending a bad effect. The trolley and the transplant cases do not fit the bill. Unsurprisingly, then, many philosophers who take these cases as illustrations of PDE, or even as the main arguments for PDE, end up dismissing PDE as superfluous or as a sign of confusion.

Another reason that the trolley and the transplant cases make poor illustrations of PDE is that they include an innocent victim. The presence of an innocent victim focuses attention away from the agent and onto the victim. This focus on the victim makes the cases well suited to challenging consequentialism, which is exactly the goal that Foot had in mind when she cited the transplant case to show the conflict between consequentialism and ordinary moral judgments.[18]

In debates about PDE, however, the focus on the victim makes these cases poorly suited to illustrating the distinction between intention and foresight. From the victim's perspective, the agent's intention does not make the action any more or less harmful to the victim. Of course, critics can present cases in which the agent's intention seems irrelevant, but one should treat these cases as challenges to PDE, not as the paradigm illustrations of PDE.

Yet another problem with using trolley and transplant cases as illustrations of PDE is that the agent's intention is not the only variable in the different cases. In the trolley and transplant cases, the agents act in different ways: turning the trolley's steering wheel, cutting out organs, throwing a switch in the tracks, and pushing someone off a footbridge. These differences make it possible to distinguish the cases by appealing to principles other than PDE. For example, someone can argue that the surgeon and the bystander on the footbridge act wrongly because they treat their victims simply as means, while the driver, the passenger, and the bystander on the switch harm their victims without treating them simply as means. The agents who seem to act wrongly need their victims, or else their plans to save people would not work. If the healthy person and the massive man vanished, the surgeon and the bystander on the footbridge would not be able to save five people, at least not in the ways that they plan. By contrast, the agents who seem to act rightly do not need their victims at all. If the people on the sidetrack vanished, the driver, the passenger, and the bystander at the switch could still divert the trolley and save the five people. Some critics conclude that Kant's categorical imperative makes PDE superfluous.[19] I respond later. For now, the important point is that confusion results when people treat trolley cases as illustrations of PDE. For example, one critic asserts that PDE "distinguishes between harming someone as a means and harming someone as a side effect" and that "Kant, like Aquinas, endorses the idea that certain actions are wrong because they involve using someone as a means."[20] This assertion is an anachronistic description of Aquinas and an imprecise summary of Kant, who opposes using a person *simply* as a means, not using a person to achieve an end that the person shares. Another problem is that someone can intend to harm a person without using the person simply as a means. Someone could see harming an enemy as an end. Someone could also treat a person simply as a means without intending harm. For example, a surgeon could seek fame by performing an operation without a patient's consent. Even if the patient is unharmed, the surgeon uses the patient simply as a means to fame.

To see a good example of the distinction between intention and foresight—one that proponents of PDE actually use—consider two cases of treating pain in a way that causes death:

- A woman suffers from a painful case of bone cancer. She takes a lethal dose of cyanide that she knows will kill her, which will relieve her suffering.
- A woman suffers from a painful case of bone cancer. The dose of narcotics that she needs to relieve her pain will slow down her heart and lungs, causing her death. She takes the narcotic to end her pain, foreseeing that she will die.

In both of these cases, a suffering woman takes a pill, which kills her and ends her suffering. According to PDE, a relevant difference between these cases is that the first woman intends her death as a means of ending her suffering, while the second woman intends to end her suffering and foresees her death as a side effect. Because these cases are similar apart from the woman's intention, they serve as a traditional illustration of PDE.[21] In contemporary debates about PDE, however, philosophers usually ignore these cases or dismiss them as irrelevant.[22] Contemporary philosophers' lack of interest in these cases, even among philosophers who debate PDE, might result from the influence of consequentialism and contemporary deontology. Consequentialism clearly makes intentions irrelevant for judging actions, but many deontologists also base moral judgments entirely on the ways that actions affect other people, not on the ways that actions form agents. Someone who accepts this view of morality will have little interest in these cases of treating pain because neither woman's action mistreats another person.

A good illustration of PDE should focus attention on the agent, not on the victims. For example, the terror bombing and the strategic bombing kill innocent victims, but the two bombings are similar from the victims' perspectives. In a real war, the pilots would need to ask whether causing civilian casualties is unjust, but philosophers can set questions about justice aside to focus on questions about the pilots' intentions. Thus, like the cases of lethal narcotics and cyanide, the two bombing cases do a good job of illustrating PDE. Proponents can point to them as cases in which differences in the agents' intentions seem to be relevant, and critics can use them to argue that the different intentions are relevant only for judging the agents, not the actions.

Given that trolley cases are not good illustrations of PDE, why discuss them at all? First, trolley cases can be interesting, even if philosophers misstate their importance for PDE. Second, many critics of PDE use trolley cases to challenge PDE, so my defense of PDE would be incomplete if I did not respond.

An Apology for Contrived Cases in Moral Philosophy

I have argued that philosophers should not treat PDE as a potential solution to the trolley problem or use trolley and transplant cases as illustrations of PDE for three reasons. First, the claim that proponents of PDE rely on these cases is a historical error. Second, all of these cases include an innocent victim who focuses attention away from the agent. Third, the cases involve principles other than PDE, which makes it easy to dismiss PDE as superfluous and to confuse PDE with other principles. Other philosophers go even further than I have. They argue that philosophers should abandon trolley and transplant cases, along with other contrived cases in which agents know that they must either allow several people to die or cause the death of one innocent person.

One objection to these contrived cases is that philosophers who use them (allegedly) assume that moral philosophers' job is to formulate principles that fit their intuitions. As one critic says: "The intent of the examples is usually to incite us to formulate principles that correspond to, or even justify, our moral intuitions."[23] The problem with this objection is that a philosopher can use intuitions about cases to introduce a topic or to explain a specific principle without seeing these intuitions as the basis of the principle. A philosopher can also use intuitions to illustrate an objection to a principle without treating those intuitions as decisive. The best proponents of PDE rely on theoretical justifications that derive their force from premises about the nature of morality, not from intuitions about specific cases. The best critics of PDE try to explain both why PDE seems plausible and why it is ultimately mistaken, as Thomson and Scanlon do. They do not rely merely on counterexamples in which PDE seems to entail counterintuitive conclusions.

A second objection to contrived cases is that they are "cartoonish" in the sense of excluding details that any real agent would have to consider, such as the different probabilities of outcomes and different relations of the agent to the victims. One critic laments "that we are usually deprived of morally relevant facts that we would often have in real life, and often just as significantly, that we are required to stipulate that we are certain about some matters which in real life could never be certain."[24] I agree that any real agent would have to consider more than what philosophers stipulate in the trolley cases. In the switch and the footbridge cases, for example, the bystander at the switch would have to consider whether any of the potential victims has a chance of escaping, and the bystander on the footbridge would have to consider the possibility that the trolley might plow through the massive man and end up killing the other five people. The bystander at the switch would also have to consider how the predicament arose. As Thomson notes, the argument for diverting the trolley would be stronger if the person on the sidetrack ignored warnings and climbed a fence to walk on the tracks, but the argument would be weaker if the person on the sidetrack was promised safety from runaway trolleys.[25] That trolley cases are unrealistic does not make them a waste of time. Moral philosophers who analyze actions in contrived cases that do not occur outside their imaginations are similar to natural scientists who perform experiments in laboratory conditions that do not occur outside the lab. Natural scientists use laboratory conditions to isolate the effects of different variables. Similarly, moral philosophers use trolley cases to isolate the effects of different variables, such as the difference between intending and foreseeing or the difference between doing and allowing. Philosophers who analyze trolley cases do not need to assume that the cases isolate the "most fundamental" aspects of living morally, as one critic alleges.[26] That the agent's intention is *a* relevant consideration does not mean that it is *the most fundamental* consideration.

A third objection to contrived cases is that philosophers who use them assume that each hard case has only one solution.[27] I agree that the right judgment about the cases may be indeterminate, but philosophers can analyze trolley cases without assuming that a case includes enough information for a final moral judgment. When Thomson poses the trolley problem, she asks why the trolley driver and the passenger *may* turn the trolley, not why they *must* turn the trolley. The trolley problem is not the problem of figuring out what a particular agent should do. After all, the agent is usually a figment of a philosopher's imagination. The trolley problem is the problem of explaining why some harmful actions (e.g., diverting the trolley) are not as clearly wrong as other harmful actions that have similar effects (e.g., cutting out the healthy person's organs or pushing the massive man onto the trolley tracks).

A fourth objection to contrived cases is that they distract philosophers from discussing more important topics: "Trolleyology is at best engaged in what amounts to a moral sideshow," according to one critic.[28] I would welcome a world with no need to make life-and-death choices in war and medicine, but I have no insights about how to achieve this goal, and I doubt that philosophers could figure out how to achieve world peace and plentiful medical care if only they spent less time analyzing trolley cases. Philosophers' attention to trolley cases surely ranks low among the causes of war and poverty. Nothing, including looking down one's nose at philosophers who debate trolley cases, will overcome the scarcity of resources and facts of human biology that produce hard cases of allocating scarce drugs and treating women with life-threatening pregnancies. I see no reason to lament the opportunity costs of spending philosophers' time on contrived cases, and analyzing trolley cases can contribute to debates about moral theory. Philosophers can analyze contrived cases without giving up debating loftier questions about moral theory and without abandoning their responsibilities as citizens.

A Minimalist Version of PDE

As noted in this book's introduction, I define PDE as the principle that the distinction between intention and foresight is relevant for judging actions, not as a sufficient set of conditions for acting rightly, because morality is too complex to fit into a short list of principles. My version of PDE does not entail any implausible conclusions about trolley cases and transplant cases for a simple reason: it does not entail any conclusions about these cases at all. It says that the agent's intention is one relevant consideration for making moral judgments, but it does not identify every relevant consideration.

Other proponents of PDE treat it as a sufficient set of conditions for acting rightly. In a widely cited article about PDE's history, Joseph Mangan describes the following statement as PDE formulated "in its full modern dress":

> A person may licitly perform an action that he foresees will produce a good effect and a bad effect provided that four conditions are verified at one and the same time: (1) that the action in itself from its very object be good or at least indifferent; (2) that the good effect and not the evil effect be intended; (3) that the good effect be not produced by means of the evil effect; (4) that there be a proportionately grave reason for permitting the evil effect.[29]

Mangan's four conditions have become a standard version of PDE.[30] Some proponents of PDE combine Mangan's second and third conditions into one condition that prohibits intending a bad effect.[31] Regardless of how many conditions are included, the important question is whether these conditions can be jointly sufficient.

To see the problem for anyone who tries to turn PDE into a sufficient set of conditions for acting rightly, consider the footbridge and the switch cases. Why may the bystander at the switch divert the trolley onto the sidetrack, where it will kill one person instead of five, even though the bystander on the bridge may not push the massive man onto the tracks so that the trolley will not kill five people? My minimalist version of PDE does not answer this question, since neither bystander intends death, at least not according to the strict definition of intended effects that I have defended. Because neither bystander intends death, my version of PDE does not solve the trolley problem. I see no problem with this conclusion, because I do not believe that PDE must solve every problem about causing foreseen harms. Someone could argue that the cases are too far-fetched to be relevant, but I could make a similar argument by focusing on the more realistic cases of stealing organs and diverting a disabled airplane from a more crowded area toward a less crowded one.

Not all proponents of PDE agree about PDE's scope. For example, one proponent of PDE writes that a version of PDE should be "sufficient to determine permissibility in the relevant hard cases."[32] To fit this description, a version of PDE must include enough conditions to distinguish the bystander's throwing a switch to divert the trolley and the bystander's pushing the massive man onto the tracks to stop the trolley.

Someone could claim that PDE distinguishes these actions because the bystander on the footbridge violates Mangan's first condition (i.e., that the action is not wrong in itself). Suppose, however, that the massive man asks the bystander to push him, saying, "Don't worry, I've stopped trolleys from this very footbridge before without any harmful effects. I would jump myself, but I tweaked my ankle yesterday, so I need some help getting over this railing." Now it no longer seems so clear that the bystander may not push the massive man. Similarly, suppose that the five potential victims are the massive man's children or that the massive man put the potential victims in danger in the first place, repented, and is now asking the bystander to help him save the victims. Now it seems more plausible to say that the bystander may push the massive man. Someone may have different intuitions about whether the bystander in these variations may push the man, but the point of these variations is that pushing someone off the footbridge is not wrong in itself. Mangan uses the first condition to rule out actions that are wrong for reasons *other than* their bad effects. Traditional examples of such actions include theft, adultery, fornication, perjury, and lying. The first condition does not rule out actions that are wrong *because of* their bad effects, such as the bystander's pushing the man off the footbridge.

A proponent of PDE could also try to solve the trolley problem by saying that the bystander on the footbridge intends to kill, or at least to harm, the massive man. This solution fails because the bystander can give a complete and honest answer to the question "What is your goal, and what are all the steps in your plan to achieve that goal?" without saying anything about killing or harming the massive man. For example, the bystander could say, "To save those five people, I will push this portly fellow onto the tracks so that the trolley will hit him and stop before it hits the five." The bystander's goal is to save five people, and the chain of causes and effects that will save the five includes the man's being hit, not his being killed or harmed.

If, however, someone assumes that PDE must solve the trolley problem, then a broad definition of intention looks tempting. For example, someone could say that an agent intends all the effects that are closely connected to the action, so the bystander on the footbridge intends the massive man's death. This appeal to closeness serves the immediate purpose of supporting the intuition that the bystander acts wrongly—although someone could modify the case in such a way that the massive man survives the impact but dies from internal bleeding days later—but this intuitive appeal comes at the steep cost of making PDE untenable. Any definition of "closeness" faces numerous counterexamples. No matter how closely one effect follows another, an agent can intend one without the other, as when a jogger runs without intending the stress on her knees. An agent can even work against an effect that constitutes the intended effect, as when a son with a speech impediment struggles against the stuttered words that constitute his testimony on behalf of his father.

So far I have argued that the bystander on the footbridge does not violate Mangan's first condition about doing something wrong in itself or any condition about intending a bad effect. Those who insist on treating PDE as a solution to the trolley problem have two options: (1) deny that the bystander on the footbridge acts wrongly or (2) revise the proportionality condition so that it solves the trolley problem. The first option would make PDE intuitively implausible, so I focus on the second option.

Proponents of PDE have offered different versions of the proportionality condition. Fortunately, I do not need to sort through all of them here.[33] The trolley and transplant cases are designed so that the proportion of people killed to people saved stays constant. Thus the proportionality condition cannot distinguish the cases.

Someone could revise the proportionality condition to say that the action must not be wrong for any other reason.[34] For example, the bystander's pushing the man onto the tracks could be right if the man is the father of the potential victims or a repentant criminal who put the potential victims in danger and wrong if the man is an innocent bystander. This revised proportionality condition differs from Mangan's first condition, which says that the action must not be wrong in itself. In Mangan's version of PDE, the first condition does not serve as a catch-all like the revised proportionality condition, which says that the action must not be wrong for another reason.

By including a catch-all condition, a proponent of PDE would give up on finding a set of principles that is sufficient to resolve hard cases because other principles are needed to determine when an action is wrong for another reason. Thus the revised proportionality condition makes PDE similar to my minimalist version. The difference is that my version leaves open the possibility that an agent may intend a harmful effect without acting wrongly, even if the rule against intending a harmful effect is stricter than the rule against causing it as a side effect. For example, I have argued that the difference between intending and knowingly causing pain is relevant even if intending pain is not always wrong.

When proponents try to turn PDE into a set of conditions that are sufficient to make an action right, they do not merely expose PDE to counterexamples. They also undermine the basis of PDE. To see why, suppose that parents leave a teenager alone for a night. The parents could say something like "Keep yourself safe" or "Don't do anything you wouldn't do if we were home" and rely on the teenager's judgment and good character. This plan might be risky, but it could work for some teenagers. Suppose, however, that the parents try to give the teenager a set of rules: "Be in bed by 11:00. Do not have more than two friends in the house at the same time. Do not allow anyone of the opposite sex to sleep over." And so on. The parents should not be surprised if the teenager regards the rules legalistically—that is, as hoops to jump through instead of rules that direct the teenager toward what is good—and starts to look for loopholes. The teenager might think, "What if I go to bed at 11:00 and get up at 11:05? What if I have twenty friends over and we stay in the garage? What if both boys and girls stay all night but nobody sleeps?" And so on. Similarly, trying to turn PDE into a complete checklist invites a legalistic view of moral rules as hurdles that stand between people and happiness. By contrast, the Socratic view of morality that I have defended treats moral rules as directions for becoming truly happy. This view can explain why the agent's character, and thus the agent's intention, is relevant for judging an action. A legalistic view cannot. Human happiness or fulfillment is too complex to be captured in a set of rules, so proponents of PDE cannot treat the rules as directions for being truly happy if they try to make PDE into a complete checklist—that is, if they try to make PDE "sufficient to determine permissibility in the relevant cases."[35]

To use another analogy about parenting, suppose that someone says to a parent, "Here are four rules that you can use to find the correct answer about what you should allow your children to do." The parent should suppose that the list is either incomplete or so general that it needs to be supplemented with other considerations about parenting. Raising a child is too complex to be captured in a list of rules. Living morally is also too complex to be captured in Mangan's four conditions or any other list of principles. To continue the analogy, suppose that the person with the list of rules says, "Of course this list can't answer every question about parenting. The list only applies when your parenting decisions will have good and bad effects." This limitation is no limitation at all, because all of a parent's decisions—or at least all the decisions that are not trivially easy—will have good and bad effects. Likewise, every significant action has good and bad effects. If I drive my car, my action causes pollution. If I stay home, my action still takes time I could have used doing something else.

By abandoning the attempt to make PDE solve the trolley problem, I am not retreating in the face of criticisms or conceding that critics are chipping away at PDE. When Aquinas analyzes self-defense, he does not list all the conditions that people must satisfy when they kill in self-defense.[36] Some proponents of PDE conclude that Aquinas does not defend a version of PDE.[37] I conclude that he does not oversimplify morality. Doing something intrinsically wrong, having a bad intention, and causing disproportionate harm are not the only ways that people can act wrongly. They also can ignore specific duties such as a parent's duty to a child, act ungrate-fully, set a bad example, and so on.

My minimalist version of PDE does not say that the driver in the original trolley case acts rightly. It says that the driver does not intend death. It also says that the driver's intention is relevant for judging whether the driver's action is right or wrong. This point about the relevance of intentions is the main point in contemporary debates about PDE, so a minimalist version still adds something to these debates even if it does not produce a final judgment about these cases. As noted in the introduction, I am not alone in treating PDE as one principle regarding the relevance of intentions rather than a set of principles that resolves hard cases, but the label "principle of double effect" is not essential to my argument. Someone could make a minimalist version of PDE more similar to a traditional version like Mangan's by saying something along the following lines:

> An agent may knowingly cause a harmful effect if and only if (1) the agent does not intend an effect that people may not intend (such as the death of an innocent human being), and (2) the action is not wrong for any other reason.

This version of PDE would resolve some cases in the literature about PDE, assuming that people may not intend the death of an innocent human being. For example, this version would distinguish between a physician's euthanizing a patient and a physician's giving a patient a lethal dose of a narcotic. It also would distinguish between the terror bombing and the strategic bombing and between drug withholding and drug rationing.

I have no substantive objection to this version of PDE, but it seems like a more obscure way of saying that the distinction between intention and foresight is relevant for judging actions. Further, I worry about creating the false impression that the agent's intention is the most important consideration for judging actions, so all other considerations can be swept up into one condition. In the original trolley case, the driver's intention is one relevant consideration, but the driver could act wrongly even without intending a harmful effect. For example:

- The situation is similar to the original trolley case, except that steering onto the sidetrack kills a convalescent instead of a track worker. The convalescent is on the sidetrack because the trolley driver and workers set up a picnic table and invited her to have lunch there, promising her that the sidetrack has been inactive for years and is perfectly safe.[38]

This driver seems to act wrongly by breaking a promise to the convalescent. Perhaps my intuition is mistaken, but the promise is a relevant detail. A version of PDE could include a condition about keeping promises, but what if the track workers have received high salaries to compensate them for the risk of being hit by a trolley? If proponents of PDE try to explain why the driver acts wrongly by appealing to the condition that the action must not be wrong in itself, then they cannot distinguish between the driver in this case, who seems to act wrongly, and the driver in the original trolley case, who seems to act rightly. The difference between the cases lies in the circumstances, not in the action itself. Proponents could add more conditions to PDE, but even if they could find a list that seemed complete, they would not rule out the possibility that a clever philosopher would find a case in which someone acted wrongly without violating any of the conditions. Instead of trying to meet the impossible demand of making PDE solve the trolley problem, proponents of PDE should appeal to PDE to distinguish between the driver's action and acts of murder and should rely on other principles to determine whether the driver acts rightly. The same strategy applies to other cases.

Someone could argue that my version of PDE makes it impossible to explain why some cases seem to be morally similar.[39] Recall the cases of the anesthesiologist who kills a patient to make organs available and the vivisecting surgeon who cuts out the patient's vital organs. According to the strict definition of intended effects that I have defended, only the anesthesiologist intends death, because the surgeon needs to take the victim's organs, not to end the victim's life. The alleged problem is that the actions seem to be wrong for the same reason, while my analysis says that only the anesthesiologist commits murder.[40] As explained earlier, however, I agree that both the anesthesiologist and the surgeon act wrongly for the same reason: they treat the victim unjustly. I also agree that this injustice is the most serious reason that they act wrongly. That the anesthesiologist also intends death explains why the action would be wrong even if it did not treat the patient unjustly—for example, if the patient were already dead—but this point does not permit the surgeon's action or lessen the surgeon's culpability in any way.

A critic could ask, "If the surgeon acts wrongly without intending harm, why is the same not true for the bystander who throws a switch on the tracks, or for the pilot who steers away from a more crowded area and toward a less populated one, or for the strategic bomber who kills innocent bystanders?" Again, I do not assume that any of these agents acts rightly. Common intuitions about all these cases may be mistaken. In fact, Thomson has changed her position and now argues that the bystander at the switch may not divert the trolley after all.[41] I see nothing implausible about a version of PDE that *does not explain* all the common intuitions about trolley cases, but a version of PDE would be implausible if it *contradicted* all these intuitions, so I will explain how someone who accepts a minimalist version of PDE still can accept common intuitions about trolley cases.

As noted earlier, someone can distinguish between the footbridge and the switch cases by appealing to the rule against treating someone simply as a means. I refer to this rule as the "Kantian rule" without trying to answer exegetical questions about Kant's categorical imperative, such as how the positive part of the rule ("Treat humanity as an end") is related to the negative part ("Do not treat humanity simply as a means"). I also focus only on actions that affect a person other than the agent, even though Kant applies the categorical imperative to actions that affect only the agent. The bystander on the footbridge forces the massive man to serve as a means of stopping the trolley, but the bystander at the switch does not use the person on the sidetrack at all. Similarly, the surgeon in the transplant case forces the healthy person to serve as a means of providing organs, but the trolley driver and the bystander at the switch do not use their victims at all. Defining which actions treat someone simply as a means is a difficult problem, but there are few clearer examples than the surgeon's cutting out the healthy person's organs and the bystander's pushing the massive man onto the tracks. Assuming that the surgeon and the bystander do break the Kantian rule, someone can accept my version of PDE and use the Kantian rule to explain common intuitions about the transplant and the footbridge cases.

Someone could argue that the Kantian rule makes my version of PDE superfluous, but not every application of PDE is a clear case of treating someone simply as a means. For example, my version of PDE explains the difference between a child's intending to incite a sibling's envy and knowingly causing a sibling's envy, but the child does not use the sibling as a means of achieving a further end. Someone could suggest that the child who intends to incite envy fails to treat the sibling's humanity as an end in itself, so that a complete version of Kant's categorical imperative does explain why the child may not intend to incite envy. I do not deny the possibility that the categorical imperative explains everything that my version of PDE explains. I also do not deny the possibility that the categorical imperative or another general rule is the basis of *all* other moral rules. My version of PDE still would not be superfluous because it would make it easier to explain why some actions violate the categorical imperative while other actions with similar effects do not. As explained in this book's introduction, I see the relation of PDE to other moral rules as similar to the relation of the principle "To calculate 25 percent of a number, divide it by four" to other mathematical principles. Even if the principle about calculating 25 percent does not add anything to the other mathematical principles, it is still true, and it makes calculating percentages easier in many cases. Analogously, my version of PDE does not modify other moral principles, but it does clarify them. For example, a physician who accepts PDE might think, "Should I ration this drug to save five people? I know murder is wrong, but is rationing the drug an example of murder? No, because the patient's death would not be part of my intention."

The physician who accepts PDE does not make an exception to the rule against murder; instead, the physician sees why rationing the drug is not an example of murder.

THE LOOP CASE

Thomson presents yet another trolley case to challenge those who use the Kantian rule to explain why the bystander may throw the switch even though the surgeon may not cut up the healthy person. She modifies the original trolley case by adding a loop in the track so that the bystander needs the one person on the sidetrack to stop the trolley:

• The case is similar to the case of the bystander at the switch, except that the sidetrack loops around and joins the main track. By itself, throwing the switch would not save five people because the trolley would loop around and hit them, but there is a massive man on the sidetrack, and his mass will stop the diverted trolley from looping around and hitting the five people on the main track.[42]

This case is a hybrid of the cases of the bystander who throws the switch to divert the trolley and the bystander who pushes the massive man into the trolley's path. The only difference between the loop case and the switch case is that the loop case includes an extra bit of track and the detail that the person on the side track is a massive man who is large enough to stop the trolley from looping around hitting the five people on the sidetrack (fig. 4.3). The only difference between the loop case and the footbridge case is that the bystanders cause the trolley to hit the massive man in different ways.

   All the trolley cases are far-fetched, but at least the cases of the trolley driver and the passenger resemble the case of a pilot who steers a disabled airplane away from a more-crowded to a less-crowded area. What is the point of adding the looping track? Thomson uses this case to challenge those who rely on the Kantian rule to explain why the bystander at the switch may divert the trolley even though the bystander on the footbridge may not push the massive man into

Figure 4.3. The loop case

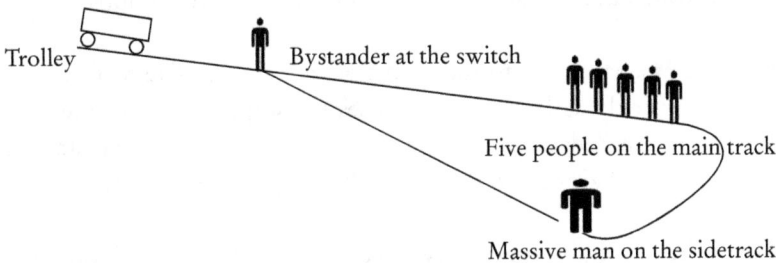

the trolley's path. In the loop case, the bystander uses the massive man simply as a means, since the bystander needs the trolley to hit the man so that it will not loop around and run over the five people. The problem for the Kantian rule, according to Thomson, is that the loop case seems similar to the original case of the bystander at the switch, so both bystanders act rightly. Seeing no reason why the looping track would be relevant, Thomson concludes that this case must be similar to the original case of the bystander at the switch.[43] If so, the Kantian rule does not distinguish between the original bystander at the switch, who seems to act rightly, and the bystander on the footbridge, who seems to act wrongly. As noted earlier, Thomson's objection to the Kantian rule does not threaten my version of PDE directly, but I respond to show that someone who accepts my version of PDE can still explain common intuitions about trolley cases.

A proponent of PDE could argue that the bystander in the loop case does not use the one person simply as a means because the bystander could intend only to delay the trolley's hitting the five. A proponent of PDE could also argue that the bystander could intend only to keep the five from being hit from the front.[44] I find these arguments unnecessary because I see nothing implausible about saying that the bystander acts wrongly. In fact, I have no clear intuition about the loop case at all, perhaps because it is even more contrived than the other trolley cases. Assuming that the bystander seeks to save the five people—not merely to prolong their lives by a few seconds or to prevent them from being hit from a specific direction—the bystander does act wrongly by using the man simply as a means to this end. To support this conclusion, consider a variation of the loop case in which the bystander's use of the man is more obvious:

- The case is similar to the loop case, but the massive man, who is surprisingly agile for his size, tries to escape. The bystander sees the attempted escape, jumps into the trolley, grabs the steering wheel, and zigzags so that the trolley hits the massive man.[45]

I see no relevant difference between this case and the other loop cases. As others have argued, it seems implausible to say that there is a relevant distinction between throwing a person at a trolley and throwing a trolley at a person.[46] I do not deny a distinction between the original trolley and zigzag cases because the original driver does not throw or steer the trolley *at* the one worker in the sense of targeting the worker. The zigzagging bystander does.[47]

I still need to explain why the footbridge and the loop cases often elicit different intuitions if both bystanders use someone simply as a means. I cannot speak with certainty about intuitions that I do not share, but I suspect that the details of the loop case obscure the bystander's use of the one person. By contrast, the bystander's use of the massive man on the footbridge is obvious. People might recognize that the bystander's pushing the massive man uses him simply as a means, and is wrong for that reason, but then fail to recognize that the bystander in the loop case uses the massive man in a morally similar, but less obvious, way.

My negative judgment of the loop case is not unusual. In one empirical study, a slim majority (56 percent) of subjects answered yes to the question "Is it morally permissible for [the bystander in the loop case] to throw the switch?"[48] In another study, only 48 percent of subjects judged the bystander's action as permissible.[49] Neither study shows a strong consensus that the bystander's action in the loop case is right or wrong. In another study, however, 81 percent of subjects judged the bystander's action as "acceptable."[50] One explanation of the different results focuses on the wording of the cases.[51] Another explanation is that different studies presented different cases to the subjects. When subjects consider the loop case in isolation, they may be more likely to find the bystander's action morally right because the bystander's use of the man is less obvious when the bystander throws a switch than when the bystander pushes the man onto the tracks. When subjects consider the loop case alongside other trolley cases, including the footbridge case, they may be more likely to find the bystander's action morally wrong because pairing the loop case with the footbridge case draws attention to both bystanders' use of the victim. Even if this explanation is incorrect, the important point is that philosophers should not simply assume that the bystander in the loop case acts rightly and dismiss any rule that does not fit this assumption.

Some critics find it implausible to say that the extra track makes a difference in the loop case so that the original bystander at the switch acts rightly while the bystander at the switch in the looping case acts wrongly.[52] The trolley cannot reach the extra track because it will either continue on the main track or run into the massive man on the sidetrack before it reaches the loop. These critics assume that the only relevant consideration is how the action affects other people. If morality consisted entirely of principles about treating others properly, then the extra track in the loop case would be irrelevant. If, however, the Socratic view of morality is correct, then the extra track can be relevant because it requires the bystanders to act in different ways to save the five workers. In the original switch case, the bystander does not need the trolley to hit the person on the sidetrack. In the loop case, the bystander does need the trolley to hit the massive man, or else the trolley will loop around and kill the five other people. The difference in the bystanders' plans does not affect the victim, but this difference means that the bystanders have different relations to their victims.

If my analysis of the loop case is correct, the basic disagreement is between those who accept some form of the Socratic view of morality and those who believe that whether an agent acts rightly or wrongly depends *entirely* on how the agent affects other people. The Socratic view can explain both why the original trolley and loop cases seem similar and also why they differ: the actions have the same effect on the victim, but they form the agent differently. I have argued that intending death can corrupt the agent whereas knowingly causing death would not. Similarly, using someone simply as a means can form habits or dispositions that are obstacles to peaceful relationships with other people. In the case of the bystander at the switch, the agent is related to the victim merely as a cause of harm. In the transplant, the footbridge, and the loop cases, the agents might not intend harm, but they do include the victims in their plans by using their bodies as tools for saving five people. Thus the agents who seem to act wrongly have a different relationship with their victims than do the agents who seem to act rightly.

As noted earlier, Thomson stresses that she does not present the trolley cases to challenge PDE.[53] She uses the loop case to argue that one cannot solve the trolley problem by appealing to the Kantian rule. Contrary to the loop case's original purpose, some critics treat the case as a counterexample to PDE. One critic asserts that PDE "famously choked on the loop case," while another describes the loop as "a general challenge to double effect."[54] I can understand why someone would see the loop case as a counterexample to the Kantian rule, but I do not understand why anyone would see the case as a counterexample to PDE. To make the loop case a counterexample to PDE, a critic must assume that the bystander intends to kill or harm the massive man. This assumption is unwarranted. In the cave case, counterfactuals about the massive man's possible survival might sound ridiculous, but there is nothing ridiculous about a counterfactual in which the massive man in the loop case survives for days or weeks instead of being killed immediately by the trolley's impact. Someone could imagine that the man is so massive that he absorbs the trolley's impact and walks away unscathed. The bystander in the loop case might foresee harm or death, but these effects are foreseen side effects, not intended effects (fig 4.4). Someone can agree with my analysis of the bystander's intention without accepting the strict definition of intended effects. In fact, Thomson introduces the loop case precisely because it seems so similar to the case of the bystander at the switch, in which the bystander clearly does *not* intend death.

I have appealed to PDE to distinguish some cases (such as the terror and the strategic bombing cases) and to the Kantian rule to distinguish others (such as the footbridge and the switch cases). Although I analyze these cases differently, I do not deny that they have something in common. I do not defend the Kantian rule here, but someone

Figure 4.4. The bystander's intention in the loop case

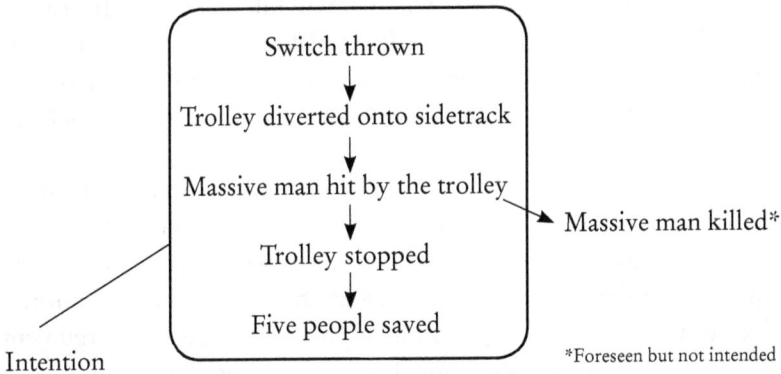

who accepts both PDE and the Kantian rule could argue that intending someone's death and treating someone simply as a means both corrupt the agent's character by distorting the agent's relationships with other people.

AN OBJECTION FROM NEUROSCIENCE AND MORAL PSYCHOLOGY

I have criticized the intuition that the bystander in the loop case acts rightly. In the next chapter I criticize some common intuitions about pregnancy cases. Critics could argue that I am cutting out the ground beneath my feet: if intuitions about these famous cases are unreliable, why trust the other intuitions that support PDE? And without these intuitions, why should anyone accept PDE? Some critics develop this challenge to PDE by citing empirical studies in neuroscience and moral psychology as evidence that PDE has no rational basis.

Arguments designed to debunk PDE include empirical evidence that automatic, emotional brain processes tend to produce nonconsequentialist judgments, such as the judgments that fit PDE, while conscious, cognitive brain processes tend to produce consequentialist judgments.[55] In one study, subjects were asked to judge different trolley cases. Functional magnetic resonance imaging (fMRI) showed increased blood flow in brain areas linked to cognition when the study's subjects judged that the bystander at the switch may divert the trolley onto the sidetrack, where it will kill one person instead of five.[56] By contrast, fMRI showed increased blood flow in brain areas linked to emotion when subjects judged that the bystander on the footbridge may *not* push the massive man onto the trolley tracks to save five people.

According to Joshua Greene, a prominent advocate of debunking arguments that rely on evidence from neuroscience, "The neuroscientific elements of my research may have been essential for getting my name in the newspaper, but they are not essential to my normative argument."[57] Evidence used to support the debunking argument against PDE does not come only from neuroscience:[58]

- Subjects are more likely to make consequentialist judgments when they have impaired emotional responses (e.g., in cases of psychopathy and brain lesions).
- Subjects are more likely to make consequentialist judgments after solving counterintuitive math problems.
- Subjects are less likely to make consequentialist judgments when they perform a distracting cognitive task.

These studies seem to confirm that consequentialist judgments result from cognitive brain processes and that nonconsequentialist judgments, including the judgments that fit PDE, result from emotional brain processes.

I do not agree that psychopaths and people with brain lesions are models of clear-headed moral reasoning, because psychopathy and brain lesions could block people from recognizing what is relevant for judging actions. I agree, however, that nonconsequentialist judgments *often* come from knee-jerk reactions and other emotional responses—for example, "The terror bombing just seems wrong!"[59] I am not surprised to hear that many people, including many professional philosophers, follow their emotions when they make moral judgments.[60] I would also not be surprised to hear that many of my judgments result from emotional responses. Why would I be immune from the nonrational influences that affect other people's judgments?

The question that matters now is whether my judgments about PDE are merely emotional responses that have no rational basis.

Moral psychologists cannot determine whether a judgment is reliable merely by identifying the brain process that produces the judgment. If I participated in a study that used fMRIs of people judging different cases, I might think something along these lines: "I don't want to be embarrassed, so I had better think carefully. This case sounds like the one from Thomson, or was it Scanlon? If I say that the action is right, I'll contradict what I've written about PDE, so I'll say that the action is wrong." My judgment results from a conscious, rational process, but the judgment is still not reliable. Perhaps my emotions first led me to accept PDE, and I am now using conscious reasoning to make sure that my judgments about specific cases fit PDE. Conversely, a judgment could be reliable even if it was produced by an automatic, emotional brain process, as when fear of pain causes people to judge that they should not touch a hot stove.

When critics try to debunk PDE, they do not reject all judgments that result from automatic, emotional responses, but they argue that these judgments are unreliable in unfamiliar cases, which one critic defines as cases in which people "have inadequate evolutionary, cultural, or personal experience."[61] A chess grandmaster's intuitions about chess are more reliable than an amateur's conscious reasoning. The grandmaster can intuit a winning move in one position because the position resembles similar positions that the grandmaster has played or studied. But the grandmaster is not born with reliable intuitions. Even a child chess prodigy needs practice and study to develop a grandmaster's intuitions, and these intuitions are reliable only because different chess games have similar positions and patterns. If a grandmaster relies on intuitions when playing poker for the first time, the grandmaster will be an easy mark for experienced poker players. A proponent of PDE could argue that people's intuitions are attuned to truths about morality even in unfamiliar cases, but I agree that it would be a "cognitive miracle" if the intuitions that people develop through familiar cases were reliable in completely different cases, as it would be a stroke of incredibly good luck if the grandmaster consistently intuited how to win while playing poker for the first time.[62] Other players would see the grandmaster's success as a sign of cheating, not of beginner's luck or well-tuned intuitions.

If critics are correct that having reliable intuitions about unfamiliar cases would be a cognitive miracle, the key question is whether PDE seems intuitively plausible only in unfamiliar cases. When people make intuitive judgments that fit PDE, are they more like the grandmaster who intuits a winning chess move or the chess grandmaster who relies on instincts to play poker for the first time? According to critics, the intuitions that support PDE come from cases of trolleys and transplants, but intuitions about these cases are unreliable because they are about killing and saving people in ways that have become possible only recently in human history, such as pushing someone into the path of a trolley that threatens five people.[63] I agree that trolley cases are unfamiliar, but people do have experience with many cases in which common intuitions seem to fit PDE. It does not take a miracle to see that a child's intending to incite a sibling's envy will form bad habits in the child or that intending to reveal a friend's secret will create an obstacle to friendship. As explained earlier, PDE was not designed to solve the trolley problem by explaining intuitions about trolley and transplant cases, so the unfamiliarity of trolley cases does not undermine PDE. Critics have not ruled out the possibility that people accept PDE, at least implicitly, because of their experience with familiar cases and that their acceptance of PDE explains their reactions to cases of trolleys and transplants.

To summarize, here is what I consider to be the strongest debunking argument against PDE that refers to empirical studies about how people make moral judgments:[64]

1. Intuitions that fit PDE are the outputs of automatic, emotional brain processes.
2. The outputs of automatic, emotional brain processes are unreliable in unfamiliar cases.
3. Intuitions that fit PDE are unreliable in unfamiliar cases. [1,2]
4. People have no reason to accept PDE apart from intuitions about unfamiliar cases.
5. People have no reason to accept PDE. [3,4]

I have said little about the first premise, as I have no expertise in psychology, and identifying problems with empirical studies that support this premise would not rule out the possibility that improved studies will confirm the premise. I agree with the second and third premises—although my defense of PDE does not require either—so my response to the debunking argument has focused on the fourth premise: that is, that PDE depends on intuitions about unfamiliar cases. Not all the intuitions that fit PDE come from unfamiliar cases, but critics would not refute PDE even if they could debunk all the intuitions that fit PDE, because not all defenses of PDE depend on intuitions. I have defended PDE by appealing to the way that intention and foresight form the agent's character, and others defend PDE by referring to the scope of moral judgments or the existence of exceptionless moral rules. To debunk PDE, critics would need to show that all these defenses of PDE fail.[65] To be fair, some critics note that empirical studies alone cannot settle any debate in moral philosophy.[66] Other critics, however, do cite empirical studies as decisive evidence against PDE.[67] At most, empirical studies of people's moral judgments could debunk some intuitions that fit PDE. These studies cannot show that every defense of PDE fails, so no empirical study can provide decisive evidence against PDE.

I should add that the cases in most of the empirical studies cited in debunking arguments are not clear illustrations of PDE. The footbridge case illustrates the Kantian rule about using a person simply as a means, not PDE. The bystander on the bridge uses the massive man as a means without intending death, but one critic conflates the Kantian rule and PDE by speaking of the "means/side-effect" distinction.[68] Further, the version of the footbridge case in one well-known study is not even a clear illustration of using someone simply as a means. This study replaces the massive man with someone who is wearing a heavy backpack.[69] This change opens up the possibility that the bystander uses the *backpack's* mass, not the *person's* mass, to stop the trolley, so someone could argue that the bystander does not act wrongly by pushing the backpack onto the tracks. I will not develop this argument because it is not essential to my defense of PDE and because it seems that the bystander uses the person as a means of getting the backpack onto the tracks. I mention the argument that the bystander uses the backpack's mass not to defend the bystander's action but to show that what seems like an irrelevant change to critics of a principle such as PDE or the Kantian principle—such as changing the massive man on the footbridge over the trolley tracks to a person wearing a heavy backpack—might be relevant after all.

In this chapter I have focused on objections to PDE that refer to trolley cases. These cases do not refute my minimalist version of PDE, which neither solves the trolley problem nor entails false conclusions about trolley and transplant cases. Other objections to PDE refer to cases in which a medical procedure saves a pregnant woman's life but also kills her unborn child. In the next chapter I analyze these cases and other alleged counterexamples from medicine and war.

Chapter Five

Hard Cases in Medicine and War

According to a view that developed in the nineteenth century, PDE distinguishes the following pair of cases of life-threatening pregnancies:

- A pregnant woman's life is in danger because her child's head is stuck in the birth canal during labor. To save the woman, the surgeon performs a craniotomy, which consists of making an incision in the child's skull and collapsing the skull. The surgeon then removes the child's body from the birth canal.
- A pregnant woman's life is danger because she has cervical cancer. To treat her cancer, a surgeon performs a hysterectomy. The woman is only four months pregnant, so the surgeon knows that the child cannot survive.[1]

The traditional view says that the craniotomy is wrong because the surgeon kills the child "directly," or as a means of saving the mother, but the hysterectomy can be right because the surgeon kills the child only "indirectly," or as a side effect. When Anglo-American philosophers criticized PDE in the twentieth century, many of them used the craniotomy case against PDE. They found it perverse to say that the surgeon must allow the woman and her child to die instead of saving at least the woman, and some of them argued that no principle distinguishes the craniotomy from the hysterectomy.

I side with the critics on both points, but problems with the traditional view of the craniotomy are not problems for PDE itself, because the surgeon can perform the craniotomy without intending the child's death. I have been described as "biting the bullet" by denying that the surgeon intends death.[2] My jaw is unclenched. I argue that my analysis of the craniotomy is both true and intuitively plausible. In the first section of this chapter I explain why the craniotomy is morally similar to the hysterectomy. In the second section I apply my analysis of the craniotomy and the hysterectomy to other pregnancy cases, including cases of ectopic pregnancy and a case of a pregnant woman with pulmonary hypertension. In the third section I look at some other cases from medicine and war that critics present as counterexamples to PDE. In the fourth section I respond to Warren Quinn's view of direct and indirect harmful agency, a view that replaces the distinction between intended and foreseen side effects and that supports the conclusion that the surgeon in the craniotomy case acts wrongly. In the fifth section I conclude my analysis of pregnancy cases and my defense of PDE by explaining why people have different intuitions about the cases discussed in this book. Before saying more on the craniotomy, I should note that, as I wrote in the introduction, caesarean sections have replaced craniotomies as remedies for obstructed labor, but the principles used to analyze the craniotomy case are still relevant.

Throughout my analyses of pregnancy cases, I use "child" to include both an embryo and a fetus and to avoid the charge of using clinical terms (e.g., "fetus" and "embryo") that obscure the gruesome details of the craniotomy and other surgeries. To focus on questions about PDE and intentions, I set aside questions about the moral status of human embryos and fetuses.[3]

THE CRANIOTOMY AND HYSTERECTOMY CASES

Many histories of PDE begin with Aquinas and his discussion of self-defense. According to Aquinas, "Moral acts take their species according to what is intended, and not according to what is beside the intention."[4] This principle does not mean merely that the agent's intention is relevant for judging the action. It means that someone must consider the agent's intention to know what sort of action is being judged. For example, an observer cannot determine whether another person is apologizing merely by looking at a set of effects. The agent's intention determines whether a set of bodily movements is an apology. Saying "I'm sorry" can be an apology for wrongdoing, but it can also be a statement of regret. Someone who says, "I'm sorry that the hurricane damaged your house" is expressing regret, not admitting wrongdoing. People can also apologize without saying a word, as by sending flowers. After stating the general principle about the species of moral actions, Aquinas argues that a person may use lethal force in self-defense only when the attacker's death is outside the agent's intention (*praeter intentionem*) or when the person acts with public authority, and only when the person does not use excessive force against the attacker.[5] This analysis of self-defense raises some interpretive questions, but I do not address them here. Unlike some proponents of PDE, I make no attempt to determine the correct interpretation of Aquinas, whose writings may be consistent with more than one interpretation. I begin with Aquinas to trace a change in the way that proponents of PDE analyze actions, not to claim his authority as evidence for my version of PDE or for my analysis of the craniotomy case.

Unfortunately, later proponents of PDE obscured the insight that the agent's intention determines an action's moral species. Consider Jean Pierre Gury's influential version of PDE from the nineteenth century:

> It is licit to bring about [*ponere*] a good or indifferent cause, from which a double effect immediately [*immediate*] follows, one good but the other bad, if there is a grave cause [*causa gravis*] and the agent's end is upright [*honestus*].[6]

Gury includes a reference to Aquinas, but his version of PDE differs from that of Aquinas in subtle, yet important, ways. The object of Gury's analysis is "bringing about" a cause, not an action defined by the agent's intention. Inanimate objects can "bring about" a cause, as when a hurricane brings about a damaged home, so Gury's term shifts the focus away from the agent and onto observable effects outside the agent. Moreover, Gury adds, "It is required that the good effect follows equally immediately [*aeque immediate*] from the cause."[7] By contrast, Aquinas says nothing about how immediately or remotely different effects follow from an action. Aquinas and Gury agree that one may not intend evil as a means, but they disagree about how to determine what the agent intends. Aquinas starts with the agent's intention to determine the action's species (murder, adultery, etc.), and then judges the action. Gury begins with observable effects, analyzes their causal relationships to determine the agent's intention, and then judges the action (or the bringing about of a cause). I refer to the first version of PDE as an "agent-based version of PDE" and to the second version as an "effects-based version of PDE."[8]

By criticizing Gury, I do not claim that the key to resolving debates about PDE is to interpret Aquinas more carefully. The main problem with an effects-based version of PDE is that it is mistaken, not that it differs from what Aquinas wrote. Suppose that a child asks a pharmacist who is giving the child a flu shot, "Why are you trying to hurt me?" The pharmacist could say, "I am not *trying* to hurt you. Your pain is a side effect." This answer might not satisfy the child, but it is correct, even though the pain follows more immediately than the good effect of being immune from the flu. In fact, the pain occurs before the vaccine enters the patient's body.

Both Gury's effects-based version of PDE and the negative judgment of the craniotomy that it supports have other sources that I do not discuss here.[9] As noted earlier, I discuss history only to explain why proponents of PDE came to oppose the craniotomy. An 1889 statement from the Holy Office of the Catholic Church says that Catholic schools may not safely teach that the craniotomy can be licit when it saves a pregnant woman's life:

> In Catholic schools, it cannot safely be taught [*tuto doceri non posse*] that the surgical operation called "craniotomy" can be licit, as declared on May 28, 1884, and the same is true of whatever surgical operation is directly lethal [*directe occisivam*] for the child or pregnant mother.[10]

This passage focuses attention on the fact that the craniotomy is directly lethal. As in Gury's version of PDE, the principle that one may not intend evil as a means to a good end remains, but as a façade that conceals the shift from an agent-based to an effects-based version of PDE. This shift turned PDE into an easy target for critics.

In the Anglo-American tradition, philosophers began analyzing PDE in the middle of the twentieth century. The legal theorist H. L. A. Hart was one of the first to do so. He summarizes the traditional view of the craniotomy and responds, "It could be argued that it is not the death of the foetus but its removal from the body of the mother which is required to save her life."[11] Hart is correct. If the child could survive the craniotomy, the surgeon's plan would not fail. Of course, no proponent of the craniotomy believes that the child has any chance of survival. The point of the fictional craniotomy case in which the child survives is that the child's death in a real craniotomy case does nothing at all to solve the problem that the surgeon seeks to solve, that is, that the child's head is too big to fit through the birth canal. Since the surgeon does not intend to kill the child as an end or as a means, the death is a foreseen side effect, not an intended effect. Hart concludes that the traditional distinction between the craniotomy and the hysterectomy is untenable. Surgeons can perform both operations without intending death.

To illustrate why the surgeon in the craniotomy case need not intend death, consider a craniotomy on a dead child, which is an actual treatment for obstructed labor, not a far-fetched thought experiment contrived by philosophers.[12] For example, suppose that a surgical resident first learns how to perform the craniotomy on dead fetuses and that the resident then asks the attending surgeon, "What different steps do I need to take to perform a craniotomy when a child is still alive?" The attending surgeon could answer truthfully by saying, "For us, a craniotomy on a living child is similar to a craniotomy on a dead child." A craniotomy on a dead child serves the same purpose as a craniotomy on a living child, and the two craniotomies consist of the same steps. In both cases, the surgeon collapses the child's skull so that the child's head will fit through the birth canal. The problem facing the surgeon is that the child's head is stuck in the birth canal, not that the child is alive. The surgeon intends to collapse the child's skull to make it smaller so that it can fit through the birth canal (fig. 5.1). When the child is alive, the surgeon knows that the child cannot survive the operation, but the similarity of the craniotomy performed on a dead child (fig. 5.2) and a craniotomy performed on a living child illustrates that the surgeon can perform both craniotomies without intending death. The two craniotomies cause different effects, because a living child differs from a corpse and a living skull differs from the head of a corpse, but the surgeon's intention—that is, the surgeon's end and the steps in the surgeon's plan to achieve that end— are the same when the child is alive and when the child is dead.

To avoid a misunderstanding about my comparison of the craniotomies, I do not claim that identical bodily movements always result in identical actions or that there is no difference between a

Figure 5.1. The surgeon's intention in the craniotomy case

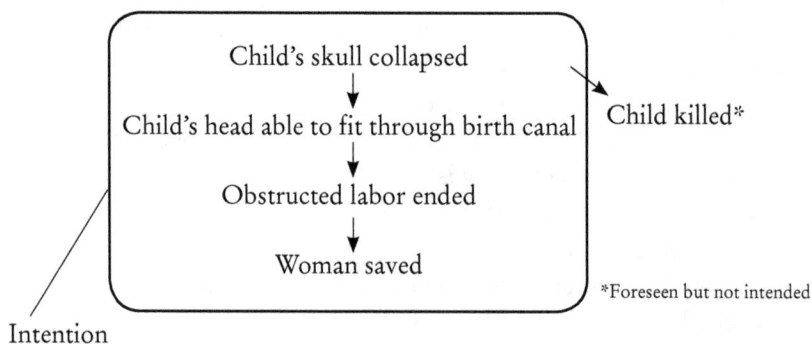

Child's skull collapsed
↓
Child's head able to fit through birth canal   Child killed*
↓
Obstructed labor ended
↓
Woman saved

*Foreseen but not intended

Intention

Figure 5.2. The surgeon's intention in the craniotomy case with a dead child

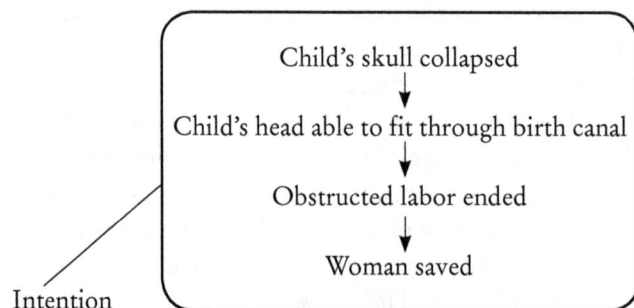

Child's skull collapsed
↓
Child's head able to fit through birth canal
↓
Obstructed labor ended
↓
Woman saved

Intention

living human being and a corpse. I compare the craniotomy on a living child and the craniotomy on a dead child only to illustrate that the child's death is irrelevant to the surgeon's plan. By describing the child's death as irrelevant, I do not mean that surgeons may disregard the child's life or that they may perform craniotomies without considering nonlethal alternatives. I mean only that the child's death is not part of the surgeon's intention, either as an end or as a means.

When the surgeon knows that the child is alive, someone could say that the surgeon intentionally causes the child's death to distinguish the surgeon from someone who unknowingly causes death. The surgeon intentionally causes death in the sense that joggers intentionally wear out their knees. Both the surgeon and joggers freely choose an action knowing full well that the action will result in death or worn-out knees. Even though they knowingly cause death or worn-out knees, the surgeon and joggers do not intend these effects as ends or as means, as the terror bomber intends death as a means of demoralizing the enemy. This sense of intended effects is the relevant one for applications of PDE, because someone must define intended effects from the agent's perspective to see why the distinction between intention and foresight is relevant.

An opponent of the craniotomy could agree that the agent's perspective is relevant and still claim that anyone who intends to collapse a living person's skull must also intend the person's death. Some variations of the case of a craniotomy on a dead child illustrate why the surgeon can intend to collapse the child's skull without intending the child's death:

- A woman's life is threatened by impacted labor, and a craniotomy is the only way to save her. The fetal heart monitor malfunctions, so nobody in the operating room knows whether the child is alive. The surgeon performs the craniotomy.
- A surgeon enters an operating room to perform three craniotomies. Someone tells the surgeon that two children are alive and that one child has already died. The surgeon approaches the nearest operating table without knowing whether the child is alive or dead. As the surgeon picks up a surgical instrument, a nurse says, "The babies on the following operating tables are still alive . . . ."

The surgeon interrupts and says, "Stop distracting me with irrelevant information!"

To assert that the surgeons intend death in these two cases entails that these agents intend effects that never cross their minds and that do nothing at all to further their plans. Someone could assert that the surgeon conditionally intends the child's death whenever the child might be alive, but this assertion is too strong given the possibility of a mistaken declaration of death. When a surgeon performs a routine hysterectomy to remove a cancerous tumor, the surgeon does not conditionally intend to kill any child who may be living inside the uterus, even if there is some chance that the woman is in the early stages of an undetected pregnancy. The same is true of the surgeon who performs the craniotomy on a child who may or may not be alive and of a surgeon who performs a craniotomy on a living child.

In contrast to the craniotomy case, suppose that a woman is close to her due date when she decides that she does not want the responsibilities of motherhood. She visits an abortionist, who agrees to help her. (I use the term "abortionist" to contrast this case with the craniotomy case, but my analysis would not change if I used the term "obstetrician" for the agents in both cases.) The abortionist dilates the cervix, collapses the child's skull, and removes the dead child from the woman's uterus. From an observer's perspective, the abortionist's action might look similar to the surgeon's action in the craniotomy case. From the agent's perspective, however, the two actions are different, because the child's death is a step in the abortionist's plan. If asked, "What is your goal, and what are all the steps in your plan to achieve that goal?," the abortionist cannot give an honest and complete answer without including the child's death. Thus the abortionist intends the child's death as a means of relieving the woman from the responsibilities of motherhood. Some counterfactuals can clarify this point. If the child survived the abortionist's action, then the plan to relieve the woman from the responsibilities of motherhood would fail. If the child were already dead, then the abortionist's action would be pointless.

The intention of an abortionist who performs a late-term abortion would be different if the goal were merely to relieve the woman from the responsibilities of pregnancy rather than the responsibilities of motherhood, because someone can intend to end a pregnancy without intending the child's death. I argue that the craniotomy case fits this description, but a less controversial example would be a case of inducing labor when the child has a good chance of survival. An obstetrician who ends a pregnancy without intending death could act wrongly by treating the child unfairly. I do not try to resolve all questions about abortion here, because my focus is on what the agent intends. As I explained earlier, an agent can act wrongly without intending death.

My analysis of a late-term abortion aimed at relieving the woman of the responsibilities of motherhood refutes a common objection to agent-based definitions of intended effects: that according to these definitions agents intend whatever they say that they intend. This objection sometimes takes the form of allegations about "redescribing" or "gerrymandering" intentions. I responded to this objection when I explained why an agent-based definition of intended effects, such as the strict definition that I defend, does not rule out truths about what an agent intends. To avoid redundancy, I do not repeat my entire response here, but I explain why a surgeon's description of an intention does not necessarily reflect what the surgeon intends. There is a truth of the matter about whether a surgeon intends death, but an observer cannot determine what the surgeon intends merely by analyzing causal relations. Analogously, there is a truth of the matter about whether a student knows a logical truth as opposed to feigning ignorance, but an observer cannot determine what the student knows merely by analyzing logical relations. Suppose that the abortionist performs a late-term abortion to relieve a woman from the responsibilities of motherhood. No matter how the abortionist describes the action—for example, "I intend only to collapse the child's skull, not to kill the child' or "I intend only to remove the child from the mother's body—the plan requires the child's death, not only the collapse of the child's skull or the removal of the child from the woman's uterus. Nothing that the abortionist *says* can change this truth about what the abortionist *intends*. In the craniotomy case, however, the surgeon's plan does not include death. This truth follows from the structure of the surgeon's plan, not what anyone says about the surgeon's intention.

Of course a surgeon *could* perform a craniotomy as a means of killing a child, just as a surgeon could perform a hysterectomy as a means of killing a child. When I speak of "the surgeon," I refer only to a specific case with specific details. I do not make claims about surgeons in general. For example, I claim only that a surgeon *can* perform a craniotomy on a living child or a hysterectomy on a pregnant woman without intending death.

By arguing that a surgeon who performs a craniotomy need not intend death, I do not deny that the rule against murder is relevant or that a surgeon should see both the mother and the child as patients.[13] That the rule against murder is relevant does not entail that the surgeon who performs the craniotomy violates the rule, and that the surgeon has obligations to two patients does not entail that the craniotomy violates any of these obligations. In the hysterectomy case, someone can agree that the rule against murder is relevant and that the surgeon has obligations to two patients and still say that the surgeon may perform the hysterectomy. Further, I doubt that any opponent of the craniotomy would agree that the woman may hire a bodyguard or other nonphysician to perform the craniotomy.

As noted earlier, appeals to directness made it easy for philosophers to reject PDE. For example, Hart notes similarities between the surgeons' intentions in the craniotomy and hysterectomy cases, so he concludes, "The differences between the cases are differences of causal structure leading to the applicability of different verbal descriptions. There seems to be no relevant moral difference between them on any theory of morality."[14] Hart is correct that the different causal structures of the craniotomy and the hysterectomy are irrelevant. Nobody denies that the craniotomy causes death more directly, in terms of time and intermediary steps, than the hysterectomy. If opponents of the craniotomy insist that the different causal structures entail different intentions, they still must define intended effects in a way that includes death in the craniotomy case but not in the hysterectomy case. Any definition that relies on causal directness invites the question, "Why is *this* sense of intended effects relevant for judging actions?"

Proponents of PDE cannot answer this question if they shift from an agent-based version of PDE to an effects-based version of PDE. How directly an action causes death might seem relevant for people who insist that the surgeon acts wrongly in the craniotomy case, but directness seems irrelevant in other cases. For example:

- A hospital's janitor learns that one patient has organs that could be used to save five other patients. The hospital's surgeons will not remove the organs as long as the patient is alive. To make the patient's organs available without being caught, the janitor rewires a circuit box so that a circuit breaker will cut off power to a machine that delivers an antibiotic that the patient needs to stay alive so that the patient's infection will worsen so that the patient will die.
- A bomber pilot has been ordered to destroy a bridge before the enemy's army can cross it. The pilot approaches the bridge and sees that a child is standing on it. The pilot does not have enough fuel to make another pass, and the enemy's army is getting closer. The pilot drops the bombs, which immediately kill the child and destroy the bridge.

From an external perspective, the janitor's rewiring the circuit box is an indirect way of killing the patient. In fact, the janitor chooses this plan precisely because it is less direct and therefore less likely to result in being caught. By contrast, the pilot's dropping bombs kills the child immediately. To explain why the janitor intends death and the pilot does not, proponents of PDE must consider the action from the agent's perspective, not from the perspective of the victim or an external observer. The patient's death is an essential step in the janitor's plan, but the child's death is not part of the pilot's plan at all. This difference, not any difference in causal directness, explains why the janitor intends death even though the pilot does not.

The shift from an agent-based to an effects-based version does not entail merely false conclusions about particular cases. This shift undermines the basis of PDE by making it impossible to explain *why* the rule against intending death is stricter than the rule against knowingly causing death. When proponents of PDE consider actions from an external perspective—by speaking of "bringing about causes" instead of actions—they cut the link between intentions and character. Without this link, proponents of PDE have no good way to explain why an agent may not directly cause death even though an agent may indirectly cause death in similar situations. Unsurprisingly, then, Hart describes PDE as "the result of a legalistic conception of morality as if it were couched in the form of a law in rigid form prohibiting all intentional killing as distinct from knowingly causing death."[15] Here I disagree with Hart. His charge of legalism is on target, but the basic problem for opponents of the craniotomy is their analysis of the surgeon's intention, not their acceptance of an exceptionless rule against intending death. Even if the rule is exceptionless, it does not rule out the craniotomy.

Opponents of the craniotomy have not given up the quest for a relevant distinction between the craniotomy and the hysterectomy. Some of them assert that collapsing a child's skull is identical to killing a child, even though removing a uterus is not identical to killing a child.[16] The problem with this assertion is that collapsing a child's skull causes death, and no effect can cause itself.[17] The skull's being collapsed and the child's being killed are two effects, not one effect described in two ways. For an example of one effect described in two ways, suppose that a prison guard executes a prisoner and then says, "I intended to execute the prisoner, not to kill the prisoner." This claim is misleading because being executed is a way of being killed, not a cause of being killed. To confirm that the prison guard could not intend to execute a prisoner without intending to kill the prisoner, note that the guard's plan to execute the prisoner would have failed if the prisoner survived. I do not try to resolve moral questions about capital punishment here. The point of the case of the executioner is to draw a contrast with the craniotomy case. Opponents of the craniotomy cannot rely on the assertion that the child's skull's being collapsed is identical to the child's being killed. They need an argument that the surgeon cannot intend to collapse the child's skull without intending the child's death.

In this section I respond to five arguments that the surgeon in the craniotomy case must have a bad intention:

1. Ordinary language shows that the surgeon intends the child's death.
2. The object of the surgeon's action includes the child's death.
3. The craniotomy cannot be part of good medical practice.
4. The surgeon operates on the child, not on the mother.
5. The surgeon intends to harm the child.

Another argument is that the child's death is too "close" to the craniotomy to be unintended.[18] I already have criticized appeals to closeness, so I do not repeat those criticisms here.

Some opponents of the craniotomy appeal to common sense or ordinary language to explain why the surgeon intends the child's death.[19] The statement "The surgeon intentionally kills the child to save the mother" seems to fit common sense, but the statement is ambiguous. It could mean that the physician *knowingly causes* the child's death, as opposed to making a mistake that kills the child. If so, the claim is true but uncontroversial. Both the surgeon in the craniotomy case and the surgeon in the hysterectomy case know full well that the operation will kill the child. The statement that the surgeon intentionally kills the child to save the mother could also mean that the physician intends the child's death as a means of preserving the mother's life. If so, the claim is exactly the controversial point about the craniotomy. My analysis of the surgeon's intention in the craniotomy case does not depend on my use of terms. I have said that the surgeon "collapses" the skull to relieve the mother's obstructed labor, but someone could also say that the surgeon "destroys" the skull to relieve the obstructed labor. I find "collapse" more accurate because the surgeon would not destroy the skull in a way that made it larger. Regardless of the terms used, the disputed question is whether the surgeon who collapses or destroys the skull must intend the child's death. To show that the answer is yes, opponents of the craniotomy need to identify the definition of intended effects that is relevant for applications of PDE and to explain why this definition supports the conclusion that a surgeon who performs the craniotomy must intend death, at least when the child is still alive.

I do not concede that my analysis of the craniotomy contradicts common sense or ordinary language. If people consider the craniotomy alongside cases in which the agent clearly does not intend death (e.g., the strategic bombing case), I suspect that many people would say that the surgeon intends the child's death. The other cases require no physical contact with the person killed, and it is physically possible to survive in similar situations. If, however, people consider the craniotomy alongside cases in which the agent clearly does intend death (e.g., the terror bombing case), I suspect that many people would see a contrast with the craniotomy. Even if most people did say that the surgeon intends the child's death in the craniotomy case, "intention" has different meanings in ordinary language. The claim that X intends Y or that X intentionally Ys can mean that X intends Y as an end or as a means as opposed to causing Y as a side effect. This claim can also mean that X voluntarily does something that causes Y, as opposed to involuntarily or accidentally causing Y. When defenders of PDE appeal to ordinary language, they risk confusing the question "When an agent does X, does an observer have good reason to infer that the agent intends Y?" with "Does an agent who does X necessarily intend Y?" A well-founded inference about an agent's intention can be mistaken in unusual cases. In the example about a soccer player that I discussed earlier, the player who appears to kick the ball through the net to score a goal might have intended to pass the ball to a teammate or to injure the goalie. Likewise, when one person knowingly crushes another person's skull, an observer has good reason to infer that the first person intended to cause death, but this inference can be mistaken in unusual cases. The craniotomy case is one of these unusual cases, so generalizations from usual cases do not settle questions about what the surgeon intends in the craniotomy case.

Some opponents of the craniotomy distinguish the object of the action from the agent's intention and then try to conjure an evil intention out of the craniotomy's object. These efforts often include appeals to St. Thomas Aquinas, but I leave exegetical questions aside.[20] Surely sound moral judgments do not require expertise in Thomistic action theory. If the surgeon acts wrongly because death is part of the surgeon's object, then opponents of the craniotomy should be able to explain why. If the surgeon's object includes death because the craniotomy inevitably kills the child, then the same is true of the surgeon in the hysterectomy case. If the surgeon's object in the craniotomy case includes death because the surgery immediately kills the child, then the same is true of the strategic bomber. Any analysis of the object that includes death in the craniotomy case will require abandoning the agent's perspective, which raises the problems identified earlier.

According to some opponents of the craniotomy, the craniotomy is wrong because it violates the standards of good medical practice.[21] One response is to say that the surgeon should ignore the standards of medicine to save a life. Asking people to sacrifice their lives for a person or for the sake of a virtue is demanding but sometimes appropriate. Asking a pregnant woman to sacrifice her life for the sake of medicine is quite different. Even this response concedes too much. When opponents of the craniotomy claim that the craniotomy cannot be part of good medical practice, they assume that the craniotomy is wrong in some way. To complete the argument, opponents of the craniotomy need to explain why good medical practice cannot include the craniotomy. The problem cannot be merely that the craniotomy causes death, because the same is true of the hysterectomy.

Some opponents of the craniotomy note that the surgeon in the craniotomy case operates on the child, while the surgeon in the hysterectomy case operates on the mother.[22] One problem with this argument is that it would rule out many acts of self-defense. If I push someone attacking me down a flight of stairs so that I will have time to escape, then I am acting on the attacker, but I can push my attacker without intending to kill or injure. (Few opponents of the craniotomy will disagree, because killing in self-defense is a standard illustration of PDE.) To see another problem with the argument that the craniotomy is wrong because the surgeon operates on the child, suppose that a physician could treat obstructed labor by giving the woman a drug that made her uterine muscles strong enough to crush the child's skull. The physician who used such a drug would act on the mother; the only difference between this fictitious case and the craniotomy case is that the physician would use a different means of crushing or collapsing the child's skull.

Some opponents of the craniotomy concede that the surgeon does not intend the child's death, but they still claim that the surgeon intends to harm the child. According to this argument, a crushed skull is a harm, so one cannot intend to collapse the child's skull without intending harm.[23] One response is that the collapsed skull cannot be identical to the harm because the collapsed skull causes harm, and no effect causes itself. Opponents of the craniotomy could insist that collapsing a person's skull is harming the person, as executing a prisoner is killing a prisoner. Still, a surgeon can perform a craniotomy on a dead child, so someone can intend to crush a skull without intending harm. A prison guard, however, cannot intend to execute a prisoner when the guard knows that the prisoner is already dead. The guard could *simulate* an execution by electrocuting or poisoning a corpse, but the guard cannot intend to execute something known to be a corpse. Opponents of the craniotomy could assert that crushing the skull of a *living* person is identical to harming the person, so that to intend one is to intend the other. As evidence against this assertion, note that a young child can intend to crush someone's skull, perhaps reenacting a scene from a violent cartoon, without realizing that doing so causes harm. A surgeon who does not know whether a child is dead or alive also can intend to crush the child's skull without intending harm. Someone could insist that to intend to crush a living person's skull is to intend harm, at least when the agent is a rational adult. With these qualifications, the assertion is no longer obviously true, and I see no way to defend it without appealing to a criterion of closeness or directness. Recall the example about a son who testifies on behalf of his father despite knowing that he will stutter. The testimony consists entirely of stuttering, but the son still intends to testify without intending to stutter. The close connection, or even the inseparability, of two events does not entail that anyone who intends one must intend the other. To my knowledge, no opponent of the craniotomy has presented a definition of intended effects that includes the child's death and excludes the man's stuttering. Even if there were such a definition, proponents of PDE would have to explain why it is relevant for judging actions.

ECTOPIC PREGNANCIES

Fortunately, modern medical technology enables surgeons to treat obstructed labor by performing caesarean sections instead of craniotomies, but the debate about the hysterectomy and craniotomy cases is similar to the debate about two treatments for ectopic pregnancy:

- A woman has an ectopic pregnancy that threatens her life. To prevent the woman's fallopian tube from rupturing, a surgeon performs a salpingotomy, which consists of making an incision into the fallopian tube and removing the embryo.
- A woman has an ectopic pregnancy that threatens her life. To prevent the woman's fallopian tube from rupturing, a surgeon performs a salpingectomy, which consists of cutting out the part of the fallopian tube that contains the embryo.

Debates about the salpingotomy and the salpingectomy follow the pattern of debates about the craniotomy and the hysterectomy. According to a common view, the surgeon who performs the salpingotomy intends or directly wills the child's death to save the woman, but the surgeon who performs the salpingectomy foresees or indirectly wills the child's death as a result of removing the damaged part of the fallopian tube, which would need to be removed even if it did not have a child growing inside.[24] This common view has the unwelcome feature of rejecting the less invasive salpingotomy in favor of the more invasive salpingectomy.

One problem with contrasting the salpingotomy and the salpingectomy is that the surgeon in the salpingotomy case could intend to remove the child from the woman's fallopian tube without intending the child's death (fig. 5.3). The problem for the surgeon is the child's growing in the fallopian tube, not the child's being alive. One difference between the craniotomy and the salpingotomy cases is that it is easy to imagine the child surviving the salpingotomy but

Figure 5.3. The surgeon's intention in the salpingotomy case

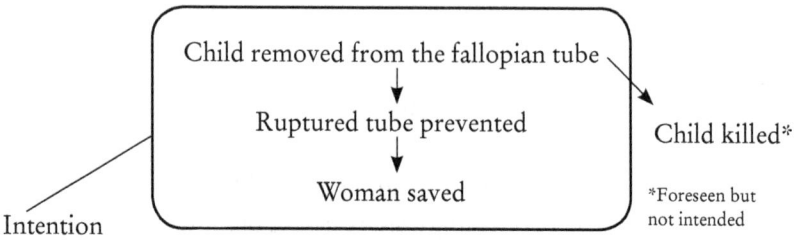

Child removed from the fallopian tube

↓

Ruptured tube prevented

Child killed*

↓

Woman saved

Intention

*Foreseen but
not intended

not the craniotomy. Obstetrics could advance to the point that the embryo could be transplanted to the woman's uterus or to an artificial womb. (There are reports, whose accuracy I am unqualified to judge, of a child's surviving a salpingotomy, but my argument does not depend on the physical possibility of the child's survival.[25])

Another problem with contrasting the salpingotomy and the salpingectomy is that the surgeon in the salpingectomy case must intend to remove the child, not only the fallopian tube (fig. 5.4). The fallopian tube does not always need to be removed after an ectopic pregnancy.[26] The problem for the woman is not only that her fallopian tube may be damaged. The problem is that the child is growing inside her fallopian tube, which will rupture the tube if left untreated. To solve this problem, the surgeon must remove the child along with part of the fallopian tube. The surgeon might claim that the child's removal is a foreseen but unintended side effect of removing the damaged tube, but this claim is false. Removing the child along with the tube is essential to the surgeon's plan, assuming that the surgeon seeks to save the woman and knows that she cannot survive if the child keeps growing inside her. This analysis of the salpingectomy again shows that an agent-based definition of intended effects does not mean that agents intend only what they claim to intend.

Another problem with contrasting the salpingotomy and the salpingectomy is that the negative judgment about the salpingectomy means that obstetricians sometimes must delay treating ectopic pregnancies for no good reason. Suppose that an obstetrician diagnoses an ectopic pregnancy early in a pregnancy, before the fallopian tube is damaged. If the negative view is correct, the obstetrician must delay

Figure 5.4. The surgeon's intention in the salpingectomy case

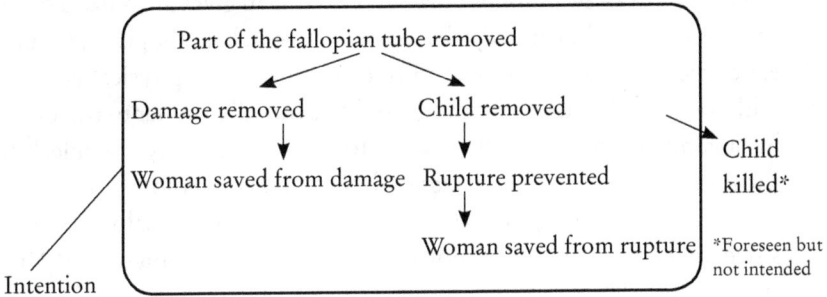

the salpingectomy until the fallopian tube becomes damaged enough to warrant surgery even apart from the pregnancy. The requirement to delay the surgery seems implausible, especially since physicians usually aim to treat diseases *before* they become life-threatening. The following case illustrates the problem:

- In January an obstetrician diagnoses an ectopic pregnancy and decides that surgery will be necessary. He schedules a salpingectomy for the first available date, which is in February. He then remembers the argument that a salpingectomy is justified because it removes a damaged part of the fallopian tube, not because it removes the child. The obstetrician reschedules the salpingectomy for March, when the tube will be severely damaged.[27]

The presence or absence of damage to the fallopian tube does not determine what the obstetrician intends. Assuming that the obstetrician decides in January that the child, not merely the tube, needs to be removed, waiting until March does not change the fact that he needs to remove the child. A drug that cured the damaged tube but left the child growing inside would not save the woman's life. By delaying the salpingectomy from February to March, the obstetrician treats moral rules as legalistic hurdles to be cleared by rearranging schedules, not as rules connected to what is good for human beings.

An opponent of the salpingotomy could note that the surgeon operates on the child, not on the woman as in the salpingectomy case. I have already responded to a similar argument against a craniotomy. To modify the example, suppose that an obstetrician gives a woman a drug that causes her white blood cells to bore a hole in her fallopian tube and expel the child. The obstetrician does not have any physical contact with the child, but using the drug would be morally similar to performing a salpingotomy. Of course such a drug is not medically possible, but the point is that physical contact with the child is not morally relevant.

I do not respond to every argument against the salpingotomy since my analysis of the craniotomy applies to the salpingotomy.[28] To summarize:

1. Nobody claims that the surgery is wrong simply because it kills the child, so opponents of the surgery must find the problem in the way that the surgeon acts.
2. The child's death might not be a step in the surgeon's plan, and the success of the surgeon's plan does not require the child's death, so opponents must find the alleged problem from an external perspective.
3. Defining the alleged problem from an external perspective invites counterexamples and leaves no good explanation as to why the alleged problem is relevant in the first place.

Proponents of PDE should conclude that the surgeon's intention does not necessarily include the child's death in the craniotomy, hysterectomy, salpingotomy, and salpingectomy cases.

THE CASE OF DILATION AND CURETTAGE AND THE USE OF METHOTREXATE

My analysis of the craniotomy and the salpingotomy applies to another case about saving a pregnant woman in a way that shortens her child's life:

• A pregnant woman has a serious case of pulmonary hypertension, which is exacerbated by her being pregnant. To prevent the pulmonary hypertension from killing her (and her unborn child), a

Figure 5.5. The surgeon's intention in the D&C case

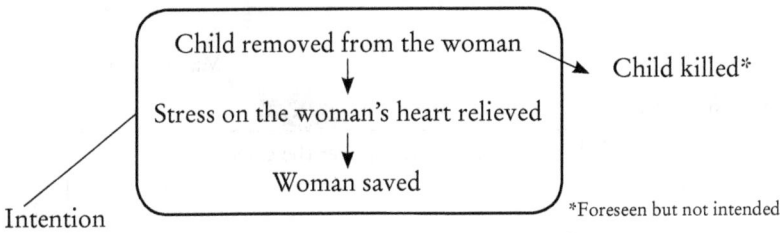

Child removed from the woman

Stress on the woman's heart relieved

Woman saved

Child killed*

Intention

*Foreseen but not intended

surgeon performs a dilation and curettage, which consists of dilating the woman's cervix and removing the child and the placenta. The surgeon knows that the procedure will kill the child.

In 2009, physicians at St. Joseph's Hospital in Phoenix performed a dilation and curettage (hereafter D&C) that fits this description. Many proponents of PDE oppose this surgery as another example of direct abortion that kills the child as a means of saving the mother.[29] My analysis of this case follows my analysis of the craniotomy and the salpingotomy. As in the other cases, the problem in the D&C case is the child's being inside the woman (along with the placenta, which I discuss below), not the child's being alive. The surgeon solves this problem by removing the child, but the child's death is not a step in the surgeon's plan (fig. 5.5). A surgeon could perform the same surgery if the child were already dead.

A lengthy analysis of the D&C would be redundant and rather dismal, given the gruesome details. Instead of a lengthy analysis of the D&C, I rely on an argument by analogy. I begin with two cases of people on a rope bridge:

- A small man and a massive man are hiking and must cross a narrow rope bridge over a deep canyon. The massive man is having an affair with the small man's wife, and the small man plans to get revenge by killing the massive man. While they are crossing the bridge, their combined weight causes one strand of the rope to snap. The massive man sees the snapped rope, panics, has a heart attack, and collapses on top of the small man (fig 5.6.a). The small

Figure 5.6. The rope bridge cases

a.

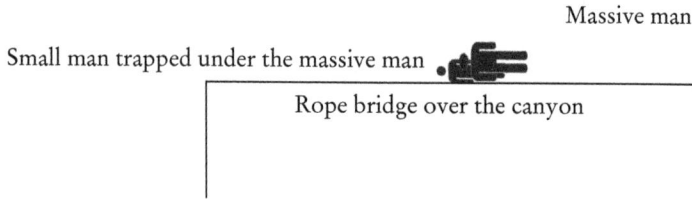

Massive man

Small man trapped under the massive man

Rope bridge over the canyon

b.

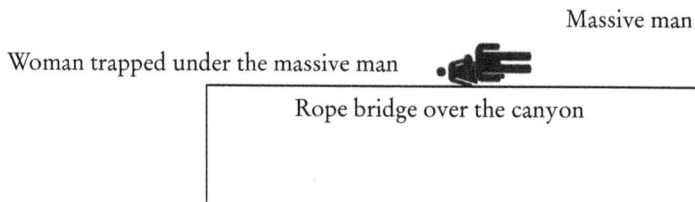

Massive man

Woman trapped under the massive man

Rope bridge over the canyon

man's wrath prevents him from noticing that the bridge is about to collapse, but he sees that his chance for revenge will vanish if the massive man dies of the heart attack. To get his revenge, the small man pushes the massive man off himself and into the canyon. The push has the unforeseen effect of making it possible for the small man to escape.

- A woman and a massive man are hiking and must cross a narrow rope bridge over a deep canyon. Their combined weight causes one strand of rope to snap. The massive man sees the snapped rope, panics, has a heart attack, and collapses on top of the woman (fig. 5.6.b). She realizes that the bridge will collapse soon. To escape before the rope snaps, the woman pushes the massive man off herself. She foresees that he will fall into the canyon, which will kill him if he has not already died from the heart attack.

Both the small man and the woman push the massive man into a canyon, which enables them to escape and also ensures that the massive man will die if he has not died already. The two cases would look identical to an observer.

Despite their superficial similarities, the small man and the woman act differently. To get his revenge, the small man needs the massive man to die from being pushed into the canyon, not from suffering a heart attack. To reach safety, the woman merely needs the massive man's body to be moved off of her. Because of this difference, only the small man intends to kill the massive man. According to my version of PDE, the surgeon's intention in the D&C is similar to the woman's intention, not the small man's intention. In the cases of the D&C and the woman on the bridge, the location of someone's body threatens a woman's life, and someone moves that body to a place where death is certain. In both cases, whether the person is alive or dead makes no difference to the success of the agent's plan.

Someone could try to distinguish the surgeon in the D&C from the woman on the bridge by noting that the curettage involved in a D&C immediately kills the child, while the woman's action does not immediately kill the massive man.[30] To illustrate the irrelevance of causal immediacy, consider another case:

- A woman and a massive man are hiking and must cross a rope bridge over a deep canyon. A small man is standing on one side of the bridge. He wants to kill the massive man as revenge for having an affair with his wife, so he shoots an arrow at the massive man. The arrow narrowly misses the massive man's heart, but it causes the massive man to collapse on top of the woman. She sees that any movement will move the arrow, which will kill the massive man immediately. She also sees that the bridge will collapse soon. To escape, she pushes the man off herself.

In this case, the woman kills the massive man more immediately than the woman in the previous case of the rope bridge, but the women in both cases intend to move a man so that they can escape the rope bridge before it collapses.

The cases of the women on the rope bridge are morally similar to the D&C case. The location of a person's body threatens a woman, and the person's body cannot be moved without causing the person's

Figure 5.7. The case of the adulterous man on the rope bridge

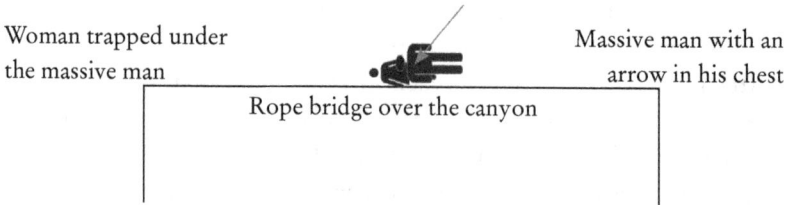

Woman trapped under
the massive man

Rope bridge over the canyon

Massive man with an
arrow in his chest

death. My argument here relies on an intuitive appeal, but my defense of the D&C depends on the same premises as my defense of the craniotomy and the salpingotomy: intended effects include nothing more or less than the effects that are part of the agent's goal or plan to achieve the goal, and neither the women on the bridge nor the surgeon who performs the D&C has a plan that includes death.

Some philosophers defend the D&C in the Phoenix case by arguing that the physicians intended to remove the placenta, which would have threatened the mother's life even if the child had already died, and killed the child as a side effect.[31] I agree that a placentectomy in these circumstances could be justified. Even if both the child's presence in the womb and the placenta threatened the woman, a surgeon could perform a D&C to remove the child without intending to kill the child. (Again, I make no claims about what the physicians in the Phoenix case intended or about whether they acted wrongly for another reason.)

So far I have not discussed a common nonsurgical treatment for ectopic pregnancy: the drug methotrexate.[32] Using a salpingotomy to remove a child from the mother's fallopian tube does not always eliminate the threat that a persistent trophoblast, which supplies nutrition to the embryo and develops into the placenta, will rupture the fallopian tube, so many physicians use methotrexate after performing a salpingectomy to stop the trophoblast's growth. Postsurgical use of methotrexate poses no difficult moral questions because it has no effect on the child, but methotrexate can also be used as alternative to a salpingectomy. Must a physician who prescribes methotrexate to treat an ectopic pregnancy intend the child's death as a means of preventing the rupture of the fallopian tube?

Figure 5.8. The case of the cuckold in the canyon

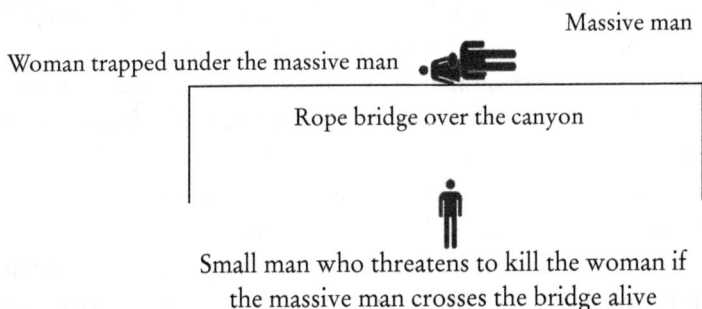

My answer is no, but this case is harder than the other cases of life-threatening pregnancies. To see why, consider one more absurdly contrived case of a woman who escapes from a rope bridge that is about to collapse:

- A woman and a massive man are hiking and must cross a narrow rope bridge over a deep canyon. The woman receives a cell phone call from a small man who is standing in the canyon. The massive man had an affair with the small man's wife, and the small man wants to watch the massive man die. To achieve his goal, the small man threatens to kill the woman on the bridge if the massive man reaches the end of the bridge alive. The massive man realizes what is happening, panics, has a heart attack, and collapses on top of the woman (fig 5.8). The woman sees that the bridge will collapse soon, killing both her and the massive man. To escape, she pushes the man off herself. She foresees that he will fall into the canyon, which will kill him if he has not already died from the heart attack.

In this case, the woman has two problems: the massive man's body is preventing her from escaping the bridge that is about to collapse, and the small man is threatening to kill her if the massive man reaches the other end of the bridge alive. Pushing the massive man off herself solves both problems. She would intend death if she reasoned, "Now that this massive man has collapsed on top of me, I have a chance to satisfy the small man's demands, so I'll push the massive man into the canyon." She would not intend death if she reasoned, "I need to escape, so I'll push this man off me even though he couldn't possibly survive the fall." Note that I have written "if she *reasons*" and not "if she *says*" or another similar term. The relevant point is what she intends, not how she describes her intention. She might feel relieved that the massive man's death satisfies the small man's demand, but her relief does not mean that she intends the massive man's death. Apart from the small man's threat, she has a good reason to roll the massive man off herself. Analogously, the trophoblast threatens the woman apart from the threat posed by a growing child, so a physician can use methotrexate to stop the trophoblast without intending the child's death.[33]

In my analysis of using methotrexate to treat ectopic pregnancy, I have assumed that the physician intends to use the methotrexate only as a means of eliminating the threat of a persistent trophoblast, not as a means of eliminating the threat from the child growing inside the fallopian tube. Suppose that the physician first plans to perform a salpingotomy and then to use methotrexate to prevent a persistent trophoblast. If the physician then realizes that giving the methotrexate first makes the salpingotomy unnecessary, performing the surgery would be pointless. In this case, the physician need not proceed with the salpingotomy in order to avoid intending the child's death. Suppose, however, that stopping the trophoblast requires X mg of methotrexate, while killing the child requires $2X$ mg. A physician who prescribes $2X$ mg most likely intends the child's death as a means of preventing the ruptured fallopian tube. (I say "most likely" because the physician could be ignorant or confused.)

I have criticized opponents of the craniotomy and the salpingotomy for relying on definitions of intended effects that face clear counterexamples and undermine the basis of PDE. A question remains: why do so many proponents of PDE set aside the agent's perspective to define intended effects? One reason is that their opposition to moral subjectivism makes them reluctant to define actions from the agent's perspective. Again, defining an action from the agent's perspective does not rule out objective judgments of the action. The relevant question is "What is the agent's goal, and what are all the steps in the agent's plan to achieve that goal?" The agent can answer evasively, incompletely, or dishonestly, but doing so does not change the correct answer. Another reason that many proponents of PDE insist on defining intentions to include death in the pregnancy cases I have analyzed may be that they worry about justifying an abortion in more typical cases, such as when a woman wants to avoid the responsibilities of motherhood. Opponents of abortion need not worry. My analysis of the craniotomy, the salpingotomy, and the D&C does not excuse procedures in which the surgeon does intend death, such as an abortion performed to relieve a woman from the responsibilities of motherhood. More importantly, my analysis of these pregnancy cases does not deny that someone can act wrongly without intending death. A surgeon could perform a craniotomy, a salpingotomy, or a D&C in a way that treats the child unfairly. Again, I claim only that a surgeon *can* perform these procedures without intending death.

More Alleged Counterexamples to PDE

Some other alleged counterexamples to PDE include that of an agent who seems to act wrongly without intending a bad effect:

- A military commander, who is well versed in PDE, wants to win a war by demoralizing the enemy's leaders without resorting to terror bombing. The commander decides to evacuate an enemy city before bombing it. The enemy leaders have fled to the mountains, so they will see the explosions and conclude that thousands of civilians have been killed. At the last minute, the civilians return to the city, but the commander gives the order to bomb the city anyway.[34]

The commander intends only to create the appearance of civilian casualties, so the casualties do not fit my definition of intended effects. The presence of civilians is not necessary for this purpose, so the commander does not seem to treat the civilians simply as a means to win the war. Still, the case seems morally similar to the terror bombing, not to the strategic bombing, so this case threatens to deprive proponents of PDE of one of their most intuitively plausible cases. Some proponents of PDE respond by claiming that the commander intends to kill innocent people because their deaths follow the explosions so closely.[35] I do not repeat my objections to appeals to closeness, but I still need to explain why the case of the repopulated city elicits different intuitions than the case of a strategic bombing. Without an explanation, the case of the repopulated city might look like a case of intending death. One relevant difference is that the strategic bomber kills only a few innocent people, while the commander in this case kills the entire population of the repopulated city. If the case of the repopulated city were revised so that only a few civilians returned before the bombing, then it would no longer seem clear that the commander acted wrongly. The point of contrasting the terror and the strategic bombings is to find cases that are morally similar in all respects except the agent's intention. Increasing the number of deaths makes the cases dissimilar. Another difference between the cases is that the commander's plan includes an implicit threat to target civilians in other cities. The strategic bomber does not make a similar threat. Because of these differences, proponents of PDE can distinguish between the case of the repopulated city and that of the strategic bombing even if the commander does not intend to kill the civilians.

I do not respond to every case in which an agent seems to act wrongly despite not intending any harmful effect or using anyone simply as a means. My response to such cases is either that the agent does in fact act wrongly but for some other reason (e.g., because of breaking a promise, as in the case of the convalescent on the sidetrack) or that the agent does not act wrongly at all. For example, Foot argues that physicians in a hospital would act wrongly by producing a gas that would save five lives but would release lethal fumes into the room of another patient who could not move.[36] I have no clear intuition about this case. Even if the physicians did act wrongly by producing the fumes, they would not break the rule against intending death.

While the last few counterexamples are designed to show that PDE is too lenient, some counterexamples are designed to show that PDE is too strict. For example, consider a bombing case in which the deaths of innocent children serve a military purpose, which one critic labels "the munitions grief case":

- A pilot bombs a munitions factory despite foreseeing the deaths of some children who live nearby. The pilot knows that the enemy citizens ordinarily would rebuild the factory, which would make the bombing pointless, but grief over the children's deaths will prevent the enemy citizens from doing so.[37]

The alleged problem is that the munitions grief case seems morally similar to the strategic bombing case, in which the bombing kills civilians without causing grief that prevents the target from being rebuilt, even though the pilot in the munitions grief case intends the children's deaths as a means of weakening the enemy. I agree that the pilot in the munitions grief case intends the children's deaths, but I deny that the case is similar to the strategic bombing case. If the pilot in the munitions grief case is asked, "What is your goal, and what are all the steps in your plan to achieve that goal?" the pilot cannot give an honest and complete answer without including the children's deaths. I have explained why an effect can motivate an action without being intended, but the children's deaths are not merely a motivating effect. They are a necessary step in the pilot's plan to weaken the enemy. By stipulation, the bombing would be pointless if the factory were rebuilt, so the pilot cannot truthfully claim that the goal is to make the factory temporarily inoperative. My minimalist version of PDE does not deliver a final verdict about this case, but it does entail the conclusion that the pilot's intention is similar to the terror bomber's intention. If the terror bomber acts wrongly, so does the pilot in the munitions grief case. Both conclusions seem plausible to me, but others may have different intuitions. To make my judgments about the case more plausible, I should add that an agent does not always intend deaths when the deaths promote the agent's purpose. In the munitions grief case, the bombing would be pointless, not merely less effective, if the children did not die. If the pilot believed that the children's survival would make the bombing less effective but not pointless, then the pilot could drop the bombs without intending death.

For another alleged counterexample to PDE, consider the following pair of cases of physicians who cope with limited resources:

- A physician lacks the resources to properly study and treat all cases of a new and deadly disease. The physician decides on a crash experimental program that leaves the stubborn cases untreated for the sake of learning more about the disease (e.g., how long it takes for the disease to be fatal). In the long run, the physician expects to save many lives. The patients do not consent to being left untreated.
- A physician lacks the resources to properly study and treat all cases of a new and deadly disease. The physician decides to focus on patients who can be cured most easily, leaving the stubborn cases untreated. The patients do not consent to being left untreated.[38]

Even if the physicians in these cases save the same number of people, their actions still seem to be morally distinct. Neither physician intends harm, since both plans could succeed even if the untreated patients immediately recovered. Even in the first case, an immediate and unforeseen recovery would show that the disease is not as serious as it first appears. Some critics agree that principles other than PDE distinguish other pairs of cases, but they see this pair of cases as a special problem for my version of PDE: "It is difficult to imagine what sort of run-of-the-mill moral principle Masek could possibly use to account for the morally relevant difference."[39] I respond in three ways. First, I have argued that a definition of intended effects should not be so esoteric that most people cannot know what is intended, but I have not argued against esoteric principles in general. Second, my version of PDE can distinguish between the two cases of leaving patients untreated. There is a relevant difference between intending exposure to harm and knowingly causing the same exposure. The first physician does not intend harm but does intend exposure to harm. The second physician intends neither harm nor exposure to harm. To illustrate the difference between the two physicians, suppose that a philanthropist steps in and treats everyone left untreated by the doctors. In the first case, the philanthropist's action will ruin the physician's plan, because the doctor intends for some patients to be untreated as a means of studying the disease. In the second case, the philanthropist's action will not ruin the physician's plan to treat the easy cases first. Third, even if my version of PDE did not distinguish between the cases of

leaving patients untreated, there is in fact a "run-of-the-mill" principle that can: the principle that physicians should act in their patients'
best interests. My physician violates her duty toward me if she leaves
my sinus infection untreated so that she can learn about sinus infec-
tions and treat other patients more effectively. This duty has limits.
My physician does not act wrongly by performing CPR on another
patient instead of keeping an appointment to look up my stuffy nose.
This pair of cases involving my physician follows the same pattern
as those of leaving patients untreated. In the first case, a physician
does not merely perform triage. Instead, the physician decides to leave
some patients untreated to benefit other patients. In the second case,
the physician cannot treat everyone and decides to focus on the easy
cases. Because of this difference, the cases are morally distinct even
though neither physician intends death or harm.

QUINN'S VIEW OF DIRECT
AND INDIRECT HARMFUL AGENCY

Warren Quinn proposes another way to distinguish between the
cases of leaving patients untreated, as well as the strategic and terror
bombings.[40] The physician who treats patients as guinea pigs turns
them into incubators of the disease, and being involved in the physician's plan harms the patients. Likewise, a bomber pilot who wants
to create the appearance of civilian casualties needs the civilians to
be near the exploding bombs, and harm results from their being
nearby. Quinn describes cases like these as "harmful direct agency":
the agent deliberately involves a victim who suffers harm as a result,
even if the agent does not intend the harm.[41] By contrast, the physician who performs triage does not need to involve the patients with
stubborn cases at all. Treating the easy cases would save lives even
if the stubborn cases did not exist. Similarly, the strategic bombing
would work just as well if the bystanders were safe and sound in a
bomb shelter. Quinn describes cases like these as "harmful indirect
agency": the agent does not deliberately involve the victims in the
way that causes harm. To explain why the distinction between direct
and indirect harmful agency is relevant, Quinn writes, "Each person

is to be treated, so far as possible, as existing only for purposes that he can share."[42] According to Quinn, direct harmful agency violates this principle because it subordinates the victims to purposes that they rightfully reject or cannot rightfully accept.[43]

My defense of PDE is not territorial. I am happy when other principles and distinctions yield similar conclusions. Further, I agree with Quinn's premises about respect for persons. I doubt the relevance of Quinn's distinction between direct and indirect harmful agency, but listing all the counterexamples that others have presented is not necessary here.[44] Perhaps Quinn's view can be modified to avoid counterintuitive conclusions, and perhaps the intuitions that contradict his view are unreliable.[45] Instead of looking to land a knockout punch with a counterexample, I focus on two differences between my version of PDE and Quinn's view.

One difference is that Quinn's view supports the common distinction between the craniotomy and the hysterectomy cases. The surgeon performs the craniotomy on the fetus, whose life is shortened as a result, but the hysterectomy need not involve the fetus at all.[46] Quinn treats this conclusion about the craniotomy as a virtue of his position. I see it as a vice, so I welcome the conclusion that the surgeon in the craniotomy case does not intend death. Quinn does not consider the salpingotomy, but it also fits the definition of harmful direct agency, so his view also distinguishes the salpingotomy from the salpingectomy. My version of PDE does not.

To see another difference between Quinn's view and my version of PDE, consider a case in which people consent to being the victims of someone's harmful direct agency:

- To capture an enemy's bunker, an officer orders soldiers to invade it, foreseeing that some of them will die. All the soldiers have volunteered and are aware of the risks.

The officer needs to involve the soldiers, who suffer harm as a result. Some critics use cases like this one as counterexamples to Quinn.[47] Quinn could modify his definition of direct harmful agency to exclude the officer's order. His view is not absolutist, so he could also say that the officer may engage in harmful direct agency. A more basic problem for Quinn's view arises when this case is paired with a similar case that is loosely based on the biblical story about David, Uriah, and Bathsheeba:

- An officer orders soldiers to invade an enemy's bunker. The officer is having an affair with a soldier's wife. The officer does not consider the military advantages of capturing an enemy's bunker. Instead, he orders the invasion so that his lover's husband will be killed. All of the soldiers, including the officer's rival, see the mission as important enough to volunteer despite their officer's bad intention.

Someone could claim that the officer does the right thing for the wrong reason, but I disagree. To an external observer, ordering an invasion to capture a bunker and ordering an invasion to kill a rival look identical, but the effects do not determine what the officer intends. The actions are as different as saying, "I'm sorry" to apologize and saying, "I'm sorry" to express regret.

Quinn's view entails that there is no relevant distinction between the two orders, which are identical apart from the officer's intention. No principle can handle all hard cases, so being unable to distinguish between these cases is not a fatal flaw for Quinn's view. This inability shows, however, that Quinn's view does not simply replace my version of PDE. Whether his view improves on my version of PDE depends on the success of my agent-based justification of PDE and of my reply to the objection about conflating different types of moral judgments.

I do not expect that my analyses of the cases in this chapter will fit everyone's intuitions. I agree with a comment that Thomson makes in a different context: "Any theory of these matters is going to have a cost in that it will draw lines at some places where intuitions differ. A good theory would be worth the cost; the best would explain why intuitions differ where they do."[48] A strict definition of intended effects supports the conclusion that the surgeons in the craniotomy, salpingotomy, and D&C cases do not need to choose between intending to kill the child and letting both the woman and her child die, a "cost" that I am happy to pay. Accepting the strict definition of intended effects requires a minimalist version of PDE, which has the cost of not explaining why some actions are wrong, such as the bystander's pushing the massive man or the surgeon's cutting out a patient's vital organs. This cost can be shifted to other moral rules, such as the rule against unjust killings. When proponents of PDE reject the strict definition and insist that the surgeons in the craniotomy, salpingotomy, and D&C cases intend death, they rely on principles that apply only in specific contexts and only to some human agents. For example, someone who appeals to the good of medical practice to analyze the craniotomy case must appeal to different principles to analyze the bombing cases, and someone who appeals to causal relations to define intentions in the D&C case needs different principles to determine whether a child chooses a toy as a means of inciting a sibling's envy or whether a fan wears a hat as a means of securing a team's victory.

Why do people have different intuitions about what agents intend in the cases I have discussed, both in this chapter and throughout this book? One hypothesis is that philosophers like me are under the spell of dualism (or Cartesianism, subjectivism, etc.) when we define intended effects from the agent's perspective. As explained earlier, however, an agent-based definition of intended effects does not entail dualism or any other view of the relation between mental states and brain states. Another problem with this hypothesis is that some defenders of the craniotomy are also critics of dualism. Why, for example, would Grisez and Boyle work at opposing dualism and explaining the subtle ways dualism corrupts views about life and death, only to forget about these arguments when they consider the craniotomy case?[49] To explain why people have different intuitions about cases like that of the craniotomy, a better hypothesis is that people focus on different perspectives when they consider these cases. From an observer's perspective or a victim's perspective, the claim that a surgeon intends to collapse a child's skull or cut a child out of the mother's womb without intending death might seem bizarre. But from the agent's perspective, this claim seems more plausible. My hypothesis has the virtue of not attributing a serious and basic mistake (as I would describe dualism) to one's opponents. If my hypothesis is correct, people are not mistaken when they treat an action's effects as relevant, but the main thesis of this book has been that the agent's perspective is also relevant, both for judging actions and for defining intended effects.

Appendix

Case Summaries

One difficulty in discussing PDE is that people disagree about the importance and purposes of different cases. In this appendix I compile descriptions of some of the most important cases that philosophers have used to explain, defend, or criticize PDE. I have not tried to find the first presentation of each case. Instead I have included the presentation of each case that has been the most influential or widely discussed in Anglo-American philosophy, at least in my rough estimation. After the presentation of each case, I include my own comments.

KILLING IN SELF-DEFENSE

AUTHOR: St. Thomas Aquinas

The case in the author's words: "Nothing hinders one act from having two effects, only one of which is intended, while the other is beside the intention. Now moral acts take their species according to what is intended, and not according to what is beside the intention, since this is accidental as explained above [reference omitted]. Accordingly the act of self-defense may have two effects, one is the saving of one's life, the other is the slaying of the aggressor. Therefore this act, since one's intention is to save one's own life, is not unlawful, seeing that it is natural to everything to keep itself in being, as far as possible. And yet, though proceeding from a good intention, an act may be rendered unlawful, if it be out of proportion to the end."

SOURCE: *Summa Theologica* 2.2.64.7.

YEAR: 1274.

PURPOSE: To explain why someone may kill an aggressor without committing murder.

My comments: Many histories of PDE cite this analysis of killing in self-defense as the first statement of PDE. Neither "doctrine of double effect" nor "principle of double effect" occurs in the text, but Aquinas does rely on the general principles that the agent's intention determines the act's species and that the agent does not intend all the action's foreseen effects. When Aquinas states the requirement about proportionality, he does not refer to the proportion of the good effect to the bad effect or try to make any type of utilitarian calculation. Instead he writes that the amount of force used must not be out of proportion to the end of saving one's life, in the sense of using more force than is necessary, not in the sense of causing more bad than good. For example, I should not save my life by shooting a two-year-old assailant who is chasing me with a knife when I can simply run away or grab the knife. Later proponents of PDE try to turn the proportionality condition into part of a set of conditions that someone must satisfy when causing bad effects.

TERROR BOMBING (A.K.A. MORALE BOMBING)

AUTHOR: G. E. M. Anscombe

The case in the author's words: "For men to choose to kill the innocent as a means to their ends is always murder, and murder is one of the worst of human actions. So the prohibition on deliberately killing prisoners of war or the civilian population is not like the

Queensberry Rules: its force does not depend on its promulgation as part of positive law, written down, agreed upon, and adhered to by the parties concerned."

SOURCE: "Mr. Truman's Degree," 64.

YEAR: 1957.

PURPOSE: To argue that Oxford should not have awarded an honorary degree to Harry Truman. According to Anscombe, Truman murdered thousands of Japanese civilians by ordering the bombings of Hiroshima and Nagasaki.

My comments: Anscombe was not the first one to apply PDE to military cases, but her analyses of cases from World War II introduced PDE to secular Anglo-American philosophy. Anscombe argues that Truman intended to kill Japanese civilians as a means of forcing Japan's unconditional surrender. The Americans did, however, drop leaflets that advised Japanese civilians to evacuate targeted cities:

> Read this carefully as it may save your life or the life of a relative or friend. In the next few days, some or all of the cities named on the reverse side will be destroyed by American bombs. These cities contain military installations and workshops or factories which produce military goods. We are determined to destroy all of the tools of the military clique which they are using to prolong this useless war. But, unfortunately, bombs have no eyes. So, in accordance with America's humanitarian policies, the American Air Force, which does not wish to injure innocent people, now gives you warning to evacuate the cities named and save your lives.[1]

These leaflets are not decisive evidence against Anscombe's argument. Truman and other Americans could have intended to kill the civilians who ignored the warning, or they could have dropped the leaflets to hide their homicidal intentions. Another possibility is that different people in the chain of command had different intentions. I mention the leaflets only to show that Anscombe's assertion about Truman's intention is not obviously true.

STRATEGIC BOMBING OR TACTICAL BOMBING

AUTHOR: G. E. M. Anscombe

The case in the author's words: "Killing the innocent, even if you know as a matter of statistical certainty that the things you do involve it, is not necessarily murder. I mean that if you attack a lot of military targets, such as munitions factories and naval dockyards, as carefully as you can, you will be certain to kill a number of innocent people; but that is not murder."

SOURCE: "Mr. Truman's Degree," 66.

YEAR: 1957.

PURPOSE: To explain why the rule against murder does not rule out killing innocent people as a side effect of attacking military targets during a just war.

My comments: The difference between a terror bombing and a strategic or tactical bombing is one of the most common illustrations of PDE. I have defended the common view that the terror bomber intends death, while the strategic or tactical bomber causes death as a foreseen side effect.

PUMPING POISONED WATER

AUTHOR: G. E. M. Anscombe

The case in the author's words: "A man is pumping water into the cistern which supplies the drinking water of a house. Someone has found a way of systematically contaminating the source with a deadly cumulative poison whose effects are unnoticeable until they can no longer be cured. The house is regularly inhabited by a small group of party chiefs, with their immediate families, who are in control of a great state; they are engaged in exterminating the Jews and perhaps plan a world war. The man who contaminated the source has calculated that if these people are destroyed some good men will get into power who will govern well, or even institute the Kingdom of Heaven on earth and secure a good life for all the people; and he has revealed the calculation, together with the fact about the poison, to the man who is pumping."

SOURCE: *Intention*, 37.

YEAR: 1957.

PURPOSE: To analyze the question "Is there any description which is *the* description of an intentional action, given that an intentional action occurs?"

My comments: Anscombe uses the case to illustrate different descriptions of the man's action (e.g., moving his arm, pumping water, poisoning the people inside the house, etc.). Her project is larger than defining intended effects in order to apply PDE in specific cases. Part of her analysis is the observation that the man can intend to pump the water to earn a salary without intending to poison the people inside the home (pp. 41–42). I do not know how to reconcile this observation with her assertion that the cave explorers and the surgeon in the craniotomy case must intend death. Her analysis of the case about pumping water also includes this observation: "The idea that one can determine one's intentions by making a little speech to oneself is obvious bosh" (p. 42). Someone can agree that this idea is "bosh" and still define intended effects from the agent's perspective.

WITHDRAWING CHILD SUPPORT

AUTHOR: G. E. M. Anscombe

The case in the author's words: "Let us suppose that a man has a responsibility for the maintenance of some child. Therefore deliberately to withdraw support from it is a bad sort of thing for him to do. It would be bad for him to withdraw its maintenance because he didn't want to maintain it any longer; and also bad for him to withdraw it because by doing so he would, let us say, compel someone else to do something.... But now he has to choose between doing something disgraceful and going to prison; if he goes to prison, it will follow that he withdraws support from the child."

SOURCE: "Modern Moral Philosophy," 11.

YEAR: 1958.

PURPOSE: To criticize Sidgwick and others who hold the thesis that "it does not make any difference to a man's responsibility for an effect of his action which he can foresee, that he does not intend it." According to Anscombe, if the man refuses to perform the disgraceful act (which she does not specify but which could be something like having sexual relations with a judge who is threatening him with a prison sentence) and is imprisoned, he is "not responsible" for the bad effect of his child's being unsupported.

My comments: Anscombe published this case in 1958, after the first editions of *Intention*, which includes the case of pumping poisoned water, and "Mr. Truman's Degree," which includes the bombing cases. The case of child support may not be as widely discussed as the others, but Anscombe's analysis of this case provides an example of using PDE to clarify other moral principles. I agree that there is a relevant distinction between intending the withdrawal of child support and accepting the withdrawal of child support as a side effect of refusing to do something disgraceful. Anscombe may overstate her point by saying that someone "is not responsible for the bad consequences of good actions." She could say instead that someone is not responsible for the bad consequences of good actions in the same way that someone is responsible for the bad consequences of bad actions.

THE HYSTERECTOMY

AUTHOR: F. J. Connell

The case in the author's words: "A pregnant woman bearing a nonviable fetus is found to have a cancerous womb that will cause her death if it is not excised as soon as possible. The operation of hysterectomy is morally lawful, for this operation is permissible in itself as a normal means of saving the woman's life. She does not positively will the death of her child, but permits it as an unavoidable evil. Both the benefit to her health and the death of child follow from the surgery with equal directness or immediacy in the order of causality, though the death of the child is prior in the order of time. The woman's chance of restoration to health (the good effect) is sufficiently desirable to compensate for the death of the fetus (the bad effect), which would probably not survive even if the operation were not performed."

SOURCE: *The New Catholic Encyclopedia*, 1021.

YEAR: 1967.

PURPOSE: To explain PDE and to distinguish the hysterectomy from other procedures that, according to Connell, violate PDE because the woman's improved health results from the abortion, "not directly as an effect of the surgery" (ibid).

My comments: Many philosophers cite Connell's article as a presentation of the traditional version of PDE. Like most proponents of PDE, I agree that the surgeon in the hysterectomy case could act rightly and that the surgeon need not intend the child's death. Still, I disagree with Connell's principle about causal directness or immediacy, which results in his restrictive analysis of the other pregnancy cases.

TERMINAL SEDATION (A.K.A. PALLIATIVE SEDATION) AND EUTHANASIA

AUTHOR: H. L. A. Hart

The case in the author's words: "The doctrine [of double effect] has its most interesting application where doctors may consider taking steps which will accelerate a patient's death. The simplest case is that of the administration of drugs to relieve the pain of a person slowly dying in agony. According to the latest Papal pronouncements, a distinction must be drawn between the case where the drug is given and the patient ceases to feel pain, but as a further consequence his death is accelerated, and the case where he ceases to feel pain because a drug has been administered to kill him as the only way of saving further pain."

SOURCE: "Intention and Punishment," 122.

YEAR: 1967.

PURPOSE: To illustrate PDE before criticizing it.

My comments: Hart's analysis of the hysterectomy and craniotomy cases is cited by Foot, who—with the possible exceptions of Anscombe and Thomson—did more than anyone to introduce PDE to moral philosophers and legal theorists outside of the Catholic tradition. Compared to cases of trolleys, the cases of terminal sedation and euthanasia do a better job of illustrating PDE because the actions have more similar effects in the cases about terminal sedation and euthanasia than do the actions in the cases about trolleys.

THE CRANIOTOMY (A.K.A. THE OBSTETRIC CRANIOTOMY)

AUTHOR: H. L. A. Hart

The case in the author's words: "If a woman is found to have cancer of the womb of which she will die unless the womb is removed, the surgeon may, according to Catholic doctrine, remove the womb with the foreseen consequence that the foetus dies. On the other hand, he is not permitted to perform a craniotomy killing an unborn child to save a woman in labour who would die if the head of the foetus is not crushed."

SOURCE: "Intention and Punishment," 123.

YEAR: 1967.

PURPOSE: To explain PDE before criticizing it.

My comments: Hart's analysis of the craniotomy sets up a common objection to PDE: that any definition of intended effects is either absurdly strict or arbitrary. I will not repeat my analysis of the craniotomy here, but one should not take the hysterectomy and craniotomy cases as illustrations of PDE. The craniotomy always has been controversial, even among proponents of PDE.

THE CAVE

AUTHOR: Philippa Foot

The case in the author's words: "A party of potholers [cave explorers] have imprudently allowed the fat man to lead them as they make their way out of the cave, and he gets stuck, trapping the others behind him. Obviously the right thing to do is to sit down and wait until the fat man grows thin; but philosophers have arranged that flood waters should be rising within the cave. Luckily (luckily?) the trapped party have with them a stick of dynamite with which they can blast the fat man out of the mouth of the cave. Either they use the dynamite or they drown. In one version the fat man, whose head is *in* the cave, will drown with them; in the other he will be rescued in due course. Problem: may they use the dynamite or not?"

SOURCE: "The Problem of Abortion and the Doctrine of Double Effect," 21.

YEAR: 1967.

PURPOSE: To provide "light relief" from the craniotomy case and to show how "odd" or "ridiculous" it would be to say that the surgeon in the craniotomy case intends to crush the child's skull but does not intend the child's death. Foot asserts that proponents of PDE would reject the explorers' claim that they intended to blast the man out of the cave, not to kill him. She adds, however, "What is to be the criterion of 'closeness' if we say that anything very close to what we are literally aiming at counts as if part of our aim?"

My comments: Foot's question has come to be known as the problem of closeness. She is correct that there is no good answer to her question about closeness, but there is nothing ridiculous about noting that the man's death contributes nothing at all to the explorers' plan. Any apparent oddity results from setting aside the agent's perspective and analyzing intentions in terms of causal relations.

THE SCAPEGOAT

AUTHOR: Philippa Foot

The case in the author's words: "Suppose that a judge or magistrate is faced with rioters demanding that a culprit be found for a certain crime and threatening otherwise to take their own bloody revenge on a particular section of the community. The real culprit being unknown, the judge sees himself as able to prevent the bloodshed only by framing some innocent person and having him executed."

SOURCE: "The Problem of Abortion and the Doctrine of Double Effect," 23.

YEAR: 1967.

PURPOSE: To present a case in which someone seems to act wrongly by intending to kill one innocent person as a means of saving several people. Foot first pairs this case with the case of a pilot who steers a disabled airplane away from a crowded area and toward a less crowded area. She then presents the case about diverting a runaway trolley.

My comments: Foot is correct that the judge intends death. Even if an unexpected turn of events could prevent the riots in some other way, the judge plans to execute the scapegoat to appease the mob. This case is a common counterexample to consequentialism because many people have the intuition that the judge acts wrongly even if the judge successfully prevents the riots.

THE ORIGINAL TROLLEY CASE
(A.K.A. THE TROLLEY DRIVER)

AUTHOR: Philippa Foot

The case in the author's words: "Beside this example [of the judge who frames the innocent person to prevent riots] is placed another in which a pilot whose aeroplane is about to crash is deciding whether to steer from a more to a less inhabited area. To make the parallel as close as possible it may rather be supposed that he is the driver of a runaway tram [trolley] which he can only steer from one narrow track on to another; five men are working on one track and one man on the other; anyone on the track he enters is bound to be killed."

SOURCE: "The Problem of Abortion and the Doctrine of Double Effect," 23.

YEAR: 1967.

PURPOSE: To explain why PDE seems plausible before criticizing PDE. According to Foot, "The question is why we should say, without hesitation, that the driver should steer for the less occupied track, while most of us would be appalled at the idea that the innocent man could be framed. . . . The doctrine of double effect offers us a way out of the difficulty, insisting that it is one thing to steer towards someone foreseeing that you will kill him and another to aim at his death as part of your plan" (23). She finally concludes "that the distinction between direct and oblique intention plays only a quite subsidiary role in determining what we say in these cases, while the distinction between avoiding injury and bringing aid is very important indeed" (29).

My comments: Foot is correct that the driver does not intend death in this case. Contrary to a common view, however, this trolley case and the other trolley cases that follow it make poor illustrations of PDE because they focus attention on the victim. Foot later changes her position and accepts PDE.[2]

JIM AND THE PRISONERS

AUTHOR: Bernard Williams

The case in the author's words: "Jim finds himself in the central square of a small South American town. Tied up against the wall are a row of twenty Indians, most terrified, a few defiant, in front of them several armed men in uniform. A heavy man in a sweat-stained khaki shirt turns out to be [Pedro,] the captain in charge and, after a good deal of questioning of Jim which establishes that he got there by accident while on a botanical expedition, explains that the Indians are a random group of the inhabitants who, after recent acts of protest against the government, are just about to be killed to remind other possible protestors of the advantages of not protesting. However, since Jim is an honoured visitor from another land, the captain is happy to offer him a guest's privilege of killing one of the Indians himself. If Jim accepts, then as a special mark of the occasion, the other Indians will be let off. Of course, if Jim refuses, then there is no special occasion, and Pedro here will do what he was about to do when Jim arrived, and kill them all. Jim, with some desperate recollection of schoolboy fiction, wonders whether if he got hold of a gun, he could hold the captain, Pedro and the rest of the soldiers to threat, but it is quite clear from the set-up that nothing of the sort is going to work: any attempt at that sort of thing will mean that all the Indians will be killed, and himself. The men against the wall, and the other villagers understand the situation, and are obviously begging him to accept. What should he do?"

SOURCE: "A Critique of Utilitarianism," 98–99.

YEAR: 1973.

PURPOSE: To criticize utilitarianism by illustrating the view that people have different responsibilities for what they do and for what other people do. Williams takes the question about what Jim should do as a difficult one, but the question would be easy if utilitarianism were true.

My comments: I used the case to explain the link between PDE and exceptionless moral rules, such as the rule against murder. To explain why Jim may not kill a prisoner, absolutists cannot focus on the harm to the prisoner, who will die anyway and who is begging Jim to pull the trigger. Instead, absolutists must focus on the corruption of Jim. PDE does not depend on exceptionless moral rules, but both PDE and exceptionless moral rules arise from a view of morality that treats the agent's character as relevant for judging actions.

THE TRANSPLANT

AUTHOR: Judith Jarvis Thomson

The case in the author's words: "David is a great transplant surgeon. Five of his patients need new parts—one needs a heart, the others need respectively, liver, stomach, spleen, and spinal cord—but all are of the same, relatively rare, blood type. By chance, David learns of a healthy specimen with that very blood type. David can take the healthy specimen's parts, killing him, and install them in his patients, saving them. Or he can refrain from taking the healthy specimen's parts, letting his patients die."

SOURCE: "Killing, Letting Die, and the Trolley Problem," 206.

YEAR: 1976.

PURPOSE: To set up the trolley problem, which Thomson defines as the problem of explaining why the trolley driver may divert the trolley onto a sidetrack where it will kill one instead of five even though the surgeon may not cut up the healthy person (or "healthy specimen" to use Thomson's label) to save five people.

My comments: Thomson does not use the case to challenge PDE, so she does not specify whether the surgeon kills the healthy person before taking organs. If not, the surgeon could intend to cut out the organs without intending the healthy person's death. Even though the surgeon does not intend death, the surgeon can do something as seriously wrong as someone who does intend death because the surgeon treats the victim unjustly.

THE TROLLEY PASSENGER

AUTHOR: Judith Jarvis Thomson

The case in the author's words: "Frank is a passenger on a trolley whose driver has just shouted that the trolley's brakes have failed, and who then died of the shock. On the track ahead are five people;

the banks are so steep that they will not be able to get off the track in time. The track has a spur leading off to the right, and Frank can turn the trolley onto it. Unfortunately there is one person on the right-hand track. Frank can turn the trolley, killing the one; or he can refrain from turning the trolley, letting the five die."

SOURCE: "Killing, Letting Die, and the Trolley Problem," 207.

YEAR: 1976.

PURPOSE: To criticize Foot's principle about the distinction between killing and letting die. According to Thomson, "If a driver of a trolley drives it full speed into five people, he kills them, even if he only drives it into them because his brakes have failed. But it seems to me that if Frank does nothing, he kills no one. He at worst lets the trolley kill the five; he does not himself kill them, but only lets them die. . . . Yet I take it that anyone who thinks Edward [the trolley driver] may turn his trolley will also think that Frank may turn his" (207).

My comments: I agree with Thomson that there is no morally relevant distinction between the trolley driver and the trolley passenger. The passenger knowingly causes death but does not intend death. Someone could use this case to illustrate PDE, but other cases work better for that purpose.

THE FOOTBRIDGE (A.K.A. THE FAT MAN, THE BYSTANDER ON THE BRIDGE)

AUTHOR: Judith Jarvis Thomson

The case in the author's words: "George is on a footbridge over the trolley tracks. He knows trolleys, and can see that the one approaching the bridge is out of control. On the track back of the bridge there are five people; the banks are so steep that they will not be able to get off the track in time. George knows that the only way to stop an out-of-control trolley is to drop a very heavy weight onto its path. But the only available, sufficiently heavy weight is a fat man, also watching the trolley from the footbridge. George can shove the fat man onto the track in the path of the trolley, killing the fat man; or he can refrain from doing this, letting the five die."

SOURCE: "Killing, Letting Die, and the Trolley Problem," 207–8.

YEAR: 1976.

PURPOSE: To challenge attempts to distinguish the cases of diverting trolleys from the case of the surgeon who steals organs. According to Thomson, "If the one has no more claim against the bad thing than any of the five has, he cannot complain if we do something to *it* in order to bring about that it is better distributed: i.e., it is permissible for Edward and Frank to turn their trolleys. But even if the one has no more claim against the bad thing than any of the five has, he can complain if we do something to him in order to bring about that the bad thing is better distributed: i.e., it is not permissible for George to shove his fat man off the bridge into the path of the trolley."[3]

My comments: Contrary to a common view, this case was not designed to analyze PDE. Unfortunately, many contemporary philosophers take it as an illustration of PDE, sometimes even the paradigmatic illustration. I agree that the bystander acts wrongly by pushing the man onto the track, even though the bystander does not intend to kill or even to harm the man. My defense of PDE does not require a final judgment about the bystander's action, but it seems that the bystander would act wrongly by forcing the man to serve the end of stopping the trolley against the man's will. If the man consented to being pushed onto the track (e.g., if he were the father of the five people and wanted to save his children's lives), then the bystander might not act wrongly.

THE CONVALESCENTS

AUTHOR: Judith Jarvis Thomson

The case in the author's words: "The five on the track ahead are regular track workmen, repairing the track—they have been warned of the dangers of their job, and are paid specially high salaries to compensate. The right-hand track is a dead end, unused in ten years. The Mayor, representing the City, has set out picnic tables on it, and invited the convalescents at the nearby City Hospital to have lunch there, guaranteeing them safety from trolleys. The one on the right-hand track is a convalescent having his lunch there; it would never have occurred to him to have his lunch there but for the Mayor's invitation and guarantee of safety."

SOURCE: "Killing, Letting Die, and the Trolley Problem," 210.

YEAR: 1976.

PURPOSE: To show that someone can act wrongly by diverting a trolley away from five people and toward one person. According to Thomson, "It isn't permissible for Edward and Frank to turn their trolleys in every possible instance" (211).

My comments: This case poses a problem for versions of PDE that are supposed to provide a complete set of conditions. By design, the proportion of lives saved is the same in this case as in other trolley cases, and the driver in this case has the same intention as the driver in the original trolley case.

THE STUTTERER

AUTHORS: Joseph Boyle and Thomas Sullivan

The case in the authors' words: "The honor of Peter's dead father has been unjustly impugned. Unwilling to suffer the attack on his father in silence, Peter rises to his defense. It is a courageous act, for Peter, a severely handicapped adult stutterer, can anticipate the results: despite desperate efforts to control the heaving of his chest and the flow of air through his quivering lips, he will vomit out every word of the defense in an agony of explosions."

SOURCE: "The Diffusiveness of Intention Principle: A Counterexample," 358.

YEAR: 1976.

PURPOSE: To give a counterexample to the diffusiveness of intention principle stated by Roderick Chisholm. According to Chisholm:

> If a rational man acts with the intention of bringing about a certain state of affairs *P*, and if he believes that by bringing about *P* he will bring about the conjunctive state of affairs, *P* and *Q*, then he does act with the intention of bringing about the conjunctive state of affairs, *P* and *Q*.[4]

My comments: Boyle and Sullivan note that Peter intends to testify but does not intend to stutter. In fact, Peter struggles not to stutter, despite knowing that he will bring about both his testifying and his stuttering. By itself, this case does not involve any moral judgments, but it is relevant for cases like the craniotomy and cave cases. Someone who defines intended effects in terms of closeness or directness will have a hard time explaining why Peter does not intend to stutter, because his testimony consists entirely of stuttered words. I know of no definition of intended effects that includes death in the craniotomy and cave cases but does not include stuttering in this case.

CRANIOTOMY ON A DEAD FETUS

AUTHOR: Joseph Boyle

The case in the author's words: "It is the dimensions of the fetus' skull being altered and not its being dead which saves the mother's life. This can be seen by considering the fact that the surgery would be required if the fetus whose position threatened the woman were already dead."

SOURCE: "Double Effect and a Certain Type of Embryotomy," 309.

YEAR: 1976.

PURPOSE: To explain why the surgeon in the craniotomy case does not intend to kill the fetus as a means of saving the mother.

My comments: I agree with Boyle's analysis of this case. The surgeon can have exactly the same plan if the fetus is dead and if the fetus is alive, so it is possible to intend to collapse or crush the child's skull without intending death. Many opponents of the craniotomy ignore the possibility of a craniotomy on a dead fetus when they assert that the surgeon intends to kill the fetus or that the surgeon directly kills the fetus as a means of saving the mother.

TWISTING A CHILD'S ARM

AUTHOR: Thomas Nagel

The case in the author's words: "You have an auto accident one winter night on a lonely road. The other passengers are badly injured, the car is out of commission, and the road is deserted, so you run along it till you find an isolated house. The house turns out to be occupied by an old woman who is looking after her small grandchild. There is no phone, but there is a car in the garage, and you ask desperately to borrow it and explain the situation. She doesn't believe you. Terrified by your desperation, she runs upstairs and locks herself in the bathroom, leaving you alone with the child. You pound ineffectively on the door and search without success for the car keys. Then it occurs to you that she might be persuaded to tell you where they are if you were to twist the child's arm outside the bathroom door. Should you do it?"

SOURCES: "The Limits of Objectivity" and *The View from Nowhere*, 176.

YEARS: 1979 and 1986.

PURPOSE: To illustrate the "deontological intuition" that intending harm is worse than allowing harm and to show that this difference seems relevant from the agent's point of view.

My comments: I agree with Nagel's analysis of this case, but not with his assertion that moral rules depend on the claims of other people. Nagel explains why intending harm and knowingly causing harm seem different from the agent's perspective, but he does not explain why the agent's perspective is relevant for judging actions.

DIRECTION OF RESOURCES
(A.K.A. RATIONING, TRIAGE)

AUTHOR: Philippa Foot

The case in the author's words: "There are circumstances in which it is morally permissible to bring something about *without* aiming at it although it would not be morally permissible to aim at it; even though the balance of benefit and harm in the consequences remained the same. That this is so is proved, I think, by some facts about the permissibility of allowing an evil to come on some for the sake of saving others. For sometimes this is a regrettable moral necessity, as in our previous examples having to do with scarce medical resources and with the person lying injured by the roadside. But it does not follow that it would be morally unobjectionable deliberately to leave someone unattended because his death would allow us to save others. We said earlier that it would be objectionable to kill even for such a good purpose, and now we must add that it would also be wrong to serve that same purpose by deliberately allowing someone to die."

SOURCE: "Morality, Action, and Outcome," 25.

YEAR: 1985.

PURPOSE: To illustrate the conflict between utilitarianism and "our ordinary morality," which includes PDE.

My comments: Foot criticized PDE in her 1967 paper, but she later came to accept it. Many people, including critics, find PDE intuitively appealing because it explains intuitions about the difference between rationing scarce medical resources and withholding treatment so that someone will die. The label "direction of resources" comes from Warren Quinn.[5]

THE BYSTANDER AT THE SWITCH
(A.K.A. SWITCH)

AUTHOR: Judith Jarvis Thomson

The case in the author's words: "You have been strolling by the trolley track, and you can see the situation at a glance: The driver saw the five on the track ahead, he stamped on the brakes, the brakes failed, so he fainted. What to do? Well, here is the switch, which you can throw, thereby turning the trolley yourself. Of course you will kill one if you do."

SOURCE: "The Trolley Problem," 1397.

YEAR: 1985.

PURPOSE: To replace the trolley passenger case with a case that looks even more similar to the bridge case and the case of stealing organs.

My comments: Contemporary philosophers commonly but mistakenly pair this case with the footbridge case to illustrate PDE. The bystander at the switch could act rightly because the bystander does not intend the one person's death, but the bystander could act wrongly for another reason, as does the driver in Thomson's case about the convalescents.

THE LOOP

AUTHOR: Judith Jarvis Thomson

The case in the author's words: "Consider now what I shall call 'the loop variant' on this case [the switch case], in which the tracks do not continue to diverge—they circle back, as in the following picture: [illustration in original] Let us now imagine that the five on the straight track are thin, but thick enough so that although all five will be killed if the trolley goes straight, the bodies of the five will stop it, and it will therefore not reach the one. One the other hand, the one on the right-hand track is fat, so fat that his body will by itself stop the trolley, and the trolley will therefore not reach the five."

SOURCE: "The Trolley Problem," 1403.

YEAR: 1985.

PURPOSE: To challenge anyone who tries to distinguish the bystander on the bridge from the bystander at the switch by arguing that the bystander on the bridge acts wrongly by using the man on the bridge simply as a means of stopping the trolley. According to Thomson, the two cases are morally similar: "We cannot really suppose that the presence or absence of that extra bit of track makes a major moral difference as to what an agent may do in these cases, and it really does seem right to think (despite the discomfort) that the agent may proceed. . . . Indeed, I should think that there is no plausible account of what is involved in, or what is necessary for, the application of the notions 'treating a person as a means only,' or 'using one to save five,' under which the surgeon [in the transplant case] would be doing this whereas the agent in this variant of *Bystander at the Switch* would not be" (1403).

My comments: I do not share Thomson's intuition that the bystander may divert the trolley onto the looping track. Instead I see this case as morally similar to the footbridge case. Both bystanders make their victims serve the end of stopping the trolley, even if the bystander's use of the man is less obvious in the loop case than in the footbridge case. Thomson's intuition that the cases are morally similar is popular among philosophers who write about the trolley problem, but much less popular among subjects in empirical studies. Thomson does not use the loop case to criticize PDE, but some critics see the case as a decisive refutation of PDE, even though neither the bystander on the bridge nor the bystander at the switch in the looping track intends death.

OVERDETERMINED SURRENDER

AUTHOR: Michael Bratman

The case in the author's words: "[The strategic bomber] is told that once he kills the children [by bombing the factory] there will in fact be a terrorizing effect on the enemy populace, and so that by killing the children he will be weakening Enemy."

SOURCE: *Intention, Plans, and Practical Reason*, 156.

YEAR: 1987.

PURPOSE: To resolve the "problem of the package deal," which says that agents who choose an overall scenario must intend a "package deal" that includes all the foreseen effects in that scenario.

My comments: Bratman argues that the bomber can intend to bomb the factory without intending to kill the children because the bomber can have a general commitment to try not to kill children and that this general commitment is incompatible with an intention to kill the children in the modified case. My analysis of the case supports Bratman. The bomber does not see the children's deaths as part of the causal sequence that makes the action worthwhile.

GUINEA PIG

AUTHOR: Warren Quinn

The case in the author's words: "Another pair of cases involves medicine: In both there is a shortage of resources for the investigation and proper treatment of a new, life-threatening disease. In the first scenario doctors decide to cope by selectively treating only those who can be cured most easily, leaving the more stubborn cases untreated. Call this the Direction of Resources Case (DR). In the contrasting and intuitively more problematic example, doctors decide on a crash experimental program in which they deliberately leave the stubborn cases untreated in order to learn more about the nature of the disease. By this strategy they reasonably expect to do as much long-term medical good as they would in DR. Call this the Guinea Pig Case (GP). In neither case do the nontreated know about or consent to the decision against treating them."

SOURCE: "Acts, Intentions, and Consequences," 336.

YEAR: 1989.

PURPOSE: To explain PDE's intuitive appeal before offering an alternative to traditional versions that focus on the agent's intention.

My comments: Contrary to some critics, my version of PDE can distinguish this case from the direction of resources case, in which the physicians do not intend to expose patients to any harm. The physicians in the guinea pig case do not need the patients to suffer harm, but they do need the patients to be exposed to harm so that the physicians can learn more about the disease. By contrast, the physicians in this case do not need the patients to be exposed to any harm. Another difference between the cases is that only the physicians in the guinea pig case violate their duty to act in their patients' best interests.

EXPLOSION ABOVE A CITY
(A.K.A. LEWIS BOMBER)

AUTHOR: Warren Quinn, who attributes the case to David Lewis

The case in the author's words: "Suppose that another terror bomber wishes to demoralize enemy leaders by bombing a major center of population, and suppose he knows that these leaders will be convinced that the city is destroyed by seeing, from afar, the explosion of his bombs over it. The explosion occurs an instant before the fatal effects below."

SOURCE: "Acts, Intentions, and Consequences," 343n16.

YEAR: 1989.

PURPOSE: To illustrate problems with versions of PDE that refer to the agent's intention and to illustrate Quinn's distinction between direct and harmful agency. According to Quinn, the bomber does not intend to blow up the civilians, but the bomber's action is an example of direct harmful agency because he aims at exploding bombs in the vicinity of the civilians.

My comments: I agree that the bomber in this case does not intend to kill the civilians, so my version of PDE does not explain why the case seems similar to the terror bombing rather than the strategic bombing. Even if neither the bomber in this case nor the strategic bomber intends death, their actions differ in two ways. First, the bomber in Quinn's case kills all the people in the city, while the strategic bomber kills an unspecified number of people near the weapons factory. If the strategic bomber also destroyed a whole city, then the two bombings would seem more similar. Second, the bomber in Quinn's case needs the enemy leaders to fear that thousands of people have been killed, but the strategic bomber does not. If intending to terrorize an enemy is wrong apart from causing casualties, then the bomber in Quinn's case also acts wrongly for this reason.

EISENHOWER AND D-DAY

AUTHOR: Andrew Kleinfeld

The case in the author's words: "When General Eisenhower ordered American soldiers onto the beaches of Normandy, he knew that he was sending many American soldiers to certain death, despite his best efforts to minimize casualties.... The majority's theory of ethics would imply that this purpose was legally and ethically indistinguishable from a purpose of killing American soldiers."

SOURCE: *Compassion in Dying v. State of Washington*, 79 F.3d 790 (C.A. 9 1996), 858.

YEAR: 1996.

PURPOSE: To explain Judge Kleinfeld's dissent from the majority ruling that struck down a state law against physician-assisted suicide. The majority dismissed PDE by finding "little, if any, difference for constitutional or ethical purposes" between a physician's using a painkiller that has the side effect of causing death and a physician's using a lethal painkiller to end the patient's pain by killing the patient.

My comments: Kleinfeld has the better argument here, and he was vindicated when the Supreme Court used his example to overturn the Ninth Circuit and uphold the statute. Proponents of PDE could be more precise by referring to Eisenhower's intention rather than referring only to his purpose.

HOMICIDAL EISENHOWER

AUTHOR: Judith Jarvis Thomson

The case in the author's words: "Suppose we are there at the time of Eisenhower's ordering the invasion to begin and he whispers to us, 'If truth be told, all I'm really intending in issuing the order is to cause the deaths of a lot of American soldiers.' And suppose we believe him. Presumably we should telephone Roosevelt and say, 'Cancel it!' For if that's all Eisenhower is intending in issuing the order, then there is real ground for worry about his planning of the invasion, and thus about what will go on in it: it is likely that there will be more deaths than are needed, not more than are needed for his purpose, of course, but more than are needed for the liberation of Europe. But if, perhaps per impossible, these concerns could be proved groundless, if, i.e., we could become convinced that all will go exactly as it would go if that were not his intention, then there would be no reason to cancel the order. If which intention he acts with will make no difference to what happens, then his intention bears, not on whether he may act, but only on him."

SOURCE: "Physician Assisted Suicide," 516n19.

YEAR: 1999.

PURPOSE: To argue that the distinction between intention and foresight is relevant for assessing agents but not for assessing actions and that PDE seems plausible because people overlook this distinction.

My comments: I have described Thomson's objection as the strongest objection to PDE. In presenting her objection, Thomson assumes that an observer can identify the action to be judged (i.e., "ordering the invasion") without referring to Eisenhower's intention and still have enough information to conclude that the action is right. Proponents of PDE should argue, however, that different intentions make for different actions, so that Eisenhower's ordering the invasion to liberate Europe is a different action than Eisenhower's ordering the invasion to kill Americans. According to my version of PDE, Eisenhower's intention is relevant for assessing both his action and his character. I agree with Thomson, however, that Roosevelt does not need to cancel the bombing simply because of Eisenhower's bad intention.

MUNITIONS GRIEF

AUTHOR: Frances Kamm

The case in the author's words: "In the well-known case, we foresee that if we bomb a crucial munitions plant during a just war, children next door will die from the plant exploding. This, it is said, is permissible. However, it is impermissible to terror-bomb the children in order to produce grieving parents who will surrender. My variant is that the bombed-out munitions plant would be immediately rebuilt by the parents, if they were not consumed by grief over the deaths of their children next door (Munitions Grief Case). In this case, we would not expend effort to bomb the plant unless we believed the children next door would be killed and the parents' grief thereby was caused, for this alone sustains the damage to the plant. Yet, I believe, it is permissible to bomb in this case consistent with its being impermissible to terror bomb."

SOURCE: *Morality, Mortality,* 179–80.

YEAR: 1996.

PURPOSE: To illustrate Kamm's principle of permissible harm, which she presents as an alternative to PDE.

My comments: I agree with Kamm that agents do not intend all the effects that motivate their actions, but I do not share her intuitions about this case. By hypothesis, the pilot in Kamm's case believes that the bombing will serve no military purpose apart from the children's deaths. Because the children's deaths and the enemy's grief are necessary steps in the pilot's plan to weaken the enemy's military, the children's deaths are an intended effect, not merely a motivating side effect. If, however, the pilot believed that the action would be worthwhile even without the children's deaths and the resulting grief, then the pilot would not intend the children's deaths.

THE PARTY CASE

AUTHOR: Frances Kamm

The case in the author's words: "I intend to give a party in order for me and my friends to have fun. However, I foresee that this will leave a big mess, and I don't want to have a party if I will be left to clean it up. I also foresee a further effect of the party: if my friends have fun, they will feel indebted to me and help me clean up. I assume that a feeling of indebtedness is something of a negative for a person to have. I give the party because I believe my friends will feel indebted and (so) because I will not have a mess to clean up."

SOURCE: "The Doctrine of Triple Effect and Why a Rational Agent Need Not Intend the Means to Her End," 26.

YEAR: 2000.

PURPOSE: To distinguish doing something *because it will have an effect* from doing something *in order to cause an effect*. Kamm uses this distinction to analyze the loop case. According to her, the bystander in the loop case diverts the trolley because it will hit the man on the sidetrack, but the bystander does not intend the trolley to hit the man:

> The only threat which faces the five that prompts my act to help them is the trolley heading toward them from one direction. This is the first problem. If this threat is not taken care of, they will die; to save them, it must be taken care of whatever else, though that does not mean that it is sufficient to save them. The problem that would exist (if the one on the side track were not there) of the

trolley coming at the five from a somewhat different direction *only arises* because I turn the trolley away from the five: One way to see this *new problem* is as a second threat facing the five because I have taken care of the only threat that faced them to begin with.[6]

Kamm concludes that the bystander in the loop does not intend to hit the man.[7] More generally, she concludes that a rational agent need not intend the means to her end.[8]

My comments: Regarding Kamm's analysis of the party case, I agree that she does not intend her friends' feelings of indebtedness and that someone can act because of an effect without intending the effect. Still, I do not see this case as a counterexample to the principle that agents intend every means to their ends. When Kamm throws the party, her end is to have fun, not to avoid a messy house. The messy house enters her deliberations only as a possible reason against the party. As I explain in chapter 2, I classify effects such as the friends' feeling indebted as motivating side effects, not as intended effects or as part of complex ends. Regarding Kamm's comparison of the party and the loop cases, I do not share Kamm's intuition that the bystander acts rightly, and I have argued that the bystander's intention includes the man's being hit by the trolley. The bystander could have the end of saving the five momentarily by saving them from being hit from one direction, but a more plausible assumption is that the bystander intends to save the five indefinitely by saving them from being hit from both directions. To save them indefinitely, the bystander needs the trolley to hit the man.

THE CHAIRMAN AND THE ENVIRONMENT

AUTHOR: Joshua Knobe

The case in the author's words: "The chairman of the board of a company has decided to implement a new program. He believes:

1. that the program will make a lot of money for his company and
2. that the program will also produce some other effect *x*.

But the chairman doesn't care at all about effect x. His sole reason for implementing the new program is that he believes it will make a lot of money for the company. In the end, everything proceeds as anticipated: the program makes a lot of money for the company and also produces effect x."

SOURCE: "Intentional Action and Side Effects in Ordinary Language," 190.

YEAR: 2003.

PURPOSE: To determine whether people ordinarily believe that a side effect can be brought about intentionally. Knobe tested the hypothesis that whether people believe that an agent brought about a side effect intentionally depends on whether the effect is good or bad. He found that when effect x is harming the environment, most subjects say that the chairman brought about the effect intentionally. When effect x is helping the environment, most subjects say that the chairman did not bring about the effect intentionally.

My comments: Knobe does not cite the results of his study as evidence against PDE, but some critics cite the results as evidence that PDE is nothing more than a tool for rationalizing moral judgments. As I explained in chapter 2, studies like Knobe's do not give evidence against PDE. Terms such as "intentionally" can be used in different ways, so the claim that the chairman intentionally harmed the environment is ambiguous. Further, even if many people define intended effects to fit their moral judgments, it would not follow that no definition of intended effects can be morally neutral.

REPOPULATED CITY

AUTHOR: William FitzPatrick

The case in the author's words: "Suppose someone wishes to demoralize the enemy government during a war, and knows he could do so by creating the belief that large numbers of civilians have been killed. He is reluctant to bring this about by deliberately killing civilians, but thinks he sees a way around this. It turns out that a major population center has been evacuated unbeknownst to the central government, so that if it is bombed they will believe that there have been massive casualties, simply viewing it from afar. He thus plans to go ahead and bomb the empty city. At the last minute, however, he discovers that the population has returned. Now suppose he goes ahead with the mission anyway."

SOURCE: "The Intend/Foresee Distinction and the Problem of Closeness," 612.

YEAR: 2006.

PURPOSE: To criticize Quinn's appeal to direct and indirect harmful agency. Quinn argues that the bomber who explodes bombs above the city is guilty of direct harmful agency. FitzPatrick argues that the bomber's action does not fit Quinn's description of direct harmful agency because the bomber does not need the civilians to be involved at all (pp. 612–13). In Quinn's case, the civilians are never evacuated, but adding the evacuation and repopulation highlights the irrelevance of the civilians' presence to the bomber's plan.

My comments: I agree with FitzPatrick's analysis of what Quinn's view entails about this case, but I do not agree that the deaths of the civilians follow the action so closely that the bomber must intend to kill the civilians. Like the bomber in Quinn's case, the bomber in FitzPatrick's variation does not intend death but still acts wrongly by killing thousands of civilians and by terrorizing the enemy. By contrast, the strategic bomber kills only a few bystanders and seeks to weaken the enemy's military, not to demoralize the enemy.

THE DILATION AND CURETTAGE (A.K.A. THE PHOENIX CASE, THE PHOENIX ABORTION CASE)

AUTHOR: Therese Lysaught

The case in the author's words: "On November 3, 2009, the woman was admitted to St. Joseph's Hospital and Medical Center with

worsening symptoms. At this time, the woman was 11 weeks pregnant. A cardiac catheterization revealed that the woman now had
'very severe pulmonary arterial hypertension with profoundly
reduced cardiac output'; in another part of the record, a different
physician confirmed 'severe, life-threatening pulmonary hypertension,' 'right heart failure' and 'cardiogenic shock.' . . . There was one
possibility for treating and reversing the pathology of the emergent
conditions of right heart failure and cardiogenic shock. The intervention for treating this pathology was to eliminate the cause of the
increased blood volume and increased demand for cardiac output.
The cause of this increased blood flow and cardiac demand was not
the fetus but rather the placenta—an organ in its own right. . . . Based
on these facts, the ethics committee at St. Joseph's Hospital and Medical Center was asked for a determination of whether the intervention
to address the placental issue via a dilation and curettage would be
morally appropriate according to Catholic teaching. . . . The ethics
committee determined that the intervention would not be considered
a direct abortion. They therefore approved the intervention, which
was carried out on November 5, 2009."

SOURCE: "Moral Analysis of a Procedure at Phoenix Hospital."

YEAR: 2012.

PURPOSE: Lysaught summarizes a real case. She argues that the ethics
committee was correct to conclude that the dilation and curettage
(D&C) was not a direct abortion.

My comments: I agree with Lysaught's conclusion but not her arguments. To defend this conclusion, she appeals to Martin Rhonheimer's
analysis of the craniotomy case to defend the D&C. According to
Lysaught:

> Rhonheimer would claim that (a) one cannot properly in that case
> speak of the intervention as having two effects; and (b) that even
> if one could establish that the "matter" of the action of the dila-
> tion and curettage was or appeared to be a physically direct act
> of killing, morally, the death of the child would have been *praeter*

intentionem, outside the scope of the intention and therefore outside of the proper moral description of the action.[9]

Regarding (a), the intervention in this case (i.e., the D&C) may have
shortened the child's life even if the child were already dying. The
difference between intending to shorten a child's life and shortening a child's life as a foreseen side effect is relevant for determining
whether the surgeons and other hospital employees acted rightly.
Regarding (b), I find the term "physically direct" misleading for the
reasons explained in chapters 2 and 5, and I would not classify all
unintended effects as being outside "the proper moral description" of
actions. For example, someone could describe a drunk driver's action
as "endangering other people's lives" even though the driver does not
intend to put anyone in danger.

Lysaught also defends her conclusion by appealing to Grisez's
analysis of life-threatening pregnancies. According to Lysaught:

> The case clearly meets Grisez's four criteria: (i) a pathology threat-
> ened the lives of both the pregnant woman and her child, (ii) it was
> not safe to wait or waiting surely would have resulted in the death
> of both, (iii) there was no way to save the child, and (iv) an opera-
> tion that could save the mother's life would, at least prima facie,
> result in the child's death. Grisez would therefore likely hold that
> the intervention enacted at St. Joseph's ought not be categorized as
> a direct killing, for the baby's death was not what was intended.[10]

The problem with this argument is that Grisez presents four "conditions" (which Lysaught labels "criteria") to describe the type of case
he is discussing, not to determine whether an agent intends death.
After presenting the four conditions, Grisez uses the craniotomy as
an example of a case in which all four conditions are fulfilled. He then
argues that the surgeon can perform the craniotomy without intending death. He does not argue that death is unintended because all four
conditions are fulfilled. Even when all four conditions are fulfilled,
a surgeon could still intend to kill the child—for example, by using
a lethal injection— so that the child's death relieves the threat to the
mother as a means of saving the woman. Further, even if one or more

conditions were not fulfilled—for example, if it were safe to wait—a surgeon could perform a craniotomy or D&C without intending death. In such a case, the surgeon could act wrongly by treating the child unjustly even if the surgeon did not intend death. In general, an observer can make plausible inferences about a surgeon's intention, but the surgery's circumstances do not settle questions about whether the surgeon intends death.

Notes

Preface

1. For MacIntyre's view about how a moral theory can be defended against rival theories, see MacIntyre, *After Virtue*, 268–69.

2. For MacIntyre's argument that moral rules become unintelligible outside of a teleological view, see ibid., 52–55.

3. For my first article about PDE, see Masek, "The Doctrine of Double Effect, Deadly Drugs, and Business Ethics." As noted above, I now believe that my argument in that article is flawed.

4. For a critique of my first article, see Tully, "The Doctrine of Double Effect and the Question of Constraints on Business Decisions."

5. For my response to Tully, see Masek, "Deadly Drugs and Double Effect: A Reply to Tully."

6. For Nagel's acceptance of PDE, see Nagel, *The View from Nowhere*, 179. For Foot's acceptance of PDE, see Foot, "Morality, Action and Outcome," 25.

7. For Foot's self-description as an atheist, see Foot and Voorhoeve, "Natural Goodness," 35.

8. For Foot's critique of consequentialism, see Foot, "Morality, Action and Outcome." For an earlier version of her critique, see Foot, "Utilitarianism and the Virtues."

9. For my first attempt at an agent-based justification of PDE, see Masek, "Intentions, Motives and Double Effect."

Introduction

1. For a more sophisticated parody of trolley cases and other far-fetched thought experiments, see Patton, "Can Bad Men Make Good Brains Do Bad Things?"

2. This case about rationing drugs is a modified version of Philippa Foot's case. See Foot, "Morality, Action and Outcome," 23.

3. This example about a sniper is a modified version of Gilbert Harman's example. See Harman, "Practical Reasoning," 433–34 and 453–57.

4. Google searches yielded 47,000 results for "doctrine of double effect" and 54,000 for "principle of double effect," and searches of The Philosopher's Index yielded 114 results for the former and 107 for the latter.

5. For a use of "double-effect reasoning," see Cavanaugh, *Double Effect Reasoning*.

6. For a use of "principle of side effects," see Anscombe, "Medalist's Address," 21.

7. For examples of philosophers who define PDE as a single principle about the relevance of intentions rather than as a set of conditions, see Boyle, "Intention, Permissibility, and the Structure of Agency," 461–62. See also FitzPatrick, "The Doctrine of Double Effect," 183; Lippert-Rasmussen, "Scanlon on the Doctrine of Double Effect," 541; Nelkin and Rickless, "Three Cheers for Double Effect," 137; Quinn, "Acts, Intentions, and Consequences," 334n1; and Wedgwood, "Defending Double Effect," 384. I cite here only proponents of some version of PDE, but I could give many more examples if I included critics.

8. For a similar argument about the incompatibility of parenting and moral skepticism, see Hursthouse, *On Virtue Ethics*, 174–77.

One   The Rational Basis of the Principle of Double Effect

1. For Thomson's criticism of the view of morality that supports PDE, see Thomson, "Self-Defense," 296. For a similar objection, see Nye, "Objective Double Effect and the Avoidance of Narcissism," 263–64.

2. My argument about intentions and character follows John Finnis's explanation of how choosing ends and means shapes an agent's character differently than does accepting side effects. See Finnis, *Moral Absolutes*, 72–73.

3. For another argument that agents have a different relation to intended effects than to foreseen side effects, see Wedgwood, "Defending Double Effect," 393. Wedgwood notes the different degrees of "agential

involvement" when an agent intends an effect versus when an agent knowingly causes an effect. I agree, and I try to explain why the difference is relevant for judging actions.

4. For an objection to PDE based on a contrast between intending death as an end and intending death as a means, see Bennett, *The Act Itself*, 215–18.

5. For Cavanaugh's justification of PDE or double-effect reasoning, see Cavanaugh, *Double Effect Reasoning*, 135.

6. For Thomson's claim that it is "queer" to say that a bombing's permissibility depends on the agent's intention, see Thomson, "Self-Defense," 293.

7. For a description of PDE as "wildly implausible," see Norcross, "Intending and Foreseeing Death," 115.

8. For another example to illustrate how someone can admit the relevance of a category and deny the relevance of degrees within the category, see Anthony Ellis's review of Cavanaugh's *Double Effect Reasoning*, 162.

9. For an example of an intuition-based justification of PDE, see Walzer, *Just and Unjust Wars*, 151–59. For a more recent example, see Kaufman, *Justified Killing*, 89–97. Kaufman appeals both to intuitions and to the Anglo-American legal tradition.

10. For a criticism of this view that philosophers can set aside their intuitions, develop a moral theory, and then apply the theory to cases, see MacIntyre, "Does Applied Ethics Rest on a Mistake?," 498–513.

11. For an argument that using "absolute" in ethics can be misleading because of the term's political connotations, see Veatch, *Rational Man*, 40.

12. For the assertion that anyone who accepts absolute moral rules must be either confused or relying on authority rather than reason, see Bennett, "Whatever the Consequences," 84.

13. For absolutist justifications of PDE, see Boyle, "Who Is Entitled to Double Effect?," and Christopher Tollefsen, "Intending Damage to Basic Goods." See also Anscombe, "War and Murder," 58. According to Anscombe, without moral absolutes "the Christian ethic goes to pieces. Hence the necessity of the notion of double effect."

14. For a non-absolutist version of PDE, see Wedgwood, "Defending Double Effect."

15. For an argument that moral dilemmas do occur, see Sinnott-Armstrong, *Moral Dilemmas*. For an argument that they do not occur, see Donagan, "Consistency in Rationalist Moral Systems."

16. For the objection that someone can reject PDE and use the distinction between doing and allowing to make sense of exceptionless rules, see Anderson, "Boyle and the Principle of Double Effect." Anderson

criticizes Boyle's justification of PDE but does not reject PDE. For Boyle's response to Anderson, see Boyle, "The Moral Meaning and Justification of the Doctrine of Double Effect."

17. For an argument that someone who accepts an agent-based definition of intended effects can set aside the distinction between doing and allowing, see Tollefsen, "Is a Purely First Person Account of Human Action Defensible?," 455–57.

18. For Williams's case of Jim and his objection to utilitarianism, see Williams, "A Critique of Utilitarianism," 98–99.

19. For Nagel's case of twisting a child's arm, see Nagel, *The View from Nowhere*, 176.

20. For Nagel's argument that the distinction between doing and allowing does not explain intuitions about twisting the child's arm, see ibid., 180.

21. For Nagel's argument that people should treat evil as repellent, see ibid., 182.

22. For a description of Nagel's justification of PDE as metaphorical, see Lippert-Rasmussen, "Scanlon on the Doctrine of Double Effect," 543.

23. For Nagel's case of twisting a child's arm, see Nagel, *The View from Nowhere*, 182.

24. For the question that distinguishes between an effect's being phenomenologically important and an effect's being morally important, see ibid., 183.

25. For Nagel's conclusion that it is not irrational to evaluate actions from the agent's perspective, see ibid., 185.

26. For an argument that intuitions are unreliable when they prohibit actions that have good consequences, see Singer, "Ethics and Intuitions."

27. For the statement that moral requirements are based in other people's interests, see Nagel, *The View from Nowhere*, 197.

Two   An Agent-Based Definition of Intended Effects

1. For the original trolley case, see Foot, "The Problem of Abortion and the Doctrine of Double Effect," reprinted in Foot, *Virtues and Vices*, 23. The original version of Foot's paper is not widely available, so I refer to the reprinted version.

2. For Foot's claim that proponents of PDE will be unable to define closeness, see Foot, *Virtues and Vices*, 21–22.

3. For a use of "backsolve" to describe the act of relying on moral judgments about an action to determine what the agent intends, see Delaney, "To Double Business Bound," 581.

4. For the statement that someone cannot shoot, stab, crush, or blow up a person without intending death, see Fried, *Right and Wrong*, 44.

5. For Bratman's planning view of intentions, see Bratman, *Intention, Plans, and Practical Reason*. For a more recent statement, see Bratman, "Intention, Practical Rationality, and Self-Governance."

6. For the principle of event identity and spatiotemporal coordinates, see Sulmasey, "'Reinventing' the Rule of Double Effect," 131.

7. For the principle of constitutive relations, see FitzPatrick, "The Intend/Foresee Distinction and the Problem of Closeness," 593.

8. For the principle of basic powers and essential constituents, see O'Brien and Koons, "Objects of Intention," 662–63.

9. For the original version of the case of a stuttering man who testifies for his father, see Boyle and Sullivan, "The Diffusiveness of Intention Principle," 358.

10. For the case of the bank robber who strays from a plan and shoots a customer, see Marquis, "Four Versions of Double Effect," 530.

11. For the use of "strict" to label a definition of intended effects, see ibid., 529.

12. I thank Thomas Cavanaugh for calling my attention to the possibility of misusing the label "strategic bombing" as a euphemism for terror bombings.

13. The case of a bomber pilot who weakens the enemy's military by destroying a military target and demoralizes the enemy by killing innocent people comes from Michael Bratman. See Bratman, *Intentions, Plans, and Practical Reason*, 156–60.

14. In my analysis of the pilot who does not intend deaths even though the deaths promote the pilot's end, I follow Michael Bratman's analysis. See ibid., 159–60.

15. For the objection that the terror bomber needs only for the victims to appear dead, see Bennett, *The Act Itself*, 210.

16. For the objection that a strict definition of intended effects classifies death as intended only when the agent seeks death as an end in itself, see ibid., 209–12. See also Davis, "The Doctrine of Double Effect," 112–13.

17. For an explanation of how someone can use counterfactuals to analyze intentions, see Tollefsen, "Response to Koons and O'Brien's 'Objects of Intention,'" 756.

18. For the objection that my version of the strict definition of intended effects is too strict, see FitzPatrick, "The Doctrine of Double Effect," 186.

19. For the accusation of "redescribing" actions, see Jensen, "Causal Constraints on Intention." For the accusation of "gerrymandering" intentions, see Reed, "How to Gerrymander Intention."

20. The case of a gangster who slices a potential witness's neck is a modified version of Anscombe's case. See Anscombe, "Medalist's Address," 23.

21. For the claim that the example of a soccer player who scores a goal shows that agents do not have access to their intentions in a way that is unavailable to observers, see Cavanaugh, *Double Effect Reasoning*, 68.

22. For the assertion that a strict definition of intended effects depends on dualism or Cartesianism, see O'Brien and Koons, "Objects of Intention," 675.

23. For the case of a surgeon who steals organs for life-saving transplants, see Thomson, "Killing, Letting Die and the Trolley Problem," 206.

24. For the objection that I cannot explain why someone who kills to make organs available and someone who simply steals the organs and causes death act wrongly for the same reason, see FitzPatrick, "The Doctrine of Double Effect," 194n8.

25. For the objection that my analysis of cases about stealing organs depends on the assumption that agents have only one intention, see Chappell, "What Have I Done?," 100n28.

26. For Finnis's suggested legal definition of murder, see Finnis, "Intention and Side-Effects," 49.

27. For Foot's challenge to state a criterion for determining when an effect follows so closely that the agent must intend it, see Foot, "The Problem of Abortion and the Doctrine of Double Effect," reprinted in Foot, *Virtues and Vices*, 22.

28. For Anscombe's case in which cave explorers move a rock that opens a cave exit and also crushes a man's head, see "Medalist's Address," 21.

29. For Anscombe's statement that the distance between the rock and the man's end is relevant to determining the explorers' intention, see ibid., 23.

30. For Anscombe's claim that a man can pump water known to be poisoned into a home without intending to poison people, see Anscombe, *Intention*, 41.

31. For Anscombe's claims about the man who does not care about the poison in the water, see ibid., 42.

32. John Finnis also notes the difference between Anscombe's analyses of the man who pumps poisoned water and of the explorers who blow the man up. See Finnis, "Intention and Side-Effects," 58–59.

33. For the claim that a sniper who shoots through a person to hit a target behind the person must intend to kill the person, see Delaney, "Two Cheers for 'Closeness,'" 347.

34. For Anscombe's statement that intentions explain why an agent acts, see Anscombe, *Intention*, 9.

35. For the definition of intended effects in terms of the agent's motivating reasons, see Shaw, "Intention in Ethics," 205–12. See also Pruss, "The Accomplishment of Plans," 52.

36. The case of a physician who must choose between two patients, one of whom is a potential organ donor, is a variation of a case about two runaway trolleys that I present in Masek, "Intentions, Motives and Double Effect," 567.

37. For the case of a party that causes friends to feel indebted and to help clean up the mess, see Kamm, "The Doctrine of Triple Effect," 26 and Kamm, *Intricate Ethics*, 95.

38. For the proposed doctrine of triple effect, see Kamm, "The Doctrine of Triple Effect." Kamm eventually rejects both the doctrine of double effect and the doctrine of triple effect.

39. For the case of the eccentric zoo owner who tells someone to shoot a mammal, see Pruss, "The Accomplishment of Plans," 53–54. Pruss uses this example to criticize traditional versions of PDE, not to defend the strict definition of intended effects.

40. For the study in which subjects were asked about the chairman who harms or helps the environment, see Knobe, "Intentional Action and Side Effects in Ordinary Language," 190–93.

41. For people's apparently inconsistent judgments about whether the chairman brings about an effect intentionally, see ibid.

42. For the statement that PDE is merely a rationalization of people's intuitions, see Levy, "Neuroethics," 6.

43. For an analysis of how subjects in Knobe's study might resolve the ambiguity of different statements, see Guglielmo and Malle, "Can Unintended Side Effects Be Intentional?," 1643.

44. For the results in which most subjects say that the chairman "knowingly harmed" the environment, see ibid., 1642.

Three   The Strongest Objection to the Principle of Double Effect

1. For the claim that "there is little, if any, difference for constitutional or ethical purposes" between a physician's killing a patient to end pain and prescribing a lethal dose of painkillers, see *Compassion in Dying v. State of Washington*, 79 F.3d 790 (C.A. 9 1996).

2. For the claim that Eisenhower did not intend the deaths of American soldiers when he ordered the Normandy invasion, see ibid., 858. The author of the dissenting opinion was Judge Andrew Kleinfeld.

3. For the Supreme Court ruling that cites the example of Eisenhower, see *Vacco v. Quill*, 521 U.S. 793 at 808n11.

4. For Thomson's counterfactual case of Eisenhower's homicidal intention, see Thomson, "Physician-Assisted Suicide," 516n19.

5. For Thomson's argument that PDE seems plausible partly because many people conflate judging *actions* and judging *agents*, see ibid., 517.

6. For a similar argument that critics of PDE are begging the question when they argue that intentions are relevant only for judging agents, see Chappell, "Two Distinctions," 226.

7. For a critic of PDE who shares common intuitions about the drug-withholding and drug-rationing cases, see Scanlon, *Moral Dimensions*, 1–2.

8. I also present this argument about question-begging terms in Masek, "In Defense of a Minimalist, Agent-Based Principle of Double Effect," 529–30.

9. For the version of PDE that refers to what the agent could intend, not what the agent does intend, see FitzPatrick, "Acts, Intentions, and Moral Permissibility." For a defense of this view, see Neil Delaney, "Two Cheers for 'Closeness,'" 356–59.

10. For the claim that actions are intentional under some descriptions but not others, see Anscombe, *Intention*, 11. See Anscombe, "Under a Description."

11. For Scanlon's description of the basic disagreement about PDE, see Scanlon, *Moral Dimensions*, 25.

12. For Scanlon's example of stabbing a doll, see Scanlon, "Reply to Hill, Mason and Wedgwood," 492.

13. For Scanlon's explanation of disagreements about PDE, see ibid.

14. For Bennett's objection to an agent-based justification of PDE, see Bennett, *The Act Itself*, 221–22.

15. For Bennett's claims about the bombers' feelings, hopes, and desires, see ibid., 222.

16. For Scanlon's statement that agents cannot choose an action and then choose a reason or intention for the action, see Scanlon, *Moral Dimensions*, 60. For a similar objection, see Bennett, *The Act Itself*, 195–96.

17. Ralph Wedgwood also defends PDE by distinguishing between choosing an intention for an action and choosing a different action. See Wedgwood, "Scanlon on Double Effect," 468–69.

18. For a similar case of a chess player who makes the only legal move without intending the inevitable checkmate, see Christopher Tollefsen, "Response to Koons and O'Brien's 'Objects of Intention,'" 773.

19. For the book title that reveals the basic disagreement about morality, see Scanlon, *What We Owe to Each Other*.

20. For Scanlon's rule about using lethal force in war, see Scanlon *Moral Dimensions*, 21–28.

21. For critiques of Scanlon's rule about using lethal force in war, see McMahan, "Intention, Permissibility, Terrorism, and War." See also Elster, "Scanlon on Permissibility and Double Effect," and Lippert-Rasmussen, "Scanlon on the Doctrine of Double Effect."

22. For an argument that Kant does not accept the view often attributed to him, see Wood, *Kant's Ethical Thought*. According to Wood, if a deontological theory "precludes grounding a moral principle on substantive values or ends," then the aim of Kant's argument about humanity as an end in itself "is to show that no deontological theory is possible" (114).

23. For Scanlon's rule about providing or withholding medical care, see Scanlon, *Moral Dimensions*, 35.

Four   Trolley Cases and an Objection
from Neuroscience and Moral Psychology

An earlier version of some material in this chapter appears in my article "In Defense of a Minimalist, Agent-Based Principle of Double Effect."

1. For an argument against the use of trolley cases, see Barbara Fried, "What *Does* Matter?," 505–29. For a similar argument, see Wood, "Humanity as an End in Itself," 58–82.

2. For the original trolley case, see Foot, "The Problem of Abortion and the Doctrine of Double Effect," reprinted in Foot, *Virtues and Vices*, 23.

3. For the original transplant case, see Thomson, "Killing, Letting Die and the Trolley Problem," 206.

4. For Thomson's use of the label "the trolley problem" to describe the problem of distinguishing the trolley driver from the surgeon, see ibid.

5. For the case of the trolley passenger, see ibid., 207.

6. For the footbridge case, see ibid., 207–208.

7. For the switch case, see Thomson, "The Trolley Problem," 1397.

8. For Thomson's statement about causing confusion by defining the trolley problem in different ways, see Thomson, "Kamm on the Trolley Problems," 116.

9. For Thomson's statement that she did not develop the trolley and transplant cases to analyze PDE, see Thomson, "The Trolley Problem," 1407n12.

10. For examples of critics who believe that PDE's proponents see it as a solution to the trolley problem, see McIntyre, "Doing Away with Double Effect," 220. See also Liao, "The Loop Case and Kamm's Doctrine of Triple Effect," 224. For an example from moral psychology, see Kahane, "The Armchair and the Trolley," 425. McIntyre, Liao, and Kahane do not cite any proponents of PDE who appeal to the trolley problem as evidence of PDE.

11. For the statement that Aquinas was the first one to enunciate PDE, see Mangan, "A Historical Analysis of the Principle of Double Effect," 49.

12. For the quotation asserting that PDE depends entirely on intuitions about cases like that of the bystander on the bridge and the bystander at the switch, see Greene, *Moral Tribes*, 223.

13. For the quotation asserting that proponents of PDE see it as a solution to the trolley problem, see Di Nucci, *Ethics without Intention*, 78–79. Di Nucci does not cite any proponents of PDE who agree.

14. For Anscombe's absolutist justification of PDE, see Anscombe, "War and Murder," 58–59.

15. For Boyle's agent-based justification of PDE, see "Towards Understanding the Principle of Double Effect," 535–37. For his absolutist justification of PDE, see Boyle, "Who Is Entitled to Double Effect?" For his footnote about the bystander on the bridge, see ibid., 570n3.

16. For Nagel's case of twisting a child's arm, see Nagel, *The View from Nowhere*, 176.

17. For Cavanaugh's justification of PDE, see Cavanaugh, *Double-Effect Reasoning*, 134–47.

18. See Foot's use of the transplant case to criticize consequentialism. Foot, "Morality, Action, and Outcome," 89.

19. For an argument that Kant's categorical imperative makes PDE superfluous, see Donagan, "Moral Absolutism and the Double-Effect Exception," 495–509.

20. For the quotation that conflates Aquinas and Kant, see Greene, *Moral Tribes*, 300–301.

21. For an example of using cases of treating pain to illustrate PDE, see *The Catechism of the Catholic Church*, section 2279.

22. For a statement that the case of treating pain is irrelevant, see Quinn, "Acts, Intentions, and Consequences," 343n17.

23. For the statement that the purpose of trolley cases is to find principles that support intuitions, see Wood, "Humanity as an End in Itself," 67.

24. For the objection that trolley cases exclude details that would be relevant to real agents, see ibid., 70. See also Fried, "What *Does* Matter?," 507.

25. For Thomson's variations that make the argument for diverting the trolley stronger or weaker, see Thomson, "Killing, Letting Die and the Trolley Problem," 211.

26. For the statement that philosophers who use trolley cases assume that the cases isolate the most fundamental aspects of real cases, see Wood, "Humanity as End in Itself," 82.

27. For the statement that philosophers who use trolley cases assume that the cases have only one solution, see Wood, "Humanity as End in Itself," 72.

28. For the statement that trolley cases distract philosophers from more important questions, see Fried, "What *Does* Matter?," 506. For a similar objection, see Wood, "Humanity as End in Itself," 80.

29. For Mangan's version of PDE, see Mangan, "A Historical Analysis of the Principle of Double Effect," 43.

30. For another example of a version of PDE that consists of four conditions, see Connell, "The Principle of Double Effect," 1020–22.

31. For an example of a version of PDE that simplifies Mangan's four conditions, see Cavanaugh, *Double-Effect Reasoning*, 36.

32. For the statement that a version of PDE should be sufficient to determine permissibility in hard cases, see ibid., 71.

33. For a history of the condition about proportionality, see Kaczor, "Double-Effect Reasoning from Jean Pierre Gury to Peter Knauer." For attempted refinements of the proportionality condition, see Cavanaugh, *Double-Effect Reasoning*, 36. See also Connell, "The Principle of Double Effect," 1021.

34. For the version of the proportionality condition that says the action may not be wrong for any reason other than the agent's intention, see Boyle, "Who Is Entitled to Double Effect?" 476.

35. For the claim that a version of PDE should be "sufficient to determine permissibility in the relevant hard cases," see Cavanaugh, *Double-Effect Reasoning*, 71. Cavanaugh criticizes Finnis, Grisez, and Boyle for explaining why some killings are wrong by appealing to principles about justice rather than to the principle against intending death.

36. For the analysis of killing in self-defense, see Aquinas, *Summa Theologica*, 2.2.64.5.

37. For the statement that Aquinas does not present a version of PDE, see Keenan, "The Function of the Principle of Double Effect," 299.

38. For the case of a convalescent who was promised safety on the sidetrack, see Thomson, "The Trolley Problem," 1411–12.

39. For the objection that my version of PDE cannot explain why some actions are morally wrong for the same reason, see FitzPatrick, "The Doctrine of Double Effect," 186–87 and 194n8. For another statement of this objection to my version of PDE, see Nelkin and Rickless, "Three Cheers for Double Effect," 128n6.

40. For the claim that I cannot explain why killing a patient to make organs available and stealing organs from a living patient are wrong for the same reason, see FitzPatrick, "The Doctrine of Double Effect," 194n8.

41. For Thomson's change of position about the trolley cases, see Thomson, "Turning the Trolley," 359–74. Thomson says that one of her graduate students, Alexander Friedman, convinced her that the bystander may not throw the switch. See Friedman, *Minimizing Harm: Three Problems in Moral Theory*.

42. For Thomson's loop case, see Thomson, "The Trolley Problem," 1402.

43. For Thomson's conclusion that the loop case must be morally similar to the original case about the bystander at the switch, see ibid.

44. For an argument that the bystander need not intend for the trolley to hit the man in the loop case, see Shaw, "Intentions and Trolleys," 74. For another argument for this conclusion from a critic of PDE, see Kamm, *Intricate Ethics*, 94.

45. For a variation of the loop case in which the trolley driver chases down the victim so that the victim stops the trolley, see FitzPatrick, "The Doctrine of Double Effect," 189.

46. For an argument that there is no relevant difference between throwing a trolley at a person and throwing a person at a trolley, see Harris, "The Moral Difference between Throwing a Trolley at a Person and Throwing a Person at a Trolley."

47. For an analysis of the loop case that is similar to mine, see Otsuka, "Double Effect, Triple Effect, and the Trolley Problem."

48. For a study in which most subjects have a negative judgment of the loop case, see Hauser et al., "A Dissociation between Moral Judgments and Justifications," 6.

49. For another study in which most subjects have a negative judgment of the loop case, see Mikhail, "Universal Moral Grammar," 149.

50. For a study in which most subjects have a positive judgment of the loop case, see Greene et al., "Pushing moral buttons." Greene reports the 81 percent approval in Greene, *Moral Tribes*, 221.

51. For the hypothesis that different ways of presenting the loop cases results in different results, see Greene et al., "Pushing Moral Buttons," 369.

52. For an argument that the extra track in the loop case is irrelevant, see Thomson, "The Trolley Problem," 1403. For another argument for the same conclusion, see Scanlon, *Moral Dimensions*, 119–20.

53. For Thomson's statement that the trolley and transplant cases are not supposed to illustrate PDE, see Thomson, "The Trolley Problem," 1407n12.

54. For the quotation about PDE's choking on the loop case, see Greene, "Beyond Point-and-Shoot Morality," 721. For the quotation about the loop case as a general challenge to PDE, see Di Nucci, *Ethics without Intention*, 243n15.

55. According to Greene, "Characteristically deontological judgments are preferentially supported by automatic emotional responses, while characteristically consequentialist judgments are preferentially supported by conscious reasoning and allied processes of cognitive control." See Greene, "Beyond Point-and-Shoot Morality," 699.

56. For the seminal study that used fMRI on subjects who considered different cases, see Greene et al., "An fMRI Investigation of Emotional Engagement in Moral Judgment." For studies in which Greene and other researchers refined their original work, see Greene et al., "Cognitive Load Selectively Interferes with Utilitarian Moral Judgment" and "The Neural Bases of Cognitive Conflict and Control in Moral Judgment."

57. For Greene's statement that his work does not rely entirely on neuroscience, see Greene, "Notes on 'The Normative Insignificance of Neuroscience' by Selim Berker," 14.

58. For evidence that is part of debunking arguments and that does not come from neuroscience, see Greene, "Beyond Point-and-Shoot Morality," 704.

59. For a recent critique of Greene's dual process model, which says that characteristically deontological judgments usually are the products of automatic emotional brain processes while characteristically consequentialist judgments usually are the products of conscious, rational brain processes, see Kahane, "On the Wrong Track." For earlier critiques of Greene, see Berker, "The Normative Insignificance of Neuroscience," and Kamm, "Neuroscience and Moral Reasoning." For Greene's responses to Berker and Kamm, see Greene, "Beyond Point-and-Shoot Morality," 701n17, 706n48, 711n68, and 722–24.

60. For evidence that professional philosophers' deontological judgments are the products of unreliable emotional processes, see Greene, "Beyond Point-and-Shoot Morality," 719–20.

61. For the definition of unfamiliar situations in which automatic emotional responses are unreliable, see ibid., 714–15. For a similar view of unfamiliar situations, see Singer, "Ethics and Intuitions," 347–48.

62. For the claim that the reliability of intuitions in unfamiliar cases would be a "cognitive miracle," see Greene, "Beyond Point-and-Shoot Morality," 715.

63. For the argument that intuitions about trolley cases are unreliable because these cases became possible only recently in evolutionary history, see Singer, "Ethics and Intuitions," 348.

64. For what I regard as the strongest debunking argument, see Greene, "Beyond Point-and-Shoot Morality."

65. For a similar response to debunking arguments, see Lott, "Moral Implications from Cognitive (Neuro)Science?" Lott notes that empirical evidence of the basis of people's intuitions does not refute PDE or any other moral principle unless those intuitions are the only reason for accepting the principle. See ibid., 252.

66. For one critic's statement that neuroscience alone cannot settle debates in moral philosophy, see Greene, "Beyond Point-and-Shoot Morality," 716.

67. For an example of a critic who cites studies in neuroscience as decisive evidence against PDE, see Dean, "Does Neuroscience Undermine Deontological Theory?," 50.

68. For Greene's reference to the alleged "means/side-effect" distinction, see Greene, "Beyond Point-and-Shoot Morality," 709.

69. For the case of a person wearing a heavy backpack, see Greene et al., "Pushing Moral Buttons."

Five   Hard Cases in Medicine and War

1. For a history of PDE's application to the craniotomy case, see Rhonheimer, *Vital Conflicts*, 31–82. Rhonheimer rejects the traditional view, but not for the same reasons that I do.

2. For the statement that my analysis of the craniotomy case requires me to bite the bullet, see Nelkin and Rickless, "So Close, Yet So Far," 388.

3. For my views on the moral status of human embryos, see Masek, "The Moral Status of Human Embryos and Other Possible Sources of Stem Cells."

4. For the statement that the agent's intention determines the action's moral species, see Aquinas, *Summa Theologica*, 2.64.5.

5. For the claim that someone who kills in self-defense must not use excessive force, see ibid.

6. For Gury's version of PDE, see Gury, *Compendium theologiae moralis*, 1.2.9. The translation of this passage is mine, but I thank Matthew Ponesse and Michael Storck for their advice.

7. For Gury's statement that the good effect must follow as immediately as the bad effect, see ibid.

8. Nancy Davis distinguishes between the "agent-interpretation" and the "event-interpretation" of PDE. See Davis, "The Doctrine of Double Effect," 112–13.

9. For a summary and critique of some other sources of the traditional view of the craniotomy, see Rhonheimer, *Vital Conflicts*, 17–18.

10. Statement from the Holy Office, August 19, 1889, my translation.

11. For Hart's criticism of the traditional view of the craniotomy, see Hart, "Intention and Punishment," reprinted in Hart, *Punishment and Responsibility*, 123–24. The original version is not widely available, so I refer to the reprinted version.

12. For the use of a craniotomy on a dead child to analyze the intention of a surgeon who performs the craniotomy on a living child, see Finnis, Grisez, and Boyle, "'Direct' and 'Indirect,'" 21.

13. For Cavanaugh's statement about why the child's being alive is relevant for judging the craniotomy, see Cavanaugh, "Double-Effect Reasoning, Craniotomy, and Vital Conflicts," 458.

14. For Hart's statement that the craniotomy and hysterectomy are morally similar, see Hart, "Intention and Punishment," reprinted in *Punishment and Responsibility*, 124.

15. For Hart's statement that the traditional view of the craniotomy results from a legalistic view of morality, see ibid., 125.

16. For an example of the assertion that the surgeon in the craniotomy case must intend death because collapsing a child's skull is identical to killing the child, see Flannery, "What is Included in a Means to an End?," 508.

17. For an appeal to the principle that no effect causes itself, see Pruss, "The Accomplishment of Plans," 60. Pruss uses the principle to distinguish the effect of exploding bombs over civilians from the effect of killing the civilians.

18. For a statement that the child's death follows the craniotomy so closely that the surgeon "obviously" intends death, see Foot, "The Problem of Abortion and the Doctrine of Double Effect," reprinted in Foot, *Virtues and Vices*, 21.

19. For an argument that ordinary language confirms that the surgeon in the craniotomy case intends the child's death, see Cavanaugh, *Double-Effect Reasoning*, 69.

20. For conflicting interpretations of what Aquinas says about the moral object and the agent's intention, see Jensen, *Good and Evil Actions*, and Tollefsen, "Response to Koons and O'Brien's 'Objects of Intention,'" 764–71.

21. For the argument that the craniotomy cannot be part of good medical practice, see Flannery, *Acts amid Precepts*, 185.

22. For one version of the argument that the problem with the craniotomy is that the surgeon operates on the child, see Long, *The Teleological Grammar of the Moral Act*, 103.

23. For an argument that the surgeon in the craniotomy case intends harm instead of death, see Jensen, *Good and Evil Actions*, 95–96. See also Cavanaugh, *Double-Effect Reasoning*, 113.

24. For the view that the surgeon can perform the salpingectomy without intending death, see Bouscaren, *The Ethics of Ectopic Operations*, 153, cited in Rhonheimer, *Vital Conflicts*, 93–96.

25. For a claim of transplanting an embryo after a salpingotomy, see Shettles, "Tubal Embryo Successfully Transferred in Utero." For a discussion of this claim, see Grudzinskas et al., "Relocation of Ectopic Pregnancy to the Uterine Cavity."

26. For a medical description of treating ectopic pregnancy, see Gibbs et al., eds., *Danforth's Obstetrics and Gynecology*, 77–80.

27. For an analysis of the salpingectomy case that is similar to my analysis, see Rhonheimer, *Vital Conflicts*, 97–98.

28. For an argument that the salpingotomy is wrong because the surgeon directly kills the child, see Marie Anderson et al., "Ectopic Pregnancy and Catholic Morality," 73. The authors are responding to Kaczor, "The Ethics of Ectopic Pregnancy."

29. For an example of the statement that a D&C like the one in the Phoenix case is wrong because it is a direct abortion, see Roman Catholic Diocese of Phoenix, "Questions and Answers Re: The Situation at St. Joseph's."

30. For an appeal to immediacy in the D&C case, see National Catholic Bioethics Center, "Commentary on the Phoenix Hospital Situation," 550.

31. For defenses of the D&C in the Phoenix case, see Lysaught, "Moral Analysis of a Procedure at Phoenix Hospital," and Tollefsen, "Response to Koons and O'Brien's 'Objects of Intention,'" 771–74.

32. For the medical details of methotrexate as a treatment for ectopic pregnancy, see Gibbs et al., eds., *Danforth's Obstetrics and Gynecology*, 77–80.

33. For a defense of using methotrexate that is similar to mine, see Kaczor, "The Ethics of Ectopic Pregnancy."

34. For one statement of the case of a repopulated city, see FitzPatrick, "The Intend/Foresee Distinction and the Problem of Closeness," 612.

35. For an appeal to closeness to analyze the case of a repopulated city, see ibid., 613.

36. For the case of physicians who treat a patient in a way that releases toxic fumes into another patient's hospital room, see Foot, "The Problem of Abortion and the Doctrine of Double Effect," reprinted in Foot, *Virtues and Vices*, 29.

37. For a case in which the enemy's grief over the deaths of innocent people prevents a military target from being rebuilt, see Kamm, *Morality, Mortality*, 180.

38. For the case of a physician who treats patients as guinea pigs by leaving them untreated, see Quinn, "Actions, Intentions, and Consequences: The Doctrine of Double Effect," 336.

39. For the argument that my version of PDE cannot distinguish between the case of the physician who treats patients as guinea pigs and that of the physician who directs resources by treating stubborn cases first, see Nelkin and Rickless, "So Close, Yet So Far," 14.

40. For Quinn's version of PDE, see Quinn, "Acts, Intentions and Consequences."

41. For Quinn's distinction between harmful direct agency and harmful indirect agency, see ibid., 341–44.

42. For Quinn's appeal to the principle of treating persons as existing only for purposes that they can share, see ibid., 350–51.

43. For Quinn's further explanation of why the distinction between harmful direct agency and harmful indirect agency is relevant for judging actions, see Quinn, "Reply to Boyle's 'Who Is Entitled to Double Effect?,'" 511.

44. For some possible counterexamples to Quinn's distinction between harmful direct agency and harmful indirect agency, see FitzPatrick, "The Intend/Foresee Distinction and the Problem of Closeness," 611–13.

45. For defenses of Quinn's distinction, see Nelkin and Rickless, "Three Cheers for Double Effect." See also McMahan, "Revising the Doctrine of Double Effect," and Smith, "A New Defense of Quinn's Principle of Double Effect."

46. For Quinn's negative view of the craniotomy, see Quinn, "Acts, Intentions and Consequences," 342.

47. For an objection to Quinn that appeals to the case of an officer who uses soldiers to capture a bunker, see Cavanaugh, *Double-Effect Reasoning*, 64–65.

48. For Thomson's claims about conflicting intuitions and moral theories, see Thomson, "Physician-Assisted Suicide," 504n8. Thomson makes these claims while discussing cases of killing and letting die.

49. For one example of defenders of the craniotomy who argue against dualism and who identify ways that dualism corrupts views about life and death, see Grisez and Boyle, *Life and Death with Liberty and Justice*, 375–79. For a more recent example, see Lee and George, *Body-Self Dualism*.

Appendix

1. For the pamphlets dropped on Hiroshima before the atomic bomb was dropped, see Williams, "The Information War in the Pacific, 1945."

2. For Foot's acceptance of PDE, see Foot, "Morality, Action and Outcome," 25.

3. For Thomson's distinction between the trolley driver's steering onto a sidetrack and the bystander's throwing a switch, see Thomson, "Killing, Letting Die and the Trolley Problem," 207–8.

4. For the diffusiveness of intention principle, see Chisholm, "The Structure of Intentions," 636.

5. For the label "direction of resources" in the case of physicians who treat stubborn cases first, see Quinn, "Acts, Intentions and Consequences," 336.

6. For Kamm's analysis of the bystander's intention in the loop case, see Kamm, "The Doctrine of Triple Effect," 25. See also Kamm, *Intricate Ethics*, 105–6.

7. For Kamm's conclusion that the bystander in the loop case does not intend to hit the man with the trolley, see "The Doctrine of Triple Effect," 32. See also Kamm, *Intricate Ethics*, 106.

8. For Kamm's argument that a rational agent need not intend the means to her end, see Kamm, "The Doctrine of Triple Effect," 32–35. See also Kamm, *Intricate Ethics*, 104–7.

9. For Lysaught's appeal to Rhonheimer, see Lysaught, "Moral Analysis of a Procedure at Phoenix Hospital," 543–44. For Rhonheimer's argument, see Rhonheimer, *Vital Conflicts in Medical Ethics*, 122–31.

10. For Lysaught's appeal to Grisez, see Lysaught, "Moral Analysis of a Procedure at Phoenix Hospital," 544–45. For Grisez's argument, see Grisez, *The Way of the Lord Jesus*, vol. 2: *Living a Christian Life*, 500–503 (chapter 8, question D).

Bibliography

Anderson, Marie, Robert Fastiggi, David Hargroder, Joseph Howard, and C. Ward Kischer. "Ectopic Pregnancy and Catholic Morality: A Response to Recent Arguments in Favor of Salpingostomy and Methotrexate." *National Catholic Bioethics Quarterly* 11 (2011): 65–82.

Anderson, Robert. "Boyle and the Principle of Double Effect." *American Journal of Jurisprudence* 52 (2007): 259–72.

Anscombe, G. E. M. 1963. *Intention*, 2nd ed. Cambridge, MA: Harvard University Press.

———. "Medalist's Address: Intention, Action and 'Double Effect.'" *Proceedings of the American Catholic Philosophical Association* 56 (1982): 12–25.

———. "Modern Moral Philosophy." *Philosophy* 33 (1958): 1–19.

———. "Mr. Truman's Degree." Pamphlet published by Anscombe in 1957. Reprinted in *Ethics, Religion and Politics: The Collected Philosophical Papers of G. E. M. Anscombe*, vol. 3, 62–71. Minneapolis: University of Minnesota Press, 1981.

———. "Under a Description." *Noûs* 13 (1979): 219–33.

———. "War and Murder." *Nuclear Weapons: A Catholic Response*, ed. Walter Stein, 43–62. London and New York: Sheed and Ward, 1961.

Aquinas, Thomas. *Summa Theologica*, trans. Fathers of the English Dominican Province. Westminster, MD: Christian Classics, 1981.

Bennett, Jonathan. *The Act Itself*. New York: Oxford University Press, 1995.

———. "Whatever the Consequences." *Analysis* 26 (1966): 83–102.

Berker, Selim. "The Normative Insignificance of Neuroscience." *Philosophy and Public Affairs* 37 (2009): 293–329.

Bouscaren, T. Lincoln. *The Ethics of Ectopic Operations*, 2nd ed. Milwaukee: Bruce Publishing, 1944.

Boyle, Joseph. "Double Effect and a Certain Type of Embryotomy." *Irish Theological Quarterly* 44 (1977): 303–18.

———. "Intention, Permissibility, and the Structure of Agency." *American Catholic Philosophical Quarterly* 89 (2015): 461–78.

———. "The Moral Meaning and Justification of the Doctrine of Double Effect: A Response to Robert Anderson." *American Journal of Jurisprudence* 53 (2008): 69–84.

———. "Towards Understanding the Principle of Double Effect." *Ethics* 90 (1980): 527–38.

———. "Who Is Entitled to Double Effect?" *Journal of Medicine and Philosophy* 16 (1991): 475–94.

Boyle, Joseph, and Thomas Sullivan. "The Diffusiveness of Intention Principle: A Counter-Example." *Philosophical Studies* 31 (1977): 357–60.

Bratman, Michael. *Intention, Plans, and Practical Reason*. Cambridge, MA: Harvard University Press, 1987.

———. "Intention, Practical Rationality, and Self-Governance." *Ethics* 119 (2009): 411–43.

Cavanaugh, Thomas. "Double-Effect Reasoning, Craniotomy, and Vital Conflicts: A Case of Contemporary Catholic Casuistry." *National Catholic Bioethics Quarterly* 11 (2011): 453–63.

———. *Double Effect Reasoning: Doing Good and Avoiding Evil*. Oxford: Clarendon Press, 2006.

Chappell, Timothy. "Two Distinctions that Do Make a Difference: The Action/Omission Principle and the Principle of Double Effect." *Philosophy* 77 (2002): 211–33.

———. "What Have I Done?" *Diametros* 38 (2013): 86–112.

Chisholm, Roderick. "The Structure of Intention." *Journal of Philosophy* 66 (1970): 633–47.

Connell, F. J. "The Principle of Double Effect." In *The New Catholic Encyclopedia*. (New York: McGraw-Hill, 1967), 1020–22.

Davis, Nancy. "The Doctrine of Double Effect: Problems of Interpretation." *Pacific Philosophical Quarterly* 65 (1984): 107–23.

Dean, Richard. "Does Neuroscience Undermine Deontological Theory?" *Neuroethics* 3 (2011): 43–60.

Delaney, Neil. "To Double Business Bound: Reflections on the Doctrine of Double Effect." *American Catholic Philosophical Quarterly* 75 (2001): 561–83.

———. "Two Cheers for 'Closeness': Terror, Targeting and Double Effect." *Philosophical Studies* 137 (2008): 335–67.

Di Nucci, Ezio. *Ethics without Intention.* New York: Bloomsbury, 2014.

Donagan, Alan. "Consistency in Rationalist Moral Systems." *Journal of Philosophy* 81 (1984): 291–309.

———. "Moral Absolutism and the Double-Effect Exception: Reflections on Joseph Boyle's 'Who Is Entitled to Double Effect?'" *Journal of Medicine and Philosophy* 16 (1991): 495–509.

Ellis, Anthony. "*Double Effect Reasoning: Doing Good and Avoiding Evil* by T. A. Cavanaugh." *Mind* 118 (2009): 160–63.

Elster, Jakob. "Scanlon on Permissibility and Double Effect." *Journal of Moral Philosophy* 9 (2012): 75–102.

Finnis, John. "Intention and Side-Effects." In *Liability and Responsibility: Essays in Law and Morals*, ed. R. G. Frey and Christopher Morris, 32–64. Cambridge: Cambridge University Press, 1991.

———. *Moral Absolutes: Tradition, Revision, and Truth.* Washington, DC: Catholic University of America Press, 1991.

Finnis, John, Germain Grisez, and Joseph Boyle. "'Direct' and 'Indirect': A Reply to Critics of Our Action Theory." *Thomist* 65 (2001): 1–44.

FitzPatrick, William. "Acts, Intentions, and Moral Permissibility: In Defence of the Doctrine of Double Effect." *Analysis* 63 (2003): 317–21.

———. "The Doctrine of Double Effect: Intention and Permissibility." *Philosophy Compass* 7 (2012): 183–96.

———. "The Intend/Foresee Distinction and the Problem of Closeness." *Philosophical Studies* 128 (2006): 585–617.

Flannery, Kevin. *Acts amid Precepts.* Washington, DC: Catholic University of America Press, 2001.

———. "What Is Included in a Means to an End?" *Gregorianum* 74 (1993): 499–513.

Foot, Philippa. "Morality, Action and Outcome." In *Morality and Objectivity: A Tribute to J. L. Mackie*, ed. Ted Honderich, 23–38. London: Routledge and Kegan Paul, 1985.

———. "The Problem of Abortion and the Doctrine of Double Effect." *Oxford Review* 5 (1967): 143–55. Reprinted in Foot, *Virtues and Vices and Other Essays in Moral Philosophy*, 19–32. Oxford: Clarendon Press, 2002.

———. "Utilitarianism and the Virtues." *Mind* 94 (1985): 196–209.

Foot, Philippa, and Alex Voorhoeve. "Natural Goodness: An Interview with Philippa Foot." *Harvard Review of Philosophy* 11 (2003): 32–34.

Fried, Barbara. "What *Does* Matter? The Case for Killing the Trolley Problem (or Letting It Die)." *Philosophical Quarterly* 62 (2012): 505–29.

Fried, Charles. *Right and Wrong.* Cambridge, MA: Harvard University Press, 1978.

Friedman, A. W. "Minimizing Harm: Three Problems in Moral Theory." Ph.D. dissertation, Massachusetts Institute of Technology, Cambridge, MA, 2002.

Giggs, Ronald S., Beth Y. Karlan, Arthur F. Haney, and Ingrid E. Nygaard, eda. *Danforth's Obstetrics and Gynecology*, 10th ed. Philadelphia: Lippincott Williams and Wilkins, 2008.

Greene, Joshua. "Beyond Point-and-Shoot Morality: Why Cognitive (Neuro)Science Matters for Ethics." *Ethics* 124 (2014): 695–726.

———. *Moral Tribes: Emotion, Reason, and the Gap between Us and Them*. New York: Penguin Press, 2013.

———. "Notes on 'The Normative Insignificance of Neuroscience' by Selim Berker." Unpublished manuscript, 2010. Available at www .joshua-greene.net.

Greene, Joshua, Fiery Cushman, Lisa Stewart, Kelly Lowenberg, Leigh Nystrom, and Jonathan Cohen. "Pushing Moral Buttons: The Interaction between Personal Force and Intention in Moral Judgment." *Cognition* 111 (2009): 364–71.

Greene, Joshua, Sylvia Morelli, Kelly Lowenberg, Leigh Nystrom, and Jonathan Cohen. "Cognitive Load Selectively Interferes with Utilitarian Moral Judgment." *Cognition* 107 (2008): 1144–54.

Greene, Joshua, Leigh Nystrom, Andrew Engell, John Darley, and Jonathan Cohen. "The Neural Bases of Cognitive Conflict and Control in Moral Judgment." *Neuron* 44 (2004): 389–400.

Greene, Joshua, R. Brian Sommerville, Leigh Nystrom, John Darley, and Jonathan Cohen. "An fMRI Investigation of Emotional Engagement in Moral Judgment." *Science* 293 (2001): 2105–8.

Grisez, Germain. *The Way of the Lord Jesus*. Vol 2: *Living a Christian Life*. Quincy, IL: Franciscan Press, 1993. Available at www.twotlj .org.

Grisez, Germain, and Joseph Boyle. *Life and Death with Liberty and Justice*. Notre Dame: University of Notre Dame Press, 1979.

Grudzinskas, J. G., M. Palomino, P. Armstrong, and A. Lower. "Relocation of Ectopic Pregnancy to the Uterine Cavity: A Dream or a Reality?" *British Journal of Obstetric Gynaecology* 101 (1994): 672–75.

Guglielmo, Steve, and Bertram Malle. "Can Unintended Side Effects Be Intentional? Resolving a Controversy over Intentionality and Morality." *Personality and Social Psychology Bulletin* 36 (2010): 1635–47.

Gury, Jean Pierre. *Compendium theologiae moralis*. Rome: Typis Civitatis Catholicae, 1866.

Harman, Gilbert. "Practical Reasoning." *Review of Metaphysics* 29 (1976): 431–63.

Harris, John. "The Moral Difference between Throwing a Trolley at a Person and Throwing a Person at a Trolley." *Proceedings of the Aristotelian Society* (2000 Supplement): 41–57.

Hart, H. L. A. "Intention and Punishment." *Oxford Review* 4 (1967): 5–22. Reprinted in Hart, *Punishment and Responsibility: Essays in the Philosophy of Law*, 113–35. Oxford: Oxford University Press, 1968.

Hauser, Marc, Fiery Cushman, Liane Young, R. Kang-Xing, and John Mikhail. "A Dissociation between Moral Judgments and Justifications." *Mind & Language* 22 (2007): 1–21.

Hursthouse, Rosalind. *On Virtue Ethics*. Oxford: Oxford University Press, 1999.

Jensen, Steven. "Causal Constraints on Intention: A Critique of Tollefsen on the Phoenix Case." *National Catholic Bioethics Quarterly* 14 (2014): 273–93.

———. *Good and Evil Actions: A Journey through Saint Thomas Aquinas*. Washington, DC: Catholic University of America Press, 2010.

Kaczor, Christopher. "Double-Effect Reasoning from Jean Pierre Gury to Peter Knauer." *Theological Studies* 59 (1998): 297–316.

———. "The Ethics of Ectopic Pregnancy: A Critical Reconsideration of Salpingostomy and Methotrexate." *Linacre Quarterly* 76 (2009): 265–82.

Kahane, Guy. "The Armchair and the Trolley: An Argument for Experimental Ethics." *Philosophical Studies* 162 (2013): 421–45.

———. "On the Wrong Track: Process and Content in Moral Psychology." *Mind and Language* 27 (2012): 519–545.

Kamm, Frances. "The Doctrine of Triple Effect and Why a Rational Agent Need Not Intend the Means to His End." *Proceedings of the Aristotelian Society* 74 (2000): 21–39.

———. *Intricate Ethics: Rights, Responsibilities, and Permissible Harm*. New York: Oxford University Press, 2007.

———. *Morality, Mortality*. Vol. 2: *Rights, Duties, and Status*. New York: Oxford University Press, 1996.

———. "Neuroscience and Moral Reasoning: A Note on Recent Research." *Philosophy and Public Affairs* 37 (2009): 330–45.

Kaufman, Whitley. *Justified Killing: The Ethics of Self-Defense*. Lanham, MD: Lexington Books, 2009.

Keenan, James. "The Function of the Principle of Double Effect." *Theological Studies* 54 (1993): 294–315.

Knobe, Joshua. "Intentional Action and Side Effects in Ordinary Language." *Analysis* 63 (2003): 190–93.

Lee, Patrick, and Robert George. *Body-Self Dualism in Contemporary Ethics and Politics.* New York: Cambridge University Press, 2008.

Levy, Neil. "Neuroethics: A New Way of Doing Ethics." *AJOB (American Journal of Bioethics) Neuroscience* 2 (2011): 3–9.

Liao, S. Matthew. "The Loop Case and Kamm's Doctrine of Triple Effect." *Philosophical Studies* 146 (2009): 223–231.

Lippert-Rasmussen, Kasper. "Scanlon on the Doctrine of Double Effect." *Social Theory and Practice* 36 (2010): 541–64.

Long, Steven. *The Teleological Grammar of the Moral Act.* Naples, FL: Sapientia Press, 2007.

Lott, Micah. "Moral Implications from Cognitive (Neuro)Science? No Clear Route." *Ethics* 127 (2016): 241–56.

Lysaught, M. Therese. "Moral Analysis of a Procedure at Phoenix Hospital." *Origins* 40 (2012): 537–49.

MacIntyre, Alasdair. *After Virtue: A Study in Moral Theory*, 2nd ed. Notre Dame: University of Notre Dame Press, 1984.

———. "Does Applied Ethics Rest on a Mistake?" *Monist* 67 (1984): 498–513.

Mangan, Joseph. "A Historical Analysis of the Principle of Double Effect." *Theological Studies* 10 (1949): 41–61.

Marquis, Donald. "Four Versions of Double Effect." *Journal of Medicine and Philosophy* 16 (1991): 515–44.

Masek, Lawrence. "Deadly Drugs and Double Effect: A Reply to Tully." *Journal of Business Ethics* 68 (2006): 143–51.

———. "The Doctrine of Double Effect, Deadly Drugs, and Business Ethics." *Business Ethics Quarterly* 10 (2000): 483–96.

———. "In Defense of a Minimalist, Agent-Based Principle of Double Effect." *American Catholic Philosophical Quarterly* 90 (2015): 521–38.

———. "Intentions, Motives and Double Effect." *Philosophical Quarterly* 60 (2010): 567–85.

———. "The Moral Status of Human Embryos and Other Possible Sources of Stem Cells." In *Contemporary Controversies in Catholic Bioethics*, ed. Jason Eberl, 331–43. Cham, Switzerland: Springer, 2017.

McIntyre, Alison. "Doing Away with Double Effect." *Ethics* 111 (2001): 219–55.

McMahan, Jeff. "Intention, Permissibility, Terrorism, and War." *Philosophical Perspectives* 23 (2009): 345–72.

———. "Revising the Doctrine of Double Effect." *Journal of Applied Philosophy* 11 (1994): 201–12.

Mikhail, John. "Universal Moral Grammar: Theory, Evidence and the Future." *Trends in Cognitive Sciences* 11 (2007): 143–52.

Nagel, Thomas. *The Limits of Objectivity*. The Tanner Lectures on Human Values, 1979. Available at www.tannerlectures.utah.edu.
———. *The View from Nowhere*. Oxford: Oxford University Press, 1986.
———. "War and Massacre." *Philosophy and Public Affairs* 1 (1972): 123–44.
National Catholic Bioethics Center. "Commentary on the Phoenix Hospital Situation." *Origins* 40, no. 31 (January 13, 2011): 549–51.
Nelkin, Dana Kay, and Samuel Rickless. "So Close, Yet So Far: Why Solutions to the Closeness Problem for the Doctrine of Double Effect Fall Short." *Noûs* 49 (2015): 376–409.
———. "Three Cheers for Double Effect." *Philosophy and Phenomenological Research* 89 (2014): 125–58.
Norcross, Alastair. "Intending and Foreseeing Death: Potholes on the Road to Hell." *Southwest Philosophy Review* 15 (1999): 115–23.
Nye, Howard. "Objective Double Effect and the Avoidance of Narcissism." In *Oxford Studies in Normative Ethics*, vol. 3, ed. Mark Timmons, 260–86. Oxford: Oxford University Press, 2013.
O'Brien, Matthew, and Robert Koons. "Objects of Intention: A Hylomorphic Critique of the New Natural Law Theory." *American Catholic Philosophical Quarterly* 86 (2012): 655–703.
Otsuka, Michael. "Double Effect, Triple Effect, and the Trolley Problem: Squaring the Circle in Looping Cases." *Utilitas* 20 (2008): 92–110.
Patton, Michael. "Can Bad Men Make Good Brains Do Bad Things?" *Proceedings and Addresses of the American Philosophical Association* 61 (1988): 555–56.
Pruss, Alexander. "The Accomplishment of Plans." *Philosophical Studies* 165 (2013): 49–69.
Quinn, Warren. "Acts, Intentions and Consequences: The Doctrine of Double Effect." *Philosophy and Public Affairs* 18 (1989): 334–51.
———. "Reply to Boyle's 'Who Is Entitled to Double Effect?'" *Journal of Medicine and Philosophy* 16 (1991): 511–14.
Reed, Philip. "How to Gerrymander Intention." *American Catholic Philosophical Quarterly* 89 (2015): 441–60.
Rhonheimer, Martin. *Vital Conflicts in Medical Ethics: A Virtue Approach to Craniotomy and Tubal Pregnancies*. Washington, DC: Catholic University of America Press, 2009.
Roman Catholic Diocese of Phoenix. "Questions and Answers Re: The Situation at St. Joseph's." Available at https://media.npr.org/assets/news/2010/05/18/qanda.pdf.
Scanlon, T. M. *Moral Dimensions: Permissibility, Meaning, Blame*. Cambridge, MA: Belknap Press, 2008.

———. "Reply to Hill, Mason and Wedgwood." *Philosophy and Phenomenological Research* 83 (2011): 490–505.

———. *What We Owe to Each Other.* Cambridge, MA: Harvard University Press, 1998.

Shaw, Joseph. "Intention in Ethics." *Canadian Journal of Philosophy* 36 (2006): 187–224.

———. "Intentions and Trolleys." *Philosophical Quarterly* 56 (2006): 63–83.

Shettles, L. B. "Tubal Embryo Successfully Transferred in Utero." *American Journal of Obstetric Gynecology* 163 (1990): 2026–27.

Singer, Peter. "Ethics and Intuitions." *Journal of Ethics* 9 (2005): 331–52.

Sinnott-Armstrong, Walter. *Moral Dilemmas.* Oxford: Basil Blackwell, 1988.

Smart, J. J. C. "An Outline of a System of Utilitarian Ethics." In *Utilitarianism: For and Against*, ed. J. J. C. Smart and Bernard Williams, 3–74. Cambridge, MA: Cambridge University Press, 1973.

Smith, Ian. "A New Defense of Quinn's Principle of Double Effect." *Journal of Social Philosophy* 38 (2007): 349–64.

Sulmasey, Daniel. "'Reinventing' the Rule of Double Effect." In *The Oxford Handbook of Bioethics*, ed. Bonnie Steinbock, 114–49. New York: Oxford University Press, 2007.

Thomson, Judith Jarvis. "Kamm on the Trolley Problems." In *The Trolley Problem Mysteries*, ed. Frances Kamm and Eric Rakowski, 113–33. Oxford: Oxford University Press, 2015.

———. "Killing, Letting Die and the Trolley Problem." *Monist* 59 (1976): 204–17.

———. "Physician-Assisted Suicide: Two Moral Arguments." *Ethics* 109 (1999): 497–518.

———. "Self-Defense." *Philosophy and Public Affairs* 20 (1991): 283–310.

———. "The Trolley Problem." *Yale Law Journal* 94 (1985): 1395–1415.

———. "Turning the Trolley." *Philosophy and Public Affairs* 36 (2008): 359–74.

Tollefsen, Christopher. "Intending Damage to Basic Goods." *Christian Bioethics* 14 (2008): 272–82.

———. "Is a Purely First Person Account of Human Action Defensible?" *Ethical Theory and Moral Practice* 9 (2006): 441–60.

———. "Response to Robert Koons and Matthew O'Brien's 'Objects of Intention.'" *American Catholic Philosophical Quarterly* 87 (2013): 751–78.

Tully, Patrick. "The Doctrine of Double Effect and the Question of Constraints on Business Decisions." *Journal of Business Ethics* 58 (2005): 51–63.

Veatch, Henry. *Rational Man: A Modern Interpretation of Aristotelian Ethics*. Bloomington: Indiana University Press, 1962.

Walzer, Michael. *Just and Unjust Wars: A Moral Argument with Historical Illustrations*, 3rd ed. New York: Basic Books, 2000.

Wedgwood, Ralph. "Defending Double Effect." *Ratio* 24 (2011): 384–401.

———. "Scanlon on Double Effect." *Philosophy and Phenomenological Research* 83 (2011): 464–72.

Williams, Bernard. "A Critique of Utilitarianism." In *Utilitarianism: For and Against*, ed. J. J. C. Smart and Bernard Williams, 77–150. Cambridge, MA: Cambridge University Press, 1973.

Williams, Josette. "The Information War in the Pacific, 1945." CIA Studies in Intelligence 46 (2007). Available online at https://www.cia.gov/library/center-for-the-study-of-intelligence/csi-publications/csi-studies/studies/vol46no3/article07.html.

Wood, Allen. "Humanity as an End in Itself." In Derek Parfit, *On What Matters*, vol. 2, 58–82. Oxford: Oxford University Press, 2011.

———. *Kant's Ethical Thought*. Cambridge, MA: Cambridge University Press, 1999.

Index

abortion, 144–46, 157, 163
absolutism
  Catholic tradition and, 31
  definition of, 26
  label for, 26–27
  moral dilemmas and, 28
  PDE and, 27–30, 110, 182
  source of, 30–31, 182
  See also exceptionless rules
agency, direct vs. indirect, 167–69,
    193–94, 199–200
agent-based definition of intended
    effects. *See* strict definition of
    intended effects
agents
  corruption of, 13–15, 17–18,
    21–22, 81–83, 130–31
  effects, relation to, 19–20
  judgments of, 76, 84–85, 195–96
  perspective of, 34–35, 144, 170,
    188–89
  trolley cases and, 111–12, 116
  victims, relation to, 129–30
  See also character: intentions
alcoholic case, 18
allowing vs. doing, 28, 32–33

Anscombe, G. E. M.
  bombing cases, 173–74
  cave case, 59–60, 62–63
  definition of intentions, 64
  justification of PDE, 110
  principle of side effects, 9
  pumping water case, 60, 174–75
  role in introducing PDE to
    secular Anglo-American
    philosophy, 173
  under a description, 80–81
  withdrawing child support case,
    175–76
apologies, 85–86, 139
Aquinas, St. Thomas, 112, 121–22,
    138–40, 171–72
arm-twisting case, 32–33, 188–89
assessments, 77

backsolving, 39, 64
  See also Knobe effect
backpack case, 135–36
  See also footbridge case
bank robbery cases, 43, 51,
    63–64
Bennett, Jonathan, 83–84

Lawrence Masek is professor of philosophy at Ohio Dominican University.

www.ingramcontent.com/pod-product-compliance
Lightning Source LLC
Chambersburg PA
CBHW060332100426
42812CB00003B/966